ADVANCED ROCK CLIMBING
Expert Skills and Techniques

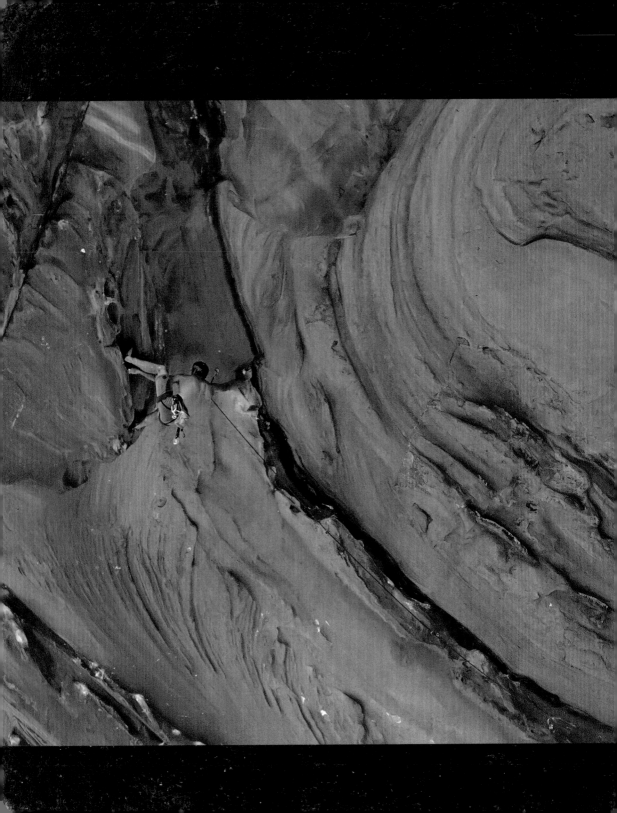

ADVANCED ROCK CLIMBING
Expert Skills and Techniques

Topher Donahue
Foreword by Tommy Caldwell

MOUNTAINEERS
BOOKS

This book is dedicated to our wild lands; the places that make
our sport a rich, beautiful, inspiring dance with nature.

MOUNTAINEERS
BOOKS

Mountaineers Books is the publishing division of The Mountaineers, an organization founded in 1906 and dedicated to the exploration, preservation, and enjoyment of outdoor and wilderness areas.

1001 SW Klickitat Way, Suite 201, Seattle, WA 98134
800.553.4453, www.mountaineersbooks.org

Printed in China
Distributed in the United Kingdom by Cordee, www.cordee.co.uk
First edition, 2016

Copy Editor: Erin Moore
Design and Layout: Peggy Egerdahl
Illustrator: John McMullen
All photographs by Topher Donahue unless credited otherwise
Cover photograph:*Tommy Caldwell on the* Dawn Wall © Corey Rich/Big UP Productions /Aurora Photo
Frontispiece: *Malcolm "HB" Matheson questioning gravity in the Grampians, Australia*
Back cover photograph: *Yuka Kobayashi enjoys a casual warm-up lap on a 5.12+ in Futagoyama, Japan.*

Library of Congress Cataloging-in-Publication Data
Names: Donahue, Topher.
Title: Advanced rock climbing : expert skills and techniques / Topher Donahue.
Description: First edition. | Seattle : Mountaineers Books, [2016] | Includes index.
Identifiers: LCCN 2016007209| ISBN 9781680510126 (trade paper) | ISBN 9781680510133 (ebook)
Subjects: LCSH: Rock climbing. | Extreme sports.
Classification: LCC GV200.2 .D66 2016 | DDC 796.522/3—dc23
LC record available at http://lccn.loc.gov/2016007209

Mountaineers Books titles may be purchased for corporate, educational, or other promotional sales, and our authors are available for a wide range of events. For information on special discounts or booking an author, contact our customer service at 800-553-4453 or mbooks@mountaineersbooks.org.

ISBN (paperback): 978-1-68051-012-6
ISBN (ebook): 978-1-68051-013-3

Contents

CHAPTER 1

Face Climbing

CHAPTER 2

Crack Climbing

CHAPTER 3

Climbing Gear

CHAPTER 12

Bouldering

CHAPTER 13

Performance

CHAPTER 14

Improvised Rescue and Epic Avoidance

Foreword

I was born in an era when rock climbing was experiencing a great divide. It was the skinny-legged sport climbers vs. the hard-core mountain climbers. The debates raged hottest in Yosemite, but my hometown of Estes Park, Colorado, had its own ethical debates. Bolts were chopped. Fights broke out. My dad sat right in the middle. He was a mountain guide who wore spandex and loved clipping bolts—a little like Arnold Schwarzenegger in a tutu. But his acceptance of all things climbing would prove to be the way forward.

My first climbs were done in a swami belt with hexentrics dangling around my ankles, but I really fell in love with climbing as a teenager, when sport climbing was all the rage. I loved the athleticism, the feeling of air beneath my feet. I liked the adventure, but I didn't want to die climbing. For a while, sport climbing was all I needed. At some point in my late teens, however, I began to feel the pull of the bigger mountains.

My dad was always my mentor, but his worldly travels were limited—and he was my dad, so I didn't always listen to him that well. I needed other mentors. That's when I started climbing with Topher Donahue. He was seven years older than I was and had a resume of wild climbs to match his wild eyes and ratted hair: huge first ascents in Alaska and Patagonia, as well as many of the most notorious climbs in Colorado. I was young, strong from sport climbing, a little cocky, and wanted to prove that even a scrawny little sport climber could hold his weight in the mountains.

I was shocked the first few times I roped up with Topher to find out that he was really conservative. He climbed slowly and methodically, put in lots of gear, and didn't seem to mind bailing at the first sign of danger. How was it then that he had done so many bad-ass climbs? His secret, I found out, was that he used his brain.

One day we headed out to a crag, below the Diamond on Longs Peak, called the Ship's Prow. It was the home to a bunch of A3+ and A4 climbs. Our goal was to try and find a way

Tommy and Mike Caldwell pitching camp in the middle of the Salathé headwall while getting schooled in big wall free climbing

to free climb it. I led first and, unable to find good gear, I punched it through some long run outs. Legs quaking and heart racing, I made it to the end of the pitch feeling darn lucky that I hadn't taken a monstrously long ledge fall. Topher's lead was next, just as the wall steepened. There was no distinct feature to follow, just a spider web of incipient seams. Topher took his time wandering back and forth, whittling gear into the most unlikely of spots. He turned his stoppers sideways to fit shallower cracks and placed large cams between opposing features. Before the crux he built a nest of good gear, carefully calculated the consequence of a big fall, decided that it would be safe, and then punched it though the crux of the climb. I was in awe of how he managed to make a climb that everyone else I knew would consider extremely dangerous legitimately safe.

For a while I viewed Topher a little like one of those genius hackers. The kid that the CIA hires to hack into the computers of a country they consider a nuclear threat. But Topher was hacking risk. Then I started to learn the systems myself. Throughout the years we did a lot of climbs together. I loved climbing with Topher because I knew that with him I could go big *and* be certain we would come home safe. And I always learned a ton. He climbed with creativity but was also hyper analytical and had a keen ability to assess risk rationally. I began to learn when to slow down and consider my options, and when to push the gas pedal to the floor. I developed a pride in doing things like using every piece of gear I had on my rack on a single pitch. I began to see places where I could cut corners to speed things up. I learned systems for being not only safe but also efficient. Combined with my training base from sport climbing and bouldering, these new skills provided a launch pad for countless great adventures.

Some people are good because they try hard, others because they are naturally talented, and some find success in their ability to run it out. Topher was good because he was smart and experienced. Also, like my dad, he accepted all things climbing. He pulled training knowledge from the community of emerging gym climbers, while using the efficiency tricks learned from alpine climbing on big walls. I have used what I know—much of it the result of Topher's teachings—to have adventures that have far surpassed my wildest dreams. I have never been the strongest climber. For me it has been a matter of learning the tricks, working hard, and loving the fact that I am outside climbing every day.

I am equally envious and excited that Topher's vast body of knowledge and the culmination of thirty-five-plus years of creative climbing experience is now compiled in a single book. When I was a teenager I had to beg Topher for the keys that unlocked the secrets of the high end of our sport. Then I spent twenty years refining the systems that grace the following pages. Well, I guess I can comfort myself in the knowledge that motivated climbers can use this book to be safer on their biggest adventures while enjoying the exhilaration of progression.

Today's expert rock climber knows that all climbers, regardless of their area of expertise, can learn from one another. The boulderer aspires to become the alpinist, and the alpinist knows that there are things to be learned from the gym climber. *Advanced Rock Climbing* is a testament to this new school idea. In Topher's own words, "Advanced rock climbing is an independent, self-ruling, intuitive, flexible, creative, anything-goes-as-long-as-it's-done-safely kind of climbing."

I have lived my entire thirty-seven years of life as a rock climber, constantly tuning and refining how I climb. I will never cease to be a student. For me, reading *Advanced Rock Climbing* is an acceleration of knowledge. Topher is not only a talented climber; he is also one of the most gifted writers and visual storytellers in our industry. This book needed to be written, and there is no better person to write it than Topher Donahue.

Tommy Caldwell
April, 2016

Acknowledgments

First and foremost, I'd like to send an enormous thank-you to the climbers and guides who took the time to contribute some of their most hard-earned and valuable knowledge to this book. Tommy Caldwell, Lynn Hill, Alex Honnold, Steph Davis, Justen Sjong, Angela Hawse, Marc Piché, Emily Harrington, Chris Schulte, Angie Payne, John Sherman, Lisa Rands, Chris Wall, Abbey Smith, and Sonnie Trotter all spent time with me, either on the phone, in the ether, over coffee, or at the crag, while I interviewed them for this book. It was an honor to spend time heart-to-heart with this group of world-class adventurers and to share a little of their combined centuries of climbing wisdom.

A big thanks to everyone who helped with the photography: the climbers who helped with the images taken specifically for this book, as well as those who are in the photos that were drawn from my thirty-year-deep archive of climbing photography. Thanks to you all, including: Airlie Anderson, Cassie Beermann, Adam Brink, Majka Burhardt, Sheyna Button, Mike Caldwell, Miguel Carasol, Toño Carasol, Vanessa Compton, Kim Csizmazia, Eric DeCaria, Kate Dooley, Robyn Erbesfield, Rich Farnham, Kristen Felix, Katie Frayler, Carolyn George, Howard Gilpin, Dave Graham, Patience Gribble, Britany Griffith, Jochen and Karina Haase, Anja and Ansgar Haberstroh, Mark Hammer, Kennan Harvey, Yuji Hirayama, Steph Johnson, Tiffany Junge, Guido Klingenberg, Angelica Lind, Enga Lokey, Craig Luebben, Malcolm "HB" Matheson, Dave Medera, Johnny Mellis, Ari Menitove, Elena Mihaly, Steve Monks, Ryan Nelson, Meg Noffsinger, Timmy O'Neill, Jeff Ofsanko, Jared Ogden, Mike Pennings, Dean Potter, Alex Puccio, Beth Rodden, Eric Rosenblum, Mike Schlauch, Vera Schulte-Pelkum, Matt Segal, Zack Smith, Mark Synott, Anna Thomas, Heidi Wirtz, and Gerald Zauner.

Thanks to Metolius, La Sportiva, Outdoor Research, and Black Diamond for product support for this book specifically, and to the outdoor industry in general, for making our sport safer and

Opposite: *Tommy Caldwell paying his dues during his first trip up the big stone of El Capitan*

more fun and for representing mountain sport so well. And to the editors at Mountaineers Books for having the vision to publish a guide that pushes the limits of climbing technique as far as this one does; with an extra shout-out to editor Erin Moore for using her own passion for the sport to provide a content edit that went beyond the basics to help express and clarify the sometimes complex lessons in this book.

Special thanks to my family, Vera, Aya, and Keahi, for helping with this project and for understanding my lifelong passion for climbing.

Finally, thank you to all the climbers with whom I've shared a rope. Those climbs with you all have made for some of the best days of my life.

Opposite: *A great reason to learn to climb hard is the places it will take you.*

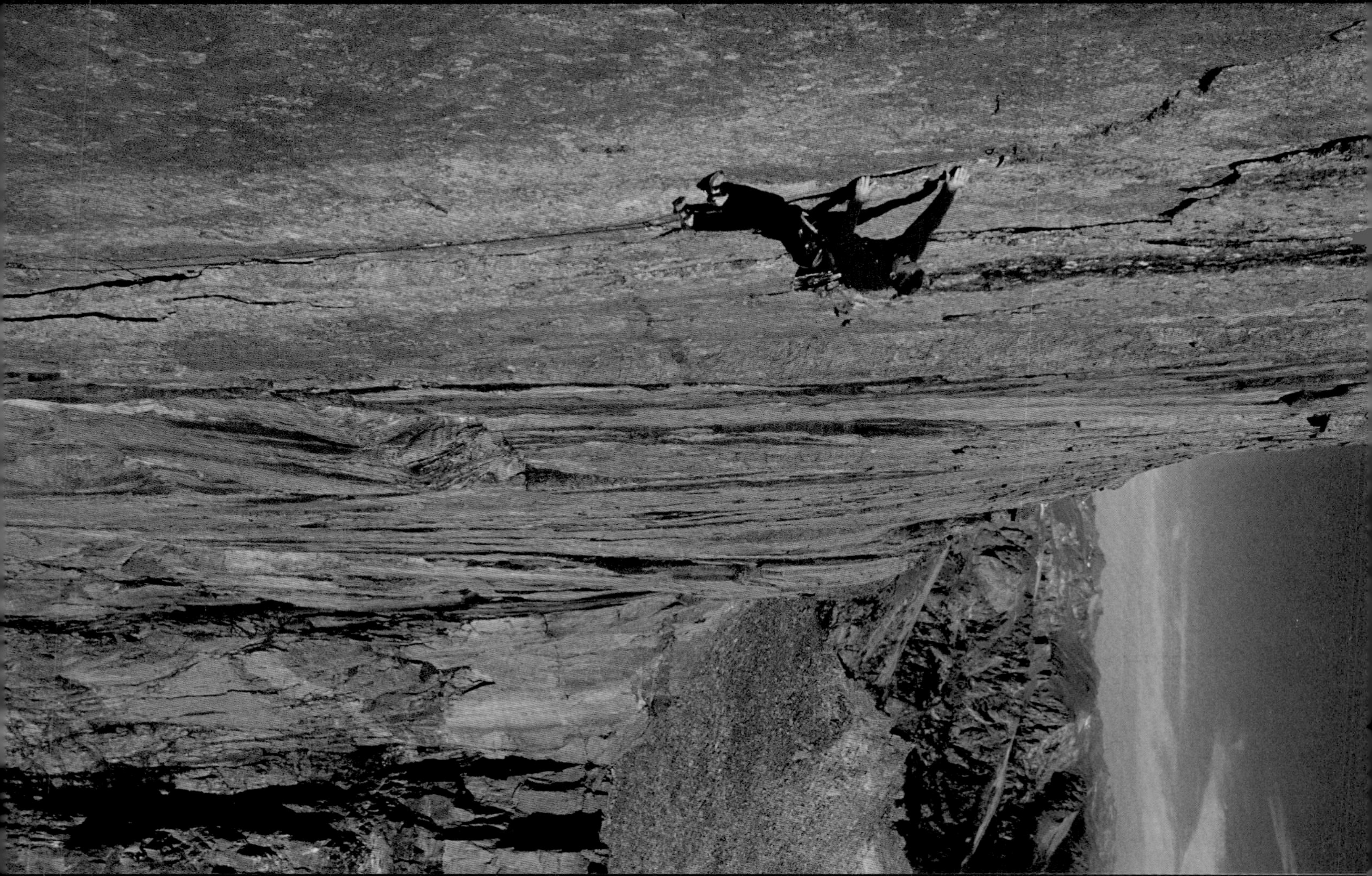

INTRODUCTION

Introduction: What Makes a Great Climber?

*"The old way of climbing was: systematic, methodical, and consistent.
Now it's anything goes, reacting to every situation differently."*

Tommy Caldwell

Some people learn the basics of rock climbing and, within just a few short years, excel to a point where they're climbing at an advanced level—5.12 trad climbing and 5.13 sport climbing. Or, on the other side, many climbers have years of experience but seem stuck forever at the same climbing plateau. There is certainly nothing wrong with either climber, provided they both have fun and stay safe. Yet what is the difference between the two? How does one climber get really good really fast while the other stays stuck at the same level? And what if you are someone itching to climb out of the plateau and who wants to go from average or good, to great? How do you climb differently?

There are age and genetic components to becoming an advanced climber, but one of the biggest reasons some people make the step up and others don't frequently boils down to mentorship. Quite often, the climber on a steep improvement curve has the opportunity to be mentored by someone in the way of advanced climbing. This way is different than textbook climbing. It is also different than having a climbing guide who takes you there. Advanced rock climbing is an independent, self-ruling, intuitive, flexible, creative, anything-goes-as-long-as-it's-done-safely kind of climbing: the kind of climbing this book is all about.

To capture the techniques and philosophy in the following pages, I interviewed some of the best climbers in the world. In the process, I tried to answer the question: How did these climbing heroes get so good? The answer I uncovered is multifaceted. Genetics help, and starting young is important to achieve the highest levels. Training is essential. Mentorship is almost mandatory. Of all the facets of climbing shared by the world-class climbers interviewed for this book, the most frequent affirmations about what makes a world-class climber were these: Top-tier climbers try really hard. They have a strong work ethic. They persevere. They commit.

"I'd already sport climbed 5.14, but I got shut down on 5.9 my first few months trad climbing."

Emily Harrington

That said, even with an Olympic athlete's work ethic and training program, we can't all be superstars and, lucky for us, we don't have to be. What matters is that some climbers have managed to reach these stratospheric levels and can now share what they've learned there in the upper sphere with the rest of us.

It's an exciting time for the sport of climbing. The techniques actively being developed by the world's best climbers are ripe for integration into systems any experienced climber can use. And while we don't need to do the world's hardest climbs, we can certainly learn from those who climb them.

THE CHANGING OF THE GAME

In January of 2015, rock climbing as we know it changed forever. With Tommy Caldwell and Kevin Jorgeson's free ascent of the

After paying his dues, Tommy Caldwell on a fast free ascent of El Cap's Zodiac

Dawn Wall, hard climbing went mainstream and the non-climbing public got a glimpse of just how incredible climbing really is. Suddenly, parents, friends, and colleagues who had never climbed were interested in our sport. Even more significant for those of us who are climbers, the unique technique and approach of the world's best climbers took center stage. For world-class climbers to incorporate techniques different from those used by average climbers is not a new phenomenon. But never before were the differences so clear—or so well publicized. The shortcuts these amazing climbers use to conserve energy, the tricks and tools they incorporate to maximize the safety provided by their pieces of protection plus their reliance on tiny protection not originally designed for free climbing, and the powerful mental attitude they exhibit steadfastly—the list goes on. Tommy and Kevin weren't the first to use these techniques, but by freeing the *Dawn Wall* so publically they dramatically raised the awareness of advanced climbing strategy and method.

It begs the question: *however did recreational, textbook climbing technique diverge so dramatically from advanced, world-class climbing technique?* A big part of the answer lies in the historical development of the guiding profession. Professional guiding originated in the European Alps, accompanied by its practice as an unregulated profession elsewhere in the world. But today, and over the last thirty years, guiding has become an established and standardized profession, and the practices of guiding have greatly influenced the accepted "textbook" climbing techniques, filtering down even to recreational climbers who have no interest in working as guides.

Guiding techniques are great, and any climber will do well to study them, but these methods are designed for expert climbers leading novices up a climb and not fashioned for a self-led climber who wants to push his or her personal limits, on lead, in challenging terrain, with a solid partner. The methods used by expert climbers pushing their limits have developed separately from guiding and instructional standards. Many of these exciting tools have gone unrecorded in the standard annals of climbing technique.

Don't get me wrong. The influence of guiding on recreational climbing has been fantastic. Bomber belays and analytic protocols that can be systematically learned by beginners have played a major role in making climbing safer and more appealing to more people. Because of the sharing of information, aspiring climbers today have volumes of well-tested climbing and guiding technique knowledge at their fingertips. Newcomers can learn more in one year than the climbers of yesteryear might have learned in a decade. As climbers gain experience, they can embark on adventures armed with exactly the right gear, dozens of trip reports from other climbers, and guidebooks using the best of modern photography and route presentation.

Then one day, we go out to push our limits—and everything changes. The wake-up call usually goes something like this: The climb that was supposed to take half a day

If you want to climb hard, climb a lot on diverse types of rock and find a mentor.

consumes us dawn to dusk. The climb with an easy grade shuts us down to the point that completing it feels impossible. Setting up anchors and belay transitions take as long as leading the pitch. Even a single-pitch climb takes us hours to prepare for, to lead, and then to follow. We carry twice as much gear as needed and arrive at the top with pounds of unused equipment. We spend as much time dealing with equipment as we do climbing. And rather than getting faster and climbing harder, we hit a plateau—a plateau in performance, efficiency, safety management, and even pleasure.

What happened? We study techniques shown in the books, taught by guides, and shared on the internet. The techniques are excellent. From this point, there are two ways we typically go as climbers. We either accept our plateau and enjoy it within its limitations. Or we find a mentor. A mentor is someone who enlightens us and changes the way we look at climbing: someone who proves that there is a way to spend more time climbing and less time fiddling with gear, who demonstrates a situation-based, rather than textbook-based, approach to safety management, and who shows us how to

Perhaps most importantly, our climbing heroes take care of the beautiful and sometimes fragile environment in which we practice our sport.

maximize our actual climbing time and make small but radical improvements and efficiencies in our climbing game.

"The more time you put in, the better you will climb—and it takes a bit more than you would expect..."

Angie Payne

HEROES AND MENTORS

The world's best climbers nearly all had mentors who helped them rise beyond the textbook. *The goal of this book,* Advanced Rock Climbing, *is to be your virtual mentor.* To achieve this goal, I recruited perspectives and

tips from some of the world's best climbers, guides, and personal trainers, and wove their words of wisdom into these pages.

These perspectives and techniques represent the pulling of the curtain on what advanced climbers really do out there. You'll be surprised. High-level performance in climbing is not always about throwing caution to the wind and just charging ahead—although there's a place for that too. Watch a world-class climber alongside an average climber. It's not that the world-class climber is necessarily climbing much faster, is not struggling, or is taking increased risks. Quite often, our climbing heroes in action appear much more human and less like superheroes than their videos, photos, or reputations would suggest. They make many of the same mistakes as ordinary climbers. They get scared, place tons of gear, do sequences wrong, fall off, get sewing-machine leg, place the wrong-size piece, and go off-route. Everyone makes mistakes.

But spend time with a world-class climber, and it doesn't take long to see that there is a world of technique, technique you won't find in a climbing class, in instructional books, in internet searches, or in guide training. In presenting a mentor-like approach to an instructional book, the following chapters are meant to bridge the gap between established climbing techniques and the improvisational, creative, limit-pushing methods that have become commonplace at the top of the climbing game.

"If climbing is an art, then creativity is its main component."

Wolfgang Gullich

THE NEXT LEVEL

If you're ready to take your climbing to the next level, this book is for you. In *Advanced Rock Climbing*, we start with motion and body language, the technique of moving over difficult rock smoothly and effectively on cracks and faces and everything in between. We'll look at how to release your inner monkey, how to do moves between the moves, when to make a move dynamic and when to make a move static, and how to use cracks beyond the basic hand and foot jams. We'll answer intriguing questions including why photos of hard climbers often show them with only one foot or hand on the rock, how to find rests in difficult terrain, and how to use alternate muscle groups to conserve energy.

Then we'll explore the limits of climbing equipment, including how to rack for different types of climbs, how to make your gear go farther, clothing choices for different types of climbing, improvised belay anchors, and planning ahead. Specific to traditional climbing, we'll talk about gear considerations for long routes versus cragging, runout strategy, nesting, and tethering delicate placements. We'll reveal the practical uses and limitations of specialized equipment including micro cams and nuts, pitons, bolt placement considerations, and improvised, alternative gear uses beyond the manufacturer's intent.

For those of us who prefer the full-throttle mind-set of sport climbing, we'll dig into the lesser-known aspects of sport climbing, including rest days, skipping bolts, cleaning steep climbs, resting mid-pitch, learning a new area, and how to plan for an onsight versus a hard redpoint.

Then we'll drop the clutch and go into the mysterious world of long route efficiency, including: methods for linking pitches, simul-climbing with a progress capture device (PCD), backup, and leading in blocks. We'll explore the mental and physical process of headpointing, or working out a dangerous climb to the point that it can be done safely. With a bulging toolbox of new skills, we'll combine it all with the game that puts it all together—big wall free climbing with instruction on PCDs for rope soloing, strategies for redpointing hard pitches on long climbs, and logistics for maximum performance on big climbs where you can't just lower back to the ground for another try.

Getting down from the climb is a dangerous part of the day, so a chapter is devoted to advanced rappelling and descending considerations, including improvised anchor backup, finding descent routes, descending from mid-pitch, and downclimbing. Anyone can rappel safely; it is hard to rappel safely every time, hundreds of times, year after year. This chapter reveals the methodology for fail-safe rappelling in even the most adverse conditions and situations.

Delving into the world of incredible difficulty, we'll uncover the tenacity, strategy, and training used by the strongest climbers in the world: boulderers. We'll look at the methods and tricks used by these power climbers to move on the tiniest holds in the steepest terrain and the training, mental strategy, and teamwork in this most social of all climbing types.

We'll look at the training needed to perform at the highest levels, including the philosophy of training weaknesses rather than strengths, utilizing cardiovascular training as part of a climbing program, and preventing overuse injury. Using insight provided by some of the world's most respected personal trainers, we will look at different training goals, including using a gym to train for climbing outdoors, and the different strategies behind training for power, mental tenacity, and power-endurance.

Finally, we'll close the circle with a chapter on improvised rescue and prevention of accidents. All advanced climbers need preplanning and fallback plans. In fact, it is the understanding of these self-rescue and rescue avoidance methods that can make it reasonable to push the limits on advanced objectives in the first place. We'll explore the simplest, yet efficient and effective, methods, with pared-down takes on standard guide techniques made appropriate for individual climbing teams.

While the chapters of this book are separated into the classical specialties—to present different skill sets unique to each genre of rock climbing—much of what *Advanced Rock Climbing* is about is applicable across all specialties in climbing. Today, the world's best boulderers are doing the hardest big wall free climbs, the strongest sport climbers are redpointing the hardest trad climbs, and the strongest free climbers are pushing the limits in alpine terrain. The objective danger is obviously higher in some types of climbing, but the skills are applicable across the board and aspiring hardmen and hardwomen will do well to learn from all the genres.

I started climbing in the 1970s as a young boy with my father, a mountain guide, so was fortunate to learn from a wide range of world-class climbers and guides. By age fourteen, I was guiding rock and alpine routes. The mentorship was incredible—but I learned from climbers of the generation who largely believed that "the leader must not fall." Which also meant, the leader should rarely, if ever,

The new school of hard climbing is blurring the lines between climbing specialties and combining the strengths of each genre to push the sport into entirely new realms.

risk a fall. This was for good reason. Bolts were of minimal climbing strength, there were no camming devices for protection, and even bouldering was sketchier without crash pads. In watching the development of sport climbing, the increased popularity of bouldering, the invention and prolifera-tion of rock gyms, the introduction of crash pads and advances in equipment, and the incredible feats of the world's best climbers, I realized that the spirit of the sport hasn't really changed much at all. The visionaries have always been equally rad. What has changed today is that far more people have discovered the rewarding practice of rock climbing, the sport has become much more popular, and technology and technique have made climbing safer.

"I draw upon my experience, but there's always new information coming out. I try to take tidbits of people's technique and see what works for me."

Emily Harrington

My motivation in writing this book was to take some tangible practices of the world's best climbers and make them available to anyone who aspires to leave the plateau and improve. *Advanced Rock Climbing* is aimed squarely at two kinds of climbers: first, it is for intermediate climbers who want to move from an intermediate to an advanced level and become comfortable on longer climbs of more sustained difficulty; and second, it is for advanced climbers who want to push their game to a new, even higher standard and experience some of the world's biggest, hardest, and most beautiful climbs.

HOW TO USE THIS GUIDE

"When I was learning to climb I read Freedom of the Hills, *and it was great. But to climb hard properly, I had to unlearn two-thirds of it."*

Alex Honnold

There may be nothing more important in a potentially high-risk sport like climbing than to drill the basics backward, forward, and inside out. Then, as Alex says, you have to unlearn part of all that and replace it with an entirely new way of looking at the game. Having the solid base is what allows you to go beyond it. But this book is about the parts of the basics you need to unlearn and the techniques to integrate in place of the basics if you really want to excel—and excel safely. If climbing were music, advanced rock climbing is free jazz, improv, and jamming. And as with music, before you can develop your own style, you must be accomplished in the basics.

It is also very worth reading through the groundwork publications of legendary climbing instructional authors like Craig Luebben, John Long, and Royal Robbins to see how our sport has progressed and changed and yet how much that is vital and elemental has remained the same. This book builds on the work done by these authors and requires that the reader already have at least an intermediate level of climbing skill and understanding.

This book is not for beginners! As noted, we assume you are already at least an intermediate climber and well versed in the climbing basics. For example, knots and techniques well explained in other climbing books or online are not covered in detail; we show a single photo of the finished knot or anchor setup instead, to focus on the pros and cons of using each. Several of the lesser-known techniques are broken down into steps, but even with these, an understanding of the basics is assumed.

Before using the techniques explained here, you must first become intimately familiar with the fundamental, textbook methods of climbing. *Before you break the rules, take shortcuts, and use equipment outside of manufacturer recommendations—you must first learn to follow the rules, avoid shortcuts, and understand the manufacturer recommendations.*

This book is not for cutting-edge athletes only! Only a few climbers need to know how to free climb one or two El Cap routes in a day. But the techniques used by these athletes can make the rest of us better, safer, more accomplished and capable climbers. We can return from our own climbs before the afternoon thunderstorms, we can bag multipitch routes after work, and we can do more than we ever thought possible. Of course, elite climbers can learn from these advanced methods too; but anyone who has learned the basics and aspires to be an expert climber will find incredible benefit from studying this book.

This book does not follow the rules! The methods shown in the following pages break, or at least bend, many of the common climbing instructional rules. Climbers have a long tradition of improvisation and creativity and bending and breaking the rules and common practices of the sport. The first portaledges were lawn chairs slung with webbing and suspended from the wall; the first nuts were machine nuts with the threads filed out and slung with cord; the first wide crack protection was cut from blocks of wood or forged from the legs of a stove; hooks and beaks designed for aid climbing have held free climbing falls; original rigid-stem cams were threaded in ways for which they were not intended in order for the cams to be strong in a horizontal placement; and the first lightweight pitons were made from pieces of wood. In fact, the evolution of climbing has been in part driven by the creativity of climbers using gear and equipment in unprecedented and unapproved ways. On top of pushing the technical limits of equipment, climbers have shattered the philosophical "rules" over and over. Simul-climbing, climbing in the dark, pulling on gear if the going gets hard, hangdogging, rehearsing, placing bolts for protection, and free soloing have all bent the rules and changed the game in dramatic ways.

Rules aside, this book will make you a safer climber in more disparate situations. Rather than focus on making your climbing systems look like what you see in the pages of textbooks, you'll focus on making your systems appropriate to the situation. Rather than assuming the rope will keep you safe, you'll make decisions that keep you safe. There will be times it will be safer to climb without a rope; safer to use gear in ways for which it was not designed; safer to simul-climb rather than set up a belay at a poor anchor; safer to take shortcuts in areas with a wide margin for safety so that you will have time to work parts of the climb with narrow safety margins—safely. There will be belays where you need far more than three pieces to make a good anchor, and others where a single bomber piece will make a perfect belay anchor for the situation—such as on ledges or in steep terrain at the start of routes where many teams don't place any anchors at all.

This book is for teams, not just for individuals! The methods shown in this book can certainly be applied on an individual level. But many of these more advanced techniques are built around the climbing team, not just the leader. The communication methods, the rope systems, the advanced belay techniques, the improvised anchors, and self-rescue know-how all are aimed at a team working together. This aspect of this book also differs from the guiding and instructional standards well-known up to this point. Classic guiding and climbing technique is designed for an experienced leader climbing with one or

Learning new techniques can make you stronger and more confident on more types of climbs.

more partners who are beginners. While an experienced leader will certainly benefit from the skills and philosophy covered in this book, the material in *Advanced Rock Climbing* will be most beneficial if undertaken as a team effort—an effort between you and your strongest partners.

The skills in this book need to be practiced! As Alex Honnold says, "By the time you use these techy techniques, it should seem like second nature." You don't want to go out on the biggest climb you've ever done and experiment for the first time with the techniques in this book. Instead, you want to practice these skills on smaller, easier climbs until you are familiar with their practical uses and probable limitations and you become efficient in the systems. We don't often think of world-class climbers spending time on lowly moderate routes, but the reality is that many of the world's best climbers have done hundreds or thousands of moderate climbs and several of the climbers interviewed for this book emphasized the importance of spending time on moderate terrain. Practice and time on rock is so important to the safe application of advanced climbing skills that an aspiring hardman or hardwoman will do well to back off from their limit, crank up the mileage, and spend some days doing ten or twenty moderate pitches while practicing the advanced skills in this book, rather than exclusively working one or two hard pitches as is so popular today.

A great coach once told me: *If you're going to add a new technique, your game is going to get worse at first—but then you'll get better than you ever were before.* This is true in many sports, but in climbing the focus on performance isolates us to the learning that is available at a given difficulty level. If you are a 5.11 climber, you probably spend most of your time on 5.10 and 5.11—missing the opportunity to learn from long, beautiful 5.8 climbs. Conversely, gym-trained young climbers are able to go climbing outside for the first time with such incredible power and endurance that they enter the trad or sport climbing game at very high levels without climbing much moderate terrain at all. It is not uncommon for a gym-trained climber to redpoint 5.12 outdoors before they ever climb a 5.9. Sure, the 5.12 is way harder, but 5.9 can improve speed, movement, and intuition in ways that are difficult to find on 5.12.

On the other hand, climbing only moderate routes will also limit your climbing. If you want to excel at rock climbing, you need to play around on terrain that is harder than anything you've ever climbed and push yourself beyond your perceived limits. The skills revealed in this book will allow you to feel more comfortable getting in over your head in terms of pure difficulty. Knowing how to improvise a mid-pitch retreat, how to use a few simple aid climbing moves to cheat past sections that are too difficult, and how to accurately assess the risk and commitment of a climb regardless of the grade will make it far more comfortable for you to try a climb much harder than anything you've ever done before.

This book will change the way you look at climbing. Like a health practitioner who learns the function of individual body parts as preamble to discovering the interrelationship between the parts, by the time you read through this book, and practice these skills on dozens of pitches, you will no longer look at climbing skills as singular techniques that exist in isolation from each other but rather as interconnected and complete systems dependent on no one element alone.

This book will not make climbing absolutely safe. (Nothing can.) In *Rock Climbing: Mastering Basic Skills,* both Craig and I included a list of the most fundamental elements of climbing safety. Blunders are equally important to avoid, regardless of your experience, skill level, or finger strength. While every other aspect of this book moves beyond the basics, the basics of staying safe as you climb remain the same. (These are the rules you don't want to bend.) Seven rules to live by:

- Always make sure your harness is completely buckled and your knot is tied.
- Always tie a knot in both ends of the rope when climbing and use a backup when rappelling.
- Make sure you are clipped into an anchor-quality system or that you are on belay at all times.
- Don't trust any piece of fixed gear (even preplaced quickdraws and bolts) without first looking at all gear with a critical eye.
- Don't make a habit of putting just one piece of gear between you and severe

consequences—even while sport climbing.

- Don't make a habit of risking extremely long falls, with or without a rope, even on easy terrain.
- Belay like your partner's life depends on it—for indeed it does.

This book will make climbing more fun, challenging, lively, and enjoyable. In the end, this is what it's all about. Following a rigid set of protocol in any outdoor adventure, especially climbing, isn't as exhilarating as improvising, being flexible, and adjusting technique and mind-set to fit the situation. In many ways, if we were to compare climbing to its sister gravity sport—skiing—climbing is where skiing was in the 1970s and '80s, when ski racing (running gates with specific, rigid technique) was the only game in town for skiers interested in the most advanced performance. Yet on the elite fringe, an entirely different game was being developed: free skiing and the unlimited creativity and interaction with the natural environment that comes with it. The techniques shown in this book will do for the fun of climbing what the big mountain free-skiing revolution has done for the fun of skiing.

The mind shifts to be found in the following pages include:

- A more creative approach to technique and sequence
- Ways to easily adapt to both longer and shorter pitches than suggested by the guidebook
- Ways for the belayer to catch the leader softly and to strategically adjust the length of the climber's fall
- What can make seemingly perfect protection fail
- How easy it can be to break or unintentionally unclip from a carabiner
- How the location of an anchor can dramatically affect the safety of the next pitch
- Why performance is so much more than just training
- Why taking strategic risks can be safer than attempting to take no risk
- When to go for it and when to hold back.
- A greatly diversified definition of a "belay"
- When to use gear as it's designed to be used—and when to bend or break the rules

"It's ok to be afraid. Pushing fear back has never worked for me – work on it, accept it, understand it."

Emily Harrington

Studying the technique, art, and capability of the world's best climbers doesn't require climbing at their level. It means climbing better than you ever dreamed. It means going up long climbs with the confidence to finish the climb in the daylight or being comfortable completing it in the dark. It means picking climbs for your team with the knowledge that you have the skills to give everyone the best chance to have a good time and stay safe throughout. It means handling unknown situations or minor epics with a toolkit and a perspective that allow you to safely operate outside the guidebook or textbook recommendations. It means being comfortable changing plans mid-move, mid-climb, mid-day, or mid-trip to do something safer, more rewarding, and more suitable for you and your partner.

Climbing with the technique and philosophy of the world's best means being the most competent, versatile, adaptable, and safest climber and climbing partner you can be.

While I was writing this book on the methodology unique to advanced climbing, and interviewing some of the world's greatest climbers in the process, this endeavor became more than a compilation of techniques. It evolved into a quest to explain what it takes to excel in the vertical arena. Researching and writing this book has made me a better climber; I hope reading it will do the same for you.

WARNING! READ THE FOLLOWING BEFORE USING THIS BOOK

Climbing is a dangerous sport. You can be killed or seriously injured while rock climbing. No book can describe or predict all the hazardous and complex situations that can occur while rock climbing, and the techniques described here are not appropriate for all climbing situations.

This book is intended to supplement formal, competent instruction. Do not rely on this book as your primary source of rock climbing information—a simple misinterpretation could be disastrous. Climbing safely requires good judgment based on experience, competent instruction, and a realistic understanding of your personal skills and limitations. Even if you do everything right you can still be injured or killed.

This book contains only the personal opinions of the author. The author and publisher make no warranties, expressed or implied, that the information contained in this book is accurate or reliable, and they are not responsible for any adverse consequences resulting directly or indirectly from information contained in this book. Use of this book implies that you understand the inherent dangers in rock climbing and assume responsibility for your own climbing actions, risks, and safety.

Opposite: *Steve Monks, inches from the summit of Castleton Tower, Utah*

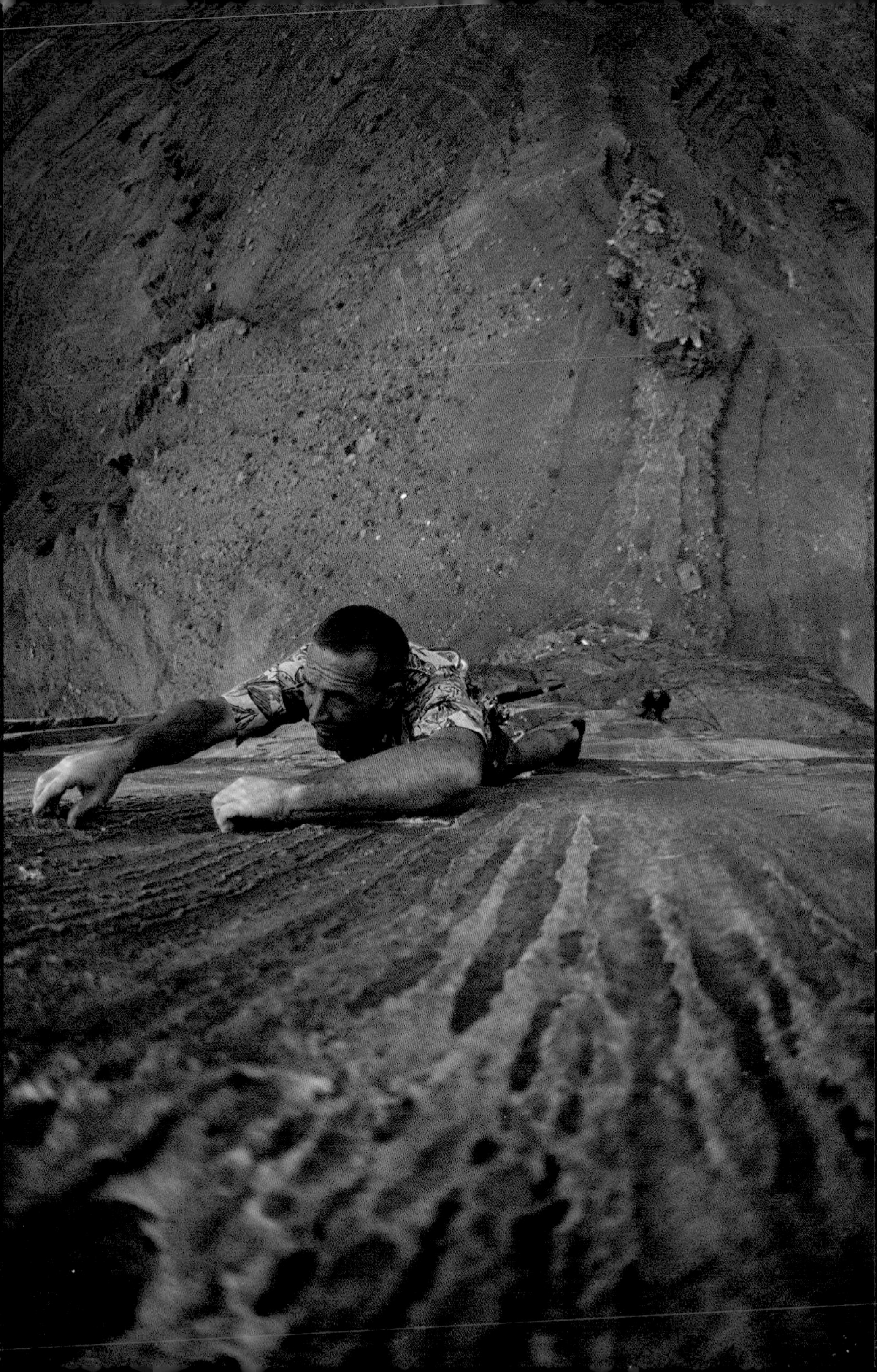

CHAPTER 1

Face Climbing

"Think of your entire body like a hand. Learn to climb in a really three-dimensional style. Use your head, shoulders, knees, everything."

Tommy Caldwell

To explain advanced face climbing skills in a book is similar to explaining how to perform a complicated dance like the tango; printed words and still photographs are clumsy ways to convey motion. The philosophy of motion, however, can be mentally learned through reading. It's then up to the reader to go out and put the philosophy into physical practice. The unlimited variety of possible moves dictated by the rock, in combination with the flowing energy of a climber moving powerfully with just a few points of contact, make face climbing the most dance-like of all types of climbing.

As beginners most of us viewed climbing as a mechanical series of correct body positions held in place by correct hand and footholds. We progress as climbers to learn that the act of climbing is much more like a monkey swinging through the trees in a succession of continuous motion than it is a robotic series of stilted positions. It is in this movement where the magic of hard climbing happens.

Yet the motion can be hard to see. To those watching, climbing seems an almost static sport. Despite moments of all-points-off dynos and other dramatic moves, much of the movement of the sport is subtle and self-contained. When a skilled climber moves, the shift of hips and spine, followed by shoulders, arms, and finally fingertips can be almost invisible from a spectator's view. But inside the climber, muscles and momentum are flowing like water. That meditative movement is partly why we love to climb. It also explains why climbing has never really caught on as a spectator sport—most of the game happens on the *inside.*

Watching a great climber dance their way up a face of water-, ice-, or wind-sculpted stone is a thing of beauty: the power, grace, and discipline, the smooth motion of the muscles shifting under the skin, the aesthetics of the cliff. And it's while climbing faces that most of us fall in love with climbing. (Of course, crack climbs can be inspiring too, but it takes a bit more of a connoisseur to find the beauty in wedging yourself between sharp edges of unforgiving rock.) Face climbing is also a mandatory skill for hard crack climbing, and quite often the crux of a crack climb is a few moves of difficult face climbing where the crack becomes almost entirely unusable.

Any climber who wants to advance in the sport will do well by paying their dues at a world-class face climbing area. Kentucky's Red River Gorge, Colorado's Rifle, California's Tuolumne Meadows, and Nevada's Red Rocks all are great places to hone face climbing skills. And anyone who wants to master face climbing should visit its epicenter, the incomparable limestone crags of southern Europe. However, "face climbing" is incredibly diverse, and the skills needed to ascend faces are as remarkably varied as the rock comprising those faces. A test piece face in Tuolumne is as different from a face climb in the Red River Gorge as an off-width in Indian Creek is from a boulder problem in Hueco Tanks. Yet, while most climbers prefer one style of rock and route over another, it is hugely beneficial to practice both steep and slabby face climbs.

No matter the angle of the rock, bouldering—ideally with climbers who are better than you—is the best way to learn face climbing skills. The close-to-the-ground action makes it much easier for you to play with movement and to study how other climbers move, use holds, and apply power to get through difficult sections. Trying the same moves multiple times and learning to execute difficult sequences is also easier when you're near the ground than when you're fiddling with gear and distracted by exposure on a high, roped climb. These are

the reasons why, for forty years, climbers have considered bouldering the ideal training for climbing. However, bouldering doesn't teach you everything you need to know to be a skilled face climber. It's also important to learn pace, resting, efficiency on easier terrain, mental endurance, and how to quickly read rock sequences. These are skills best learned by climbing many hundreds of long pitches right near your onsight limit.

Face climbing is how most of us are introduced to climbing, and due to the enormous number and variety of climbable faces around the world, face climbing is the most popular style of climbing. The skills needed for climbing sheer walls, overhanging caves, and smooth slabs are climbing's foundation: applying solid footwork, using handholds in creative and efficient ways, reading sequences, developing rock awareness, knowing how to channel powerful movement, using the friction potential of the rock, and understanding your own unique body dimensions and power are all best learned by face climbing.

FOOTWORK

"Footwork. That's one thing that's hard to get through training. You gotta just go climbing. Spend time on technical terrain."
Tommy Caldwell

When photos and videos of a young Chris Sharma first appeared in climbing media, climbers were skeptical. Commonly overheard comments included: "He doesn't

Practice looking over a shoulder to see your footholds from a better angle—looking straight down underneath you provides a limited angle of view.

swinging, carrying momentum, and finding balance in the wildest of motions.

Coaching for basic climbing footwork includes trusting each foothold, placing each foot precisely and then not moving that foot as you weight it, and trying to get as much weight as possible on the feet at all times with as much of the body's weight oriented over the feet as you can. For hard climbing, these fundamentals become even more important because small holds become increasingly difficult to trust and handholds get too small to always use with arm and finger power alone. Fortunately, there are a few footwork techniques that are unique to advanced climbing.

Use your feet like a ballerina en pointe—on the tip of the toe for maximum versatility, reach, and power.

even use his feet!" "His footwork sucks!" "How does he climb so hard?" Obviously, Chris got better at using his feet, but he never gave up on his signature climbing style, and in the process showed us a better way to move: a way that isn't limited to always needing to keep both hands and feet on the rock. Channeling Chris, we use a leg or arm more like the tail of a monkey,

Feet supporting center: Use core tension to adjust the hips away from the rock on slabs, directly over the feet on vertical, or tucked in over the feet on overhanging rock. In each case, keep body weight over the feet as much as possible.

FOOT POWER

It is easy to equate climbing power with the upper body. Get very far into a sustained section of footwork-intensive climbing, however, and the power of the lower body becomes critical. One of the physical aspects that differentiates experienced climbers from greenhorns is the strength of the feet. As beginners, we are using holds that are big enough that we can often simply stand on them as if we're on a small ledge. As the holds get smaller, however, it becomes necessary to press our feet onto much smaller holds, using toe, foot, and leg power combined with body angle to maintain pressure on a really small patch of rock.

To best channel foot power, you want to move beyond the concept of simply standing on your feet to use them far more dynamically and powerfully. Some mental visuals to consider in developing powerful footwork include:

- Use positive edges as if you are trying to pull the holds off the rock with your toes.
- On different angles of rock, adjust your hips to put more weight over your feet as shown in the illustration above.
- Use pockets and depressions aggressively, almost as if you are digging or screwing your toes into the hold.
- Press with power and precision comparable to an *en pointe* ballet move where the dancer stands with full body weight on the very tips of the toes.
- Use core strength to keep your weight centered over your feet, even if your

body is off to one side or you are faced not directly into, but to one side or the other of, the rock.

THE SWEET SPOT

"You should be able to determine where you want your feet without even looking at them. After you've decided where you want your feet, then look for a foothold at that spot."

Justen Sjong

On the terrain we learn to climb on and in climbing gyms there are usually footholds of some sort. On harder terrain on natural rock, there are many passages without any significant footholds at all, or footholds in places where they are difficult to use. A section of rock requiring a lieback is an obvious example: Every climber just leans back and walks their feet up the wall, using sweet spots—rather than any specific footholds—that best fit them and their body dimensions. The less obvious occasions when placing the foot in the sweet spot helps immensely include:

- High steps, where smearing one foot on a poor or nonexistent hold allows you to get your other foot onto a better, higher hold.
- Sections with poor handholds, where you can still smear a foot against a blank section of rock in just the right spot to make the handholds usable.
- On dynamic moves, where you're jumping off one foothold like a sprinter starting a race, and the other foot just goes in the sweet spot rather than on any particular hold.

- In opposition to other holds as in a stem: When there is a good hold facing left, many times all you need is something to push against to the right, even if it is just a smooth face.

One of the biggest differences between 5.9 footwork and 5.12 footwork is this: *It's more important for a foot to be in the right place relative to your body than it is for your foot to be on the biggest hold!*

Setting up, with your feet in the right spot for the next move (rather than the current move), is a key to unlocking harder moves.

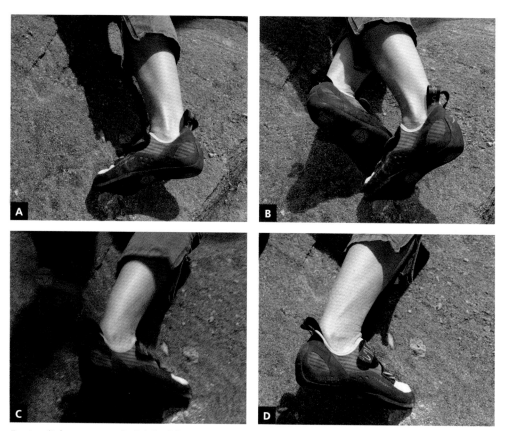

Foot switch sequence: A. Original foot position. B. Position new foot directly above original foot.
C. Hop slightly, pulling the original foot off the hold while dropping the new foot into position.
D. Stand fully on the hold.

EXPERIMENT

*"Watch climbers who have better footwork
than you do. Watch how they move. Then
try to move like they do."*

Sonnie Trotter

When watching someone with excellent
footwork their first time on a climb, it
often appears as if they know exactly what
they are going to do next—as if they've
been there before. In reality, they are
often experimenting with foot positions
as they go, adjusting their feet to better
reach handholds, switching feet frequently
to adjust balance, and trying one foothold
before moving to another. They move with

conviction from one foothold to the next, but experimentation is part of the dance.

In fact, experienced climbers are very good at experimenting as they go. Don't get caught in the trap of thinking that solving a difficult sequence is set in stone. *Like Tommy says at the beginning of this chapter, use your whole body like a hand.* On our first day on the rock, most of us quickly learn to experiment with hand position to most effectively grasp holds, but it is much less intuitive to experiment with body position when moving to and through those holds. The direction your body faces, the parts of your body touching the rock, the order in which you move your limbs, and how you use core strength to move are often more important than which specific holds are used.

Long-ingrained muscle memories often prevent us from moving differently. This is why so many climbers are stuck in a square-to-the-wall approach, toes pointing to either side, reaching only for straight-up holds, and struggling with holds off to one side or the other. It's also why climbers end up stuck in the same grade. To break out of this habit, climb with both feet pointing the same direction and hips turned slightly away from the wall, switching directions when it seems appropriate. Whenever possible, try to avoid the old standby of standing with both feet splayed outward. Experimenting with radical positions

FOOT SWITCH

Anyone who has been climbing, even once, has found themselves with the wrong foot on the right hold. Quite often it's easy to switch feet, but a foot switch can appear difficult at first. Sometimes, a tricky section of climbing requires switching feet twice on the same hold to execute the move. There are several different approaches to executing a quick and efficient foot switch.

- **Stutter Step**—Advance the offending foot, the one that's hogging the good hold, slightly higher (often just onto a sweet spot), and bump the lower foot onto the good hold.
- **The Twist**—Rotate one foot off of the hold while the other foot rotates into position. Rotating the entire lower body, just as you would in the 1960s Twist dance move, helps transition the weight fully onto the other foot.
- **The Hop**—It's amazing what you can do with rock shoes! Jump up, move the first foot off the hold, and land on the hold with the second foot.
- **Inside/Outside**—Flipping your foot, moving from the inside to the outside of the foot or vice versa, can also make all the difference in the world. A quick foot switch allows you to about face, helping you to use the handholds far more effectively or even to reach holds that at first seemed too far away.

A playful, experimental approach to climbing is a common trait among top climbers.

helps you to adjust your ingrained muscle memory, to calibrate your body dynamics and reach, to look at sequences with a more open mind, to break the habit of climbing in a rigid style—and to climb way harder.

FOOTWORK DRIVES REACH

"Don't just put your foot on a hold randomly. Look at the hold clearly, check the angle of the hold, and consider how you need to use it."

Lynn Hill

"If only I could get my hands on that hold!" We've all said it, looking longingly at some thank-God hold in the distance. Well, the first question to ask is not which hold do I need to grab first to reach that target handhold but instead, *where do my feet need to be to get me to that handhold?*

Once you've determined where your feet need to be, the hand sequence often follows intuitively. Try to get there with hands only, and you won't get very far. This may seem obvious, but I see climbers of all skill levels struggling with moves simply because they are trying to reach higher before first moving their feet higher. Though a big reach can save the day, overextending causes problems on all angles of rock.

Pushing the limits of reach on overhanging rock

- On overhanging rock, reaching too far positions your limbs far from your center of balance, so that when you finally do move your feet, your whole body swings like a pendulum, potentially ripping your hands off the holds—unless those holds are very good (and you are very strong).

- On vertical rock, reaching too far results in not being able to move your feet because your body is plastered against the rock, and you can neither see the next footholds nor can you bend your knees to step higher because the rock is in the way.

- On slabby, low-angle rock, reaching too far changes the angle of pressure on your feet from directly down and powerfully over, to outwardly angled and potentially off, sloping, small holds.

HANDHOLDS

"Changing how you climb is all about subtleties: subtleties of body position, alignment, and the coordination of push-pull forces between the holds."

Lynn Hill

Using the hands and upper body is the most intuitive of all climbing techniques. Put a five-year-old on the rock and they will immediately adjust their hand to match the shape of the hold. The basic face climbing techniques for using handholds are crimp, open hand, pinch, finger pocket, undercling, sidepull, mantle, and gaston. (If you're unfamiliar with any of these techniques, consult *Rock Climbing: Mastering Basic Skills*.)

On difficult terrain these basic hand techniques form the foundation for face climbing—and familiarity and practice with the basics is essential. But to advance into higher levels of difficulty, you must focus more on how you orient and move your

Thumdercling

Piano move

Fingernails

Backhand

Subtle mantle

body *relative* to the holds, and you must train your hands for the kind of climbing you plan to do. There are several handy, less intuitive, advanced tricks for using handholds that go beyond the basics. They include the thumdercling, piano move, fingernail, backhand, and subtle mantle.

LIGHT TOUCH

On our first encounter with a hard move, we grab the hold as tightly as we can, flexing our finger joints, wrist, elbow, and shoulder to put as much pressure on the hold as we can muster. It doesn't take long for this method to sap our energy and turn our arms to Jell-O. Next, we learn to use our feet better to take more of the weight; but we still hold on with a flexed posture in our arms and hands. Finally, we learn to use the minimum musculature necessary to maintain grip and execute the move. It is here, in applying our muscles as little as possible and incorporating our skeleton as much as possible, that we can most improve our efficiency at using handholds.

HAND STRENGTH

"It's easier to have good technique when you're strong."

Christian Griffith

Hand strength takes a long time to develop. (Consult Chapter 13, Performance, for specific methods to increase hand strength.) Specific training, ideally in a gym or on a hangboard, is the fastest way to develop hand strength. If you don't have access to a climbing gym, or just prefer to climb outside, climbing frequently and changing the ways you hold onto the rock will pay great dividends in hand strength.

The Holy Grail of hand strength is open hand contact strength. Though harder to develop, open hand contact strength is superior to crimp power in many situations. Climbers with good open hand contact strength have an advantage over climbers who only or always crimp, because an open hand position:

- Allows you to grasp the same holds using less force than crimping.

- Puts the hand and tendons in a less injury-prone position than a crimp because of the reduced leverage and because the climber's weight is supported by bone more than by connective tissue.
- Adjusts to more varieties of holds than does the crimp position.
- Puts more skin in contact with the rock, increasing friction and "stickiness" and decreasing the need for power.

There is certainly a place for both crimping and open hand strength, but most climbers become strong at crimping long before they develop strong open hand technique. To improve at open hand climbing takes work:

- Climb warm-ups and easy terrain while grasping every hold with an open grip. Save your crimp power for the cruxes!
- Use your feet with conviction—solid footwork supports relaxed hand positions.
- On every hold, take a moment to position your hand so the natural edges of the hold match the natural bends in your fingers.
- As part of your warm-ups and cool-downs, make sure to practice backward wrist curls and other hand exercises to help protect against possible tendon damage.

Crimping can be powerful, but it also creates leverage that can waste hand strength and increase the risk of tendon injury.

Practice an open hand grip for maximum efficiency and to conserve power.

SPEED-READING BY BRAILLE

When you grab a hold for the first time, you may need to weight the hold immediately. If possible, once you've established yourself on the hold, feel around to find the most efficient and useful way to grasp the hold. Even just a dimple where you can place a fingertip can add to the security of the hold and reduce the amount of energy needed to hang on. Also, by exploring the entirety of a hold, you may learn how useful (or not) the hold will be for resting, switching hands, and planning the next sequence.

It's a delicate balance, however, between spending time feeling each hold, and making a decision and taking a position to move quickly and efficiently. When onsighting, great climbers will quickly feel around on some of the holds, while using others in the very first spot they touch. The best way to practice this is to develop a habit of speed-reading by braille. Don't waste time and energy fondling every hold over and over; a quick tactile scan of a hold will often reveal much more than meets the eye.

- Don't let tick marks fool you—they might be on the best spot, but quite often people tick a hold before they are sure of the very best spot. Also, differences in hand size and strength between climbers, and even the difference in length between your own fingers, can challenge you to hang onto a hold differently than other climbers. Do it your way.
- Take advantage of restful stances to feel the holds around you.

Changing the orientation of your body on the same holds can allow you to use the holds in entirely different ways. With a bolt clipped waist-high, feel free to experiment.

▦ Consider how the hold will feel at the beginning and the end of a move—an undercling may feel terrible at first contact, but once you've moved your feet and body up toward it, it may be the best option you have.

▦ When the climbing gets really hard, to the point that you can barely hang onto the very best parts of the very best holds, you may need to actually weight the hold, not just braille it, to determine which part of the hold is better for you.

MENTAL MOMENTUM

There is much more to learning to climb with momentum than just the physics of movement. There is the enormous mental benefit. On long climbs, mental momentum comes from utterly crushing the first hard pitch, giving you an inner boost for the pitches ahead. On a day of sport cragging, this can mean being so efficient on the warm-up that you have to do another warm-up to get your blood flowing. On a single pitch or even a boulder problem, mental momentum comes by flowing through an opening sequence better than you ever have before.

There's also a long-term benefit to developing mental momentum. Working through the fear of falling gives you the confidence to more quickly work through the fear next time. Playing around on a climb far beyond your ability can give you incredible mental strength on climbs within your comfort zone the next time. See Chapter 13,

Performance, for further discussion on the mental aspect of climbing.

ROCK AWARENESS

One big difference between intermediate climbers and advanced climbers is that advanced climbers are aware of the rock features all around them at all times, even the holds and features they don't use. As a climber looking to develop advanced skills, you're probably already aware of nearly all of the fundamental techniques for using big rock features, including stems, liebacks, mantels, and heel hooks. The tricky part is recognizing the rock features, that allow such moves.

Rock features are not always obvious. A slight angle change to the left or right can offer a place to stem or rest, or offer the solution to a difficult problem. A roof can deliver the crux, but with a bit of creativity a roof can also offer a rest because it gives you something to press against that is not just another hand- or foothold. Push a shoulder against it. Undercling below it. Throw a kneebar into it. Even a half-inch corner 6 feet away can provide respite from a grueling section of power-endurance climbing. A sloping shelf, if you trust the friction of your shoes on the rock, can deliver a no-hands rest in the most improbable of places. Noticing a subtle scoop, even just a few degrees of opposing rock, or an equally subtle arête can often make the difference between a proud send and a pathetic wilt onto the rope.

A good rule of thumb is to always pay attention to every detail of the rock that is a full wingspan on either side of you. For sport climbing, this helps you to anticipate changes in difficulty and to plan ahead on sequences. For trad climbing, this not only helps in the gymnastics of the climbing, but also helps with routefinding, looking for protection, and noticing potential hazards like loose rock.

Rock awareness also allows you to read the path of ascent. Climbs don't always go straight up. In fact, even the climbs that follow a perfect vertical line usually deviate to the left and right in regards to the distribution of holds. Look for places where better holds can be found a body length to one side or the other of the main route. Even the most popular climbs, coated with chalk and riddled with tick marks, can have several variations—one of which is usually the easiest.

MAXIMIZING FRICTION

One of the best-kept secrets in hard climbing is that hard climbers—when they get to a new area or an area they haven't been to for a while—will experiment on warm-up pitches by using the smallest, most sloping, and improbable holds they can find. Not that they burn extra energy in testing the holds; rather, they relax their hands and max out the limits of their shoes' stick to the rock in order to dial in their estimation of friction. It is critical to become versed in the friction coefficient of a particular crag or even route; and big positive

holds will not tell you nearly as much about friction as the small, sloping holds.

BODY DIMENSIONS

A phenomenon of the sport of rock climbing is that it teaches us the precise dimensions of our bodies like nothing else, but it takes concerted effort to calibrate you brain to match your body. To climb hard face moves you need to dial in your body awareness to the point that you know *exactly* how far you can extend your fingertips while standing on your tiptoes—I'm not talking numerical measurements, but the ability to look ahead and know precisely how far you can really reach, and to look to the side and know how far you can really stem.

Beginning climbers often reach too far, skipping holds that make a section easier. They also often don't reach far enough. Either way, you have to know your own body's dimensions to make the choice.

Since it's difficult to use a hold right at the limit of our reach, advanced climbers tend to avoid the longest reaches when possible. Yet to move into really difficult climbing, we must look to the longest reaches we can possibly make. Grabbing a hold at full extension is as common in hard climbing as reaching for the chalkbag.

A problem is that most of us underestimate the absolute length of our reach. Even experienced climbers will look ahead and tell themselves, "I can't reach that hold." Then, after exhausting all other options (and their muscles), they try to reach the hold and, lo and behold, they *can* reach it!

To make your longest reach, be intimately aware of your own exact dimensions—and know how to take advantage of them.

The ability to judge accurately that a hold can be reached is one of the skills that differentiates good climbers from great climbers. This difference is so dramatic that often a shorter climber with better body awareness consistently makes *longer* reaches than a taller climber with less-tuned body awareness.

Articulation and body angle are the keys to maximizing reach. On the rock we are often positioned with most of our joints slightly articulated. We then try to extend one arm or one leg to reach a hold without extending the rest of our body. Watch a great climber extend to reach a hold and you'll see them adjust the articulation of their whole body like a cobra preparing to strike. They'll straighten backs and shoulders, elbows, wrists, knees, hips, ankles, down to even the smallest joints in their toes, to suddenly gain, like magic, several inches or more of additional reach.

To learn your dimensions while bouldering, have your spotter support you in toward the rock so you can extend fully to see if you can reach between the holds without having to support your entire weight. On a roped climb, consider aiding the next move by pulling on a bolt or the gear. Then, with the support of the rope above, try to position your body between the holds—you'll be amazed how your reach increases by having your body in the right position.

BEWARE YOUR EXCUSES

If you're shorter than average, you might be in the habit of repeating the mantra, "I'm too short to reach that hold." It might be true, but it can also become a self-fulfilling prophecy. If you recite your mantra of shortness before you've exhausted the options to reach the hold, you're only holding yourself back. While climbing with short climbers, I've seen this happen dozens of times. Yet once they move their feet up, they reach the hold, no problem. Then they have to admit, "I guess I can reach it." This psychological rollercoaster of always doubting your ability to reach a hold interferes with good climbing. Let it go. It's a rare climb that is truly impossible if you're short.

If you're taller than average, you might spend a lot of time getting overextended because you think you can reach past every difficulty. It sure must be fun to reach past sections where shorter people struggle. But the reality is that a long reach is no substitute for good technique, and becoming overextended at the wrong time has the same effect no matter how tall you are: it makes the climbing harder.

If you're weaker than average, you might spend a lot of time repeating the mantra, "If only I was stronger." On strenuous climbs, you end up expending energy trying to find work-arounds to avoid doing powerful moves, which results in even further reduced power. Instead, remember that on any given day you are as strong as you will be that day. You might as well just climb the best you can, move decisively and efficiently, and use the power you do have to its maximum potential.

If you're stronger than average, you probably don't use it as an excuse directly: but strength can also be a handicap because some people use it as an excuse for poor footwork and sloppy technique. If this is you, know that power alone will only take you so far. If you have loads of natural monkey power, seek out technical climbs, such as small-hold, smeary face climbs, that challenge your technical weaknesses, and you might just become a world-class climber.

Opposite: *Beth Rodden dressed for battle on* Anaconda *(5.13c), Lumpy Ridge*

CHAPTER 2

Crack Climbing

"Be willing to fail and fail and fail and to struggle and struggle and struggle, but once you learn crack climbing, you'll never forget it."

Sonnie Trotter

Face climbing is intuitive enough that even a three-year-old, without coaching or encouragement, can grab a series of face holds and go climbing. See hold. Grab hold. Pull on hold. Few sports get more primal or basic. Crack climbing is another matter entirely. With cracks, unlike faces, it appears at first that *you are climbing something that is not there*, a negative space. When you are face climbing, gravity lends the downward force that on many holds keeps your hand or foot on the rock; when you are crack climbing, your muscles and your technique are the opposing force that keeps you on the rock.

The complexity of forces, even on really easy crack climbing, is baffling. You have to push against the sides of the crack with enough pressure to overcome the constant downward pull of gravity using a relatively small part of your body. How do you get your hand to push in two directions at the same time? How do you jam your feet securely enough to hold your body weight but then in the next moment easily remove them from the crack?

Worse, just about the time you get the idea of how to climb a crack that fits your hands and feet perfectly: the crack changes size, the technique that was working doesn't work at all anymore, and the battle starts over again.

As you learn the basics of crack climbing and push into the harder grades, there becomes an immense overlap between the skills needed for face climbing and crack climbing. In fact, at the highest levels of difficulty, there is little reason to distinguish between the two. World-class sport climbers have been known to learn a few crack climbing basics and in just a few days go on to free climb El Cap or redpoint and even onsight the hardest cracks. It comes down to power, balance, precision, tenacity, movement, and finger strength—just as in face climbing.

As with most of the subjects covered in this book, with crack climbing we're starting from where basic instruction ends and going from there. To learn to climb cracks with advanced skills, it is important not only to learn advanced skills but to *execute basic technique with advanced effi-ciency.* So we'll start with the thinnest cracks and work our way to the widest chimneys, examining basic efficiency and advanced technique for each. We'll also cover gear, tape, and considerations for the leader in each category of crack.

SEAMS

"The best sport climbers make the best crack climbers."

Sonnie Trotter

Many of the hardest climbs of yesteryear were thin seams: cracks just wide enough to accept the thinnest protection and (some-times) fingertips. These wicked-thin crack climbs are still proud achievements that any climber would be happy to tick. Thin seams are where the line between face climbing and crack climbing is blurred the most, since seams are often little more than naturally protected face climbs. But there are still a few crack climbing skills that help even on the thinnest seams.

On many seams, the crack may be too thin to insert the fingers for a proper finger jam, but in places one edge of the crack will stick out farther than the other. This creates an offset that can be used for a creative pseudo-jam for both the hands and feet. For the hands, one sort of pseudo-jam is a thumb lever, useful where the crack opens slightly or where a vertical edge appears next to the crack. This is done by putting the fingers on the edge, or crimping the edge of the crack, and levering the thumb

Thumb lever

against the offset wall. Such an offset can also be used as a lieback. Note that before you commit to a lieback it's always a good idea to look ahead—if there are no good foot- or handholds and should the crack offset disappear, you'll find yourself stuck, with fading strength, fading holds, and no hope of letting go with either hand to place gear. Yup, the lieback to nowhere is a horri-fying experience.

For the feet, an offset edge can be pressed against, but it is often more effec-tive to do a sort of pseudo–foot jam against the offset wall. With a small hold or even slight angle change on one side, pressing the foot both onto the angle change and into the offset can create a surprisingly solid hold and turn a sphincter-tightening seam crux into a walk in the park. This method of opposing pressure to increase the security of a poor hold is a good tech-nique anytime the holds are tiny, but it is

Offset foot jam

easy to forget that you can oppose pressure on the bottom of the shoe by simply adding pressure to the side of the shoe.

The biggest problem with leading seams is that the protection is often extremely thin. Refer to Chapter 5, Traditional Gear Placement, for specific methods to maximize the security and strength of thin protection. But for long sections of thin gear, consider adjusting your racking method:

- If you know you're going to be placing a lot of micro and small nuts, rack them on single biners or singly on quickdraws to save fiddling with the racking biner and potentially dropping the cluster of small nuts.

- Place an upward, directional piece near the bottom of the seam and clip the rope in as close to the wall as possible to keep the rope pinned to the wall and prevent it from lifting outward on the small protection. This method can sometimes allow you to use single biners—rather than quickdraws—on each nut because it eliminates outward pull on each piece.

- If you know you'll be climbing sustained seams, carry an extra set of micro nuts

Leading a sustained seam can be one of the more intimidating forms of climbing.

Finger cracks are some of the most enjoyable of all crack sizes, combining crack and face climbing skills with the aesthetics of natural protection.

beyond what the guidebook recommends. Doubling up is the best way to increase the strength of a tiny placement. Micro nuts weigh next to nothing and when you want one you almost always want a whole lot more.

FINGERS

"When getting back to crack climbing after a season of sport climbing, my ligaments are tightened and crack climbing is painful. If you hate crack climbing because it hurts, do it more and it will become less painful. Give it time to let your ligaments do their thing. Then, when you're not in pain you can torque more and the climbing feels easier."

Sonnie Trotter

Finger cracks are technically the simplest to climb, and the most photographed and aesthetic of all the crack sizes. For the crack that is the perfect size for your fingers: stick 'em in and pull down—end of story. However, the cracks don't usually behave so well and it turns out that most of the hardest cracks in the world are finger cracks.

One of the difficulties with finger cracks is that, while the fingers may be locked in like a pit bull's jaw, the feet are scraping desperately. The second issue is that cracks are rarely perfect and do not provide perfect jams all along the crack length. Even at Indian Creek, land of the cartoon-perfect cracks, the rock has irregularities that make it much harder to jam with one hand than the other. The third issue is the challenge of placing gear: for even the strongest climbers, it's ridiculously strenuous to hang full body weight on even a perfect finger-lock and let go with one hand long enough to fiddle in a piece.

In the perfect world, with a perfect splitter finger crack, the most powerful jam is with the elbows out and thumbs pointed down for jam after jam to glory. We all know this rarely happens. Instead, something gets in the way. A corner juts out from one side of the crack, the crack angles slightly to one side, or a small variation between the two edges of the crack makes the thumbs-down jam useless.

To get past these places, use the thumbs-up jam strategically. Think of the thumbs-up as your secret weapon. Here's why: *the thumbs-up jam allows you to reach much, much farther than the thumbs-down jam.* To illustrate this, grasp the book you're holding with one hand, thumbs-down, and pinch it with the book held vertically. Then raise it as far as you can and lower it as far as you can before the book tips sideways or you start feeling really awkward. Now switch to thumbs-up and do the same thing. Feel it? With thumbs-down you can only move the book a couple of feet, right in front of your face, before it feels really wonky. With thumbs-up you can move it from ceiling to floor without feeling anatomically incorrect. In a crack, this means you can crank a thumbs-up jam all the way to your ankles if you need to, but a thumbs-down jam, while extremely powerful, has a very limited range. So . . . set yourself up with a thumbs-up jam at the top of the last good jam, and reach as far as your wingspan will take you.

SMEDJAMMING

For hard finger cracks, the combination of smearing, edging, and jamming is often the solution for getting some purchase with the feet. The trick to smedjamming is:

1. As high as you can step, tip the shoe vertically as if you were going to *edge* against the side of the crack.
2. Twist slightly, *smearing* your foot against the corner created by the edge of the crack. Don't twist too hard, or you'll lose it.
3. Press inward, *jamming* your foot against both edges of the crack.

Don't extend too far, or your feet will slip. Smedjamming requires inward pressure to work, and as you stand up tall, all your pressure is directed downward, which will blow out the hold on difficult terrain.

When leading any difficult-size crack, unless you're on a stance where you can extend comfortably, resist placing gear at the limit of your reach. It is far easier to place gear *below* your highest jam than it is to place it at the extension of your reach. Certainly there are times, like when there is a ledge below you or another hazard, when it is worth the extra effort to get the protection as high as possible. The rest of the time, fire the gear in right in front of you and get on with it!

OFF-FINGERS

"In the off-sizes, I'm just always thinking about the feet."

Steph Davis

Too big for finger jams but too small for hand jams, off-finger-size cracks are diabolically hard. The technique of smedjamming, as described in the previous section, is essential for this size crack because you can get a bit more rubber into the crack, which means less inward force is required to create a secure jam.

Sonnie's opening comment to the finger crack climbing section, about the need to warm up the ligaments for crack climbing, is especially applicable for the demands on feet in off-finger cracks. At first, the twisting of the ankles required for good foot purchase in these cracks feels anatomically awkward to the nth degree. Don't lose heart. Even stretching your ankles before the pitch will help, but a few shorter sessions in sustained hand

Thumb stack

cracks will get you there (and if you don't have cracks where you live, woman up for that sculpted crack in your local rock gym for some ligament stretching before your crack climbing road trip). Other suggestions to make off-fingers feel less impossible include:

- Think of a thumb stack as a fingerlock against your thumb. Try to relax your hand and let your finger twist secure the jam.
- For a finger stack, position your middle finger slightly above your index finger, then pull mostly on the middle finger so it wedges against the index finger.
- Practice using finger stacks and thumb stacks on easier terrain, when the footholds are good, so you will know how to use these techniques when there is no other option.

- Tape strategically: on the index finger, middle finger, and perhaps lower thumb knuckle.
- Don't wear shoes that cramp or bunch up your toes. A comfy slipper is the best shoe for off-fingers jamming because you can get the tips of your toes into the crack.

Three words describe a common strategy for leading off-finger-size cracks: Run. It. Out. This may hold true with any bad-size section of climbing. But if the off-size section isn't too long, and the fall is safe, the best way to crush this horrible size is to avoid placing gear in the middle of it. Place a piece (or two) as high as you can at your last good jam and carefully estimate how far you can safely go without placing gear. If the off-size section is so long that you must place pro in the middle of it, look for pods and footholds to place from. While an off-finger crack is by definition desperate, a slightly wider part can deliver a pretty good thin hand jam and an even better foot jam. Look ahead and go for it.

Footwork in thin cracks requires strong feet and attention to optimizing the subtle changes and variations in crack size.

THIN HANDS

"I mix my jams a lot—finger stack one hand, thin hands with the other. Then switch for awhile."

Alex Honnold

Thin hand cracks are where every crack climber with little hands sends their first 5.12. That's because most of these pitches aren't really 5.12 if you have small hands. The same is true for guys with huge hands on off-finger cracks who get solid finger locks where everyone else is thumb-stacking. My favorite climbing team for crack climbing is a group of three—a person with tiny hands who can lead the thin cracks, a person with huge hands for the meaty pitches, and someone with average hands for everything else. So as it relates here, we're talking about thin hands for *you*, not what the guidebook says.

Anyone who can hand jam can climb thin hand cracks. Much of the technique is the same, but the demand on efficiency and strategy increases. Many times, a wide finger stack will also fit a thin hand jam. Remember what Alex says about switching jams; changing it up allows you to use different muscles, which conserves energy and also increases your skill set diversity when the climbing gets more difficult.

Experiment with the half-jam, a method of aligning the side of your hand vertically and using only half of your hand in the crack. This can work thumbs-down, by expanding the fat part of your thumb pad tightly in the crack, but a half-jam is usually more secure and fits a slightly smaller crack with the thumbs up and out. To do a thumbs-out half-jam, slide the outer edge of your hand into the crack, then expand the meaty part of your hand below the pinky. For this method to work, you must keep your elbow flush with the rock; lifting the elbow will pop the jam like it was lifted with a crowbar. For this reason, the half-jam usually works best with the bottom hand.

Thin hand jams are desperate for the upper body but generally secure for the feet; so while leading thin hand sections, keeping one foot high and one foot low creates a leverage advantage. You can almost sit on the higher foot while the lower foot acts as a sort of cantilever. This is the position you want to be in to place gear. So, to place gear on thin hand cracks:

1. Find a spot with a slightly better hand jam—but don't place gear immediately!
2. Look down at your feet and raise one as high as is reasonable and see if you can get a jam that allows you to

For the thinnest cracks you can still fit your hands into, try to avoid using any tape at all to allow you to fit as much of your hand as possible into the crack.

sit with more of your weight on the high foot. There is a sweet spot—not too high so it tips you off the rock, but not too low so all your weight ends up on your hands.
3. Quickly shake out the hand you are about to hang from to place the gear.
4. Replace the most solid jam and fire in the piece and clip with the other hand.

Placing protection quickly, "on the fly," can be used in any sustained situation, trad or sport, where the holds are all similar; but it is particularly useful in sustained thin hand cracks because each hold tends to be equally poor. Placing gear while hanging from poor jams requires discipline and body awareness. It often works best to integrate the movements of placing the gear or clipping the bolt into the movement and flow of the climb instead of stopping in one position to execute the entire sequence of placing gear and clipping the rope. To most efficiently place gear in a strenuous thin hand crack:

1. Look ahead to anticipate the gear placement a move or two early.
2. As you climb past the placement, fire it in with one hand—but instead of clipping the rope immediately, move on to the next jam or handhold.
3. Pull the rope up and clip with the opposite hand with which you placed the piece.

This may seem like a minor change on paper, but on the rock it is significant; it effectively cuts in half the amount of time you must hang on one hand to place and clip each piece. Over the course of a long, sustained pitch, this makes a big difference. It also preserves momentum and encourages movement—keys to climbing hard.

HANDS

"Part of the painfulness of crack climbing is the fit of your shoes. What's the point of a really soft shoe if you can't jam in it?"
                                        Alex Honnold

Once you know how to do a hand jam, there is no more secure hold; even a huge jug requires more effort to hang onto than a perfect hand jam. Foot jams in hand cracks are almost too good—for beginning crack climbers, one of the lessons is to avoid placing the feet too deeply in the crack, which is tempting but impedes progress. With solid technique, hand cracks are so secure that they are a favorite among soloists and also can be perfect places for strategic

---

MICRO-REST

For the most continuous thin hand cracks, as well as other sustained cracks (and also sustained face climbing), a method for conserving energy is the micro-rest. This requires practice and discipline but can be extremely effective. To use a micro-rest:

- Develop an acute awareness of your body's energy output.
- When you are passing through a move requiring less energy, take advantage of it.
- Drop your arm and hand for a moment, even if the rest of your body is still making upward progress.
- If you can't drop the hand, even just opening your fingers gives your hand a split second of rest.
- In cracks, using a micro-rest gives your hand a moment of respite from the cramped position of jamming.

runouts to save gear for later on the pitch. Because the jams are so secure, the key to advanced hand crack method is typically not in making the jam stick, but in using the jams with as little effort as possible.

The hand jam is a misleading name, because you don't really "jam" the hand into the rock. This simple misnomer may be part of the reason why many inexperienced crack climbers find crack climbing so painful; they try to jam their hand as hard as they can when much less force is necessary. There are two actions that create the hand jam, and neither one of them is really a jam, but instead more of an expansion of the hand into a custom shape to fit the rock. Think of it more like blowing up a hand-size balloon inside the crack—not jamming the hand like a nut.

At the advanced level, there are two big mistakes strong climbers often make when climbing hand cracks. The first is that they overgrip each jam. The thing about jamming is that it takes place between two immobile walls of rock, so the strongest climber can quickly sap his or her energy by squeezing as hard as they can when only a small amount of pressure is enough. The second mistake is forgetting to release the jam entirely before rotating out of the jam to move up the crack. This creates unnecessary, cumulative friction with each move upward—not what you need on a long climb or hard pitch. To avoid this, consciously release each jam entirely before moving your hand up the crack.

Hand cracks can be a joy to climb, but they are still strenuous, and any way you can increase efficiency will help you. And

Tape protects the hands from rough cracks just as well as it ever has, but the high friction rubber of modern crack gloves makes it possible to jam in unlikely places and new, low-profile designs are gaining favor among even elite crack climbers.

while there are times you may need to reach high above a hand jam to place a piece, 90 percent of the time, if you are in a perfect hand crack, it is a colossal waste of energy to lock off and place the gear high above you. Do everything you can with straight arms.

- Always place gear hanging from a straight arm.
- Always chalk up hanging from a straight arm.
- Whenever possible, move your feet higher while hanging from a straight arm.

even a seemingly ideal crack insecure and difficult. Some rock types with great friction on the surface form smooth walls inside cracks with surprisingly poor friction. Water, completely nonexistent on the outside of the crack, can continue to run down the inside of cracks long after the last rain, creating a slippery trap for the unsuspecting leader. I speak from experience here, as on two separate occasions I have fallen out of perfect hand jams—once thanks to water and once, slippery stone on a humid day. Both occurred after I had logged many miles of climbing hand cracks, so inexperience was no excuse.

WIDE HANDS

"Go to Indian Creek and climb all the sizes—especially the off-sizes."

Tommy Caldwell

Wide hand cracks are the blue-collar labor of crack climbing—lots of work, unpleasant movement, tiring, sometimes painful, and no glory. But if you're going to be a well-rounded crack climber or get busy handling long routes, you'd better pay your dues in wide hand cracks.

The first and foremost thing to remember about wide hands is that there may be no more secure–size crack for the feet. In the most difficult sections it is possible to cantilever between the lower foot and the upper foot, carrying the support through your core to take weight off of your hands. In a wide hand crack, always use your feet like crazy.

Using straight arms whenever possible and relaxing a little with every move are the keys to succeeding at sustained crack pitches.

As mentioned, hand jams can be great places for strategic runouts, but don't make a habit of doing dangerous runouts, even on hand cracks. While hand jams can be the most secure of all jams, they can also be deceptive. A section that appeared to have perfect hand jams from below can be slightly different than it looked, making

The hand jams, however, are a different story. The classical method for climbing wide hands is called *cupped hands* and, as long as it's not too steep, cupped hands work fine; but they put a lot of pressure on a small point on the back of your knuckles, so most climbers find taping to be a big help on this size.

The *twist/jam* is less known but works far better than the cupped hand and also eliminates the need for tape if you move carefully from jam to jam. To execute a twist/jam:

1. Make your hand flat like a board and place it in the crack as if you were going to do a hand jam.

2. Instead of cupping your hand, twist it, bringing your pinky toward the outside of the crack and pressing the back of your thumb into the wall.

3. Pull *outward* against the twist rather than downward.

4. Lean back against the jam, almost like a lieback, and use your feet, which are stonking bomber in the crack, to push your body weight upward.

The key to the twist/jam is in opposing pressure with the feet. On overhanging terrain, face the palm in the direction of pull. In the perfect world, such as on an Indian Creek splitter, you can avoid doing cupped hands by using twist/jams. But most of

Wide hands is one of the most difficult to learn of the hand-size methods, but it's a critical skill for all-around climbers.

the time, a combination of cupped hands, twist/jams, and fist jams are necessary where the crack changes size and the rock's features push you into awkward positions.

When leading, wide hands are the first size where sliding a cam up the crack ahead of you becomes realistic and reasonably safe. It is also the size where the gear gets heavy, because the pieces are so large. For this reason, if you are looking to do long climbs, it is advised to practice this size enough that you become comfortable climbing it with longer runouts when the fall is safe. You just don't want to carry four cams of huge size to do the wide hands section on *Astroman* in Yosemite, the long routes in the Bugaboos of Canada, or the wide sections of the *Black Dagger* on Colorado's Diamond. To save weight, consider a couple extra hexes rather than added sets of cams in this size. The bottom line is that you're likely never going to see many Instagram posts about wide hands pitches. But if you're going to be a crack climber, you'd better roll down your sleeves, tape up, put on your hard hat and work boots, pack a lunch, and learn to climb wide hands.

FISTS

"Get really technical with your taping, wear crack gloves—and somebody needs to invent climbing-specific tape."
            Tommy Caldwell

Fist cracks have a similar culture to wide hands, but there is something more macho about a burly section of fists that makes them slightly more rewarding. Unlike wide hands, a perfect fist jam can be as secure as a hand jam. The feet are also no-brainers in fist cracks. The problem is that the difference between a secure fist jam and a horrible one is only about a bazillimeter.

The basic fist jam is simple, but making use of it in tricky spots with less than ideal crack sizes is where it gets difficult. In tight fists, the twist/jam described in the previous section can work quite well. As the crack widens beyond the perfect fist, everything becomes more difficult and begins to slip (including the climber's mood).

To get through these wide fist sections:

- Good footwork is mandatory. Put as much of your weight on your feet as possible.
- Look carefully for face climbing options; even tiny crimps and unobvious stems right in the sweet spot can allow you to take weight off your fists.
- Teacup fists, where you stick your thumb out of the side of your fist jam so it looks like the handle of a teacup, can give you slightly more purchase, but it is also one of the most insecure of all crack techniques. Taping your thumb carefully, especially on coarse rock, is nearly mandatory for this technique to work.

There are few more burly and intimidating moments in climbing than setting off to lead a sustained fist crack. Once you settle into the rhythm, however, fist cracks have their own special pleasures. For one thing, you can reach incredibly far off a fist jam because the orientation of your hand is almost like hanging onto the rung of a

Wearing crack gloves and taping the thumb help make fist jams more secure.

ladder. Second, if you pay your dues in fist cracks you become more versatile; you'll be able to take on bigger climbs with more diverse crack sizes. Many of the world's classic long routes (often first discovered and climbed because they follow larger crack systems that are visible from far away) have sections of wide crack.

Common advice for leading fist cracks is this: Don't. Instead, let your partner with bigger hands lead the pitch. As with all crack sizes, however, it is best to practice

this size and learn to climb it. Most good crack climbers can climb all sizes of crack not just the ones that fit their hands best.

OFF-WIDTHS

"Off-widths are beautiful."

Craig Luebben

Climbing off-widths will make you a better climber. Your body awareness and patience will increase dramatically. You'll also learn humility. For practicing using "your entire body like a hand" as Tommy suggests, and focusing on "the subtleties of movement" as Lynn suggests in Chapter 1, Face Climbing, there may be no better training than getting on a few off-widths.

Advanced off-width skills, like other styles of climbing, are more about movement than the specifics of static technique. In fact, not moving in an off-width is usually relatively easy—it's the moving that's hard. Pictures in a book send the wrong message because they too are static. The basic off-width techniques—arm bars, heel-toes, hand stacks, knee jams, and chicken wings—are all pretty easy to do if you just hang there frozen like a photograph. It's moving through and linking them that's challenging. If you're unfamiliar with the basic off-width technique, consult *Rock Climbing: Mastering Basic Skills*.

To understand how to move in an off-width, we're going to move beyond the basic techniques and focus on the attitude and movements that make the difference between a bloody suffer-fest and a

Steep, off-width cracks can require inversion and other advanced techniques.

beautiful, intimate experience with this least popular of all crack sizes.

USE PATIENCE AND THINK SMALL

Patience may be the single most important part of climbing wide cracks. Every other kind of climbing benefits from moving quickly, but when you're wedged inside the very womb of an ancient cliff, moving slowly is the only option. On average, climbing an off-width takes at least twice as long as any other pitch of comparable difficulty. So it's best to just accept it. When I start up an off-width, I like to pause at the first good stance (which might be with my feet still on the ground but my body in the crack) and just relax, absorb the location, and prepare my mind to just be inside for a while. I consciously push away anxiety, haste, and the desire to force my way up and replace it with patience and yoga-like relaxation and breathing. This helps bring experimentation and intuition to the fore-front of my mind.

Off-width games are won with small moves. Sure, there are places where you can bust out a few lieback moves, and the perfect crack size for "leavittation"—a method first described by California climber Randy Leavitt, where you alternate between hand

SIDEWINDER

Named by Craig Luebben, the climbing visionary who invented the Big Bro off-width protection, and inspired by the sideways movement of the snake of the same name, the sidewinder is an advanced technique for body-size off-widths. The sidewinder deserves explanation because it exemplifies the experimental attitude needed for off-width success.

- Little-by-little (of course), move your body out of the vertical position and toward the horizontal.
- Arm bar below and chicken wing above.
- Twist your hips so they jam and cam against the rock.
- Press your feet against the back wall.
- Alternate movement between the three contact points: shoulders/arms, hips, and feet.
- Hold your weight with two points while the third moves.

stacks and knee jams—can allow for making some bigger moves. But off-width climbing most often is a game of inches. The crack may be big, but the focus is on making small moves, using core strength to move your body upward.

Right now, as you sit holding this book in your hands, slump down; now sit up straight, extending your spine as far as you can. That's a big move in an off-width. Now, shrug your shoulders—another big move. Now lift one hip above the other as high as you can. Think of these as your full-extension moves in an off-width, the equivalent of powering 4 feet between hand-holds on a sport climb. And, just as with other types of climbing, most of the time something prevents you from making a full reach. In an off-width, a slight change in the rock can make it so you can only move a fraction of a shrug, a hip lift, or a back extension.

Off-width climbing is a great way to learn the subtleties of body position, as well as specific techniques like hand stacking.

When the cracks get big, think small; dial down your perception of a successful move so that even a few millimeters of upward progress is a victory.

IN TO REPOSITION, OUT TO MOVE UPWARD

In many different-size off-widths, upward movement is greatly optimized by looking at the off-width sequence in two different stages:

- Move into the crack, wedging your body, to move legs and arms.
- Move your body out of the crack, supported by arms and legs, to move your body upward.

Moving into the crack makes your position more secure, but that same security makes moving upward difficult or even impossible. Shifting your body (slightly) to the outside of the crack frees your body from the friction of the rock and greatly reduces the effort of movement. At first, the insecurity that comes with leaning out of the crack is unnerving, but the progress that results quickly outweighs any insecurity. Moving your body back into the crack allows you to take advantage of the friction of the rock on your body in order to move your hands and feet.

Watch a good off-width climber at work and you'll see that they use this concept over and over: pull into the crack and reposition hands and feet, lean out of the crack to move upward, in to reposition, out to move—and so on.

CLOTHING

With the above technique in mind, clothing is critical to off-width success and enjoyment. Obviously, protection from abrasions is a consideration, but beyond that—when you're wriggling up a man-eating crack—clothing becomes a tool in itself, similar to the rubber on the shoes.

- For extended or particularly brutal chicken wing sections, a neoprene elbow wrap works magic. Wearing it high enough to protect the back of the arm from abrasion also increases friction and traction.
- High-top climbing shoes help keep you from ripping the skin off your anklebones.
- Except for on mountain routes where cotton gives poor storm protection, low-stretch cotton clothing is far better for movement in off-widths than high-tech fabrics like polyester. The tiny fibers of tech fabrics tend to catch on every rugosity as if you're wearing Velcro; their stretch causes them to bunch up around knees; and during a good sweat, tech fabrics in an off-width make you feel like a fish in a plastic bag.
- Consider wrapping your shirtsleeve into your tape job to hold your shirt from sliding up your arm. Also tape your pant legs down.
- Modern yoga-style pants are not ideal for off-widths. They tend to bunch up around the knees, which can cause the horrifying sensation that comes with getting your clothing-wrapped knee stuck in the crack. The best off-width pants are made of a non-stretch material and are cut roomy enough to allow full mobility.

LEADING OFF-WIDTHS

Several small changes to gear and rope management are a big help for leading off-widths. It may be tempting to organize the rack and tie in as you always have, but the full-body contact encountered when off-width climbing makes a mockery of standard gear and rope management techniques.

- Wear the rack on a shoulder sling. Unless you're doing an upside-down stacking problem where your body is hanging out of the crack the entire time, clipping anything to your harness gets in the way in the crack. Using a shoulder sling also allows you to flip the rack to the other side of your body when you switch from facing one direction to facing the other.

- Tie your tie-in knot farther than normal from your harness so it hangs between your legs—believe me, the last thing you want is a knot wedging you into the crack by your crotch.

- Helmets not only make off-width climbing nearly impossible, they also create a unique hazard. On one of the first off-widths I ever led, my helmet wedged in the crack at the lip of an overhang. I was able to wriggle out of the helmet and climb on, leaving it for my second to remove, but if I had fallen while my helmet was jammed I could have badly injured my neck.

- Learn to use Big Bros on longer off-widths—they are much more space and weight efficient (one #5 Camalot takes up about the same space on your

Geared up for an off-width lead: longer tie-in knot, knee and elbow guards, everything racked on shoulder sling, high-top shoes, and no helmet

rack as four #2 Bros). Big Bros are also more stable when left behind in parallel cracks than are big cams, which have an unnerving tendency to twist and fall out of the crack if the rope bumps against them or causes the cam to rotate.

- Slide a cam above you and leave Big Bros behind for protection.

▥ Clip almost all protection with a long sling or draw—the gear is often placed deep in the crack, but generally you want the rope to stay closer to the lip of the crack. As well as reducing rope drag, this also helps keep the rope movement from dislodging the piece.

Cleaning an off-width also has some special considerations. As with leading, tie your knot with more space between the knot and the harness. Pull up on the rope to see where the knot will be while climbing—*you want the knot to be above your chest.* Anything lower will end up wedged around your stomach or chest, another scenario you want to avoid in order to enjoy off-widths.

Put the gear you clean onto a shoulder sling. It is not necessary to carry a proper gear sling, a shoulder-length runner will do. On longer routes, if you are carrying a water bottle, raincoat, approach shoes, or extra gear, and you don't have a tag line to haul, it can be easiest to hang the gear from your harness and let it drag up the crack behind you rather than clip it all around your waist as you would on more dainty terrain.

Opposite: *Kate Dooley slotting nuts in the Grampians, Australia*

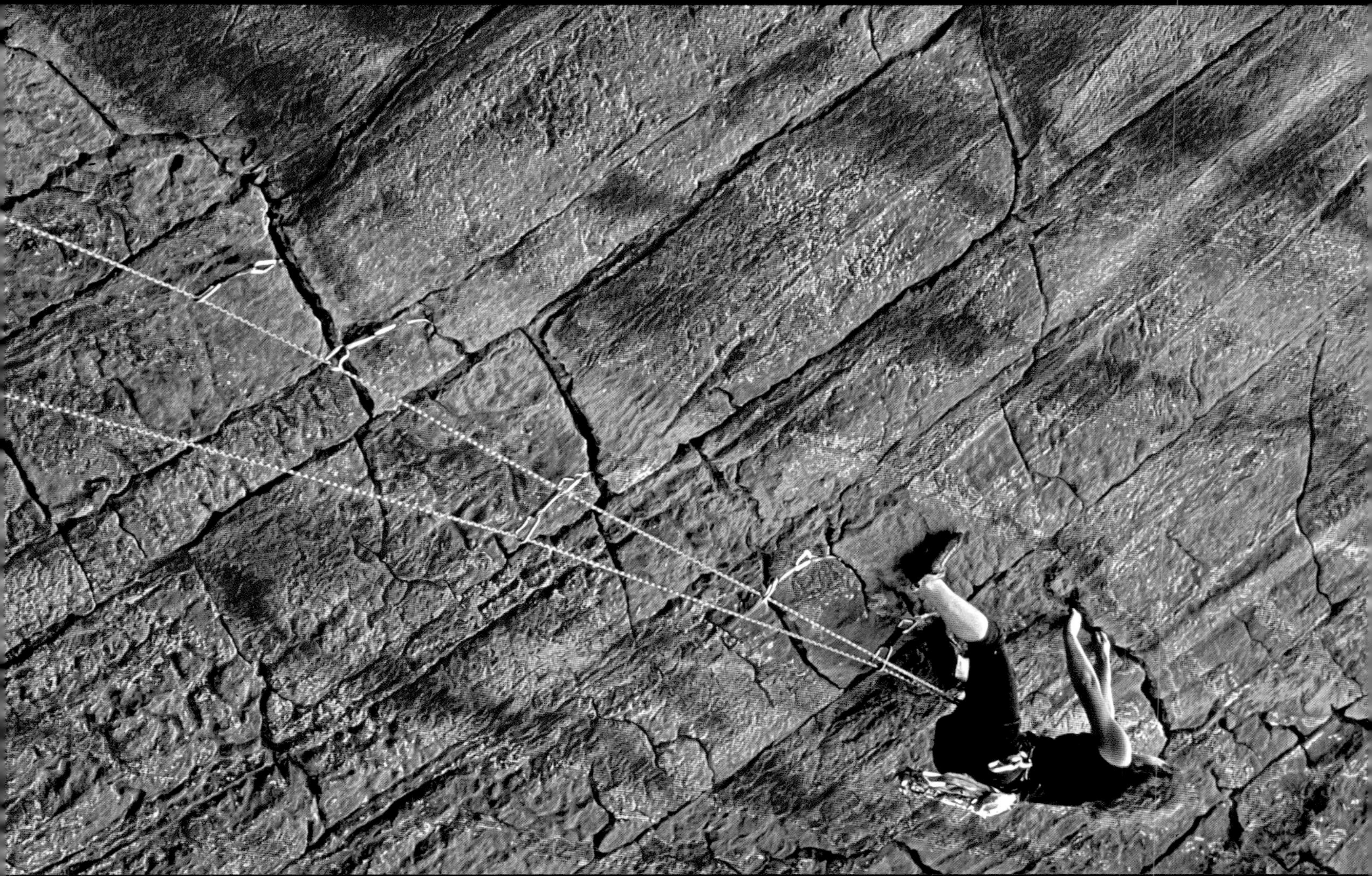

CHAPTER 3

Climbing Gear

"The gear may be somewhat pricey, but by far the biggest cost of climbing for most hard-core climbers is the huge amount of time spent climbing and not working."

—*Craig Luebben*

If you were to base your equipment choices on what's said on the online forums, it might seem that the brand you choose is the most important decision you'll ever make. However, if you were to base your equipment choices on what you see expert climbers using and wearing at the crag, you'd realize that there are many great brands out there. These brands have been copying and learning from each other for so long that the results are many options and a lot of great gear. The brand isn't what makes a piece of equipment safe or effective; it's how you use the gear that matters. In this chapter we'll discuss the pitfalls in using gear the wrong way, the tricks for using gear safely beyond its intended design, and the ways you can optimize your gear choices for particular types of climbs.

To begin with, the most crucial bit of advice in this book might be this: the gear will not keep you safe—the way you use the gear will keep you safe. There is no cam that will hold if placed too poorly, no rope that will remain whole and uncut if allowed to drop into a razor-sharp notch under force, no harness that will work if partly unbuckled, no helmet that will save you if you are hit by too huge of a rock, no carabiner that is unbreakable if levered over a bolt hanger or rock edge, no belay device that will hold every fall no matter what you do as a belayer.

Long before the invention of all the incredible gear we have available today, climbers were safely doing pretty rad things with primitive equipment. Using common sense and an acute sense of the limitations of the gear is still the best way to look at any and all climbing equipment. The gear we have today may have been optimized for rock climbing, but frankly the rock wasn't designed for the gear.

HARNESSES

In one of the most surprising accidents in climbing, Todd Skinner's belay loop broke while he was rappelling, dropping him to his death. It was an older, well-worn harness, and the accident shook the climbing community to the core. Many of us asked, "Can we trust our harnesses?"

The answer is yes, but only if the harness has been cared for properly and retired as the nylon ages. Other lesser-known but equally nerve-wracking stories include one where the stitching on a harness was compromised through contact with some kind of chemical: when weighted, the stitching simply popped when a climber leaned back on the harness in a gym. Thankfully, the climber didn't fall, was only slowly weighting the harness, and was able to hang on to be safely lowered, but the danger is obvious.

- Don't leave your harness or other nylon gear lying around in a garage or in the trunk of a car (who knows what you or the previous owner had in there, and solvents that damage nylon are not uncommon).
- Along with your harness, it is best to carry and store all your nylon climbing gear—quickdraws, ropes, etc.—in enclosed containers or bags, not lying on the floor of your closet.
- Retire your harness and other equipment according to manufacturer recommendations. Sun and time cause nylon to deteriorate no matter how gently and carefully the gear is used.

Aside from caring for your harness as if your life depended on it, there are other considerations when selecting a climbing-specific harness:

Sport climbing harness—Lightweight, no more than two gear loops, comfortable to hang in, allows unrestricted movement, adjustable leg loops optional. Some climbers use a comfortable harness for working a route but then switch to an even more stripped-down harness with no gear loops and minimal padding for the redpoint, sacrificing comfort and shaving off every possible ounce when going for the send.

Trad climbing harness—Generous padding, unrestricted movement, four gear loops minimum, adjustable leg loops helpful for changing clothing or high-angle pit stops, full-strength gear loops are useful.

Big wall harness—Same as trad harness, with haul loop, additional gear loops, overbuilt padding in waist and legs, adjustable and droppable leg loops mandatory.

Women-specific harness—Some products' gender-specific designs may be pure style, but the women's harness is a worthwhile investment for any crag diva; many are designed with the center of balance adjusted to a woman's shape. Make sure a women's harness includes droppable leg loops, or else (I'm just guessing here) it's really just a man's harness in a feminine color. . . .

BELAY DEVICES

"I carry two Mega Juls (high friction tubes) and give one to my belayer to belay me."
                    Angela Hawse

There is a bewildering selection of belay devices and they can all do the job if used properly; and they can all drop a climber in a heartbeat if used badly. For the advanced climber, there are different devices for different situations and most climbers end

There are many different brake devices to choose from. Whichever you use, learn it so well that you can operate it flawlessly in the dark, in the rain, with gloves on, and when you're exhausted.

up with a couple of belay devices in their collection: assisted lock for sport climbing and cragging, and a rappel/belay device for dynamic belays, multi-pitch routes, and rappels. High friction tubes are now changing the game, and can provide the most versatility in a single device.

In the following section, device types are broken down by functionality and explained in terms of strengths and weaknesses. Ideally, become familiar with each type of device so you know its limitations and uses. It is advisable to stick with the one or two devices you are most familiar with, but there are times when you may end up belaying with someone else's device. Additionally, it's nice to be able to observe your belayer briefly, whatever device they are using, and know if they're wielding their device correctly. No matter which belay device you use, learning the proper belay method is essential. And at its base is the fundamental technique for belaying—*never let go of the rope with the brake hand.* You must control the rope at all times. See Chapter 6, Belaying for Mastery, for the full look at belay method.

TUBES

Tubes include the Black Diamond ATC, Trango Jaws, Metolius BRD, and more.

Pros:

- Lightweight
- Inexpensive
- Good for learning to belay properly
- Easy to give a dynamic belay

Cons:

- No backup for the brake hand
- The belayer must use hand strength to hold a leader hanging on the rope
- No guide mode for belaying a second

TUBES WITH GUIDE MODE

Also called "plaquette-style" (from the flat design of the Kong GiGi, the first autoblocking—hands-almost-free—belay device), this design concept now includes the ATC Guide, Petzl Reverso, and others. For all-around climbing, these have been the most popular and versatile all-around belay devices in recent years. For belaying a leader these devices work the same as tubes: but in guide mode for belaying a second, they deliver assisted lock capabilities for belaying either one or two followers.

Pros:

- Versatile
- Inexpensive
- Lightweight
- Easy to give a dynamic belay
- In lead belay mode, functions exactly like a regular tube

Cons:

- In guide mode it is hard to lower a second who is hanging
- No backup for the brake hand in lead mode
- Grip required to hold a fallen leader

HIGH FRICTION TUBES

This type includes the Edelrid Mega Jul, the Climbing Technology Click Up, and the Mammut Smart. These devices use friction from the belay biner pinching the rope into a notch in the device when weighted to create assisted lock capabilities in a simple, lightweight device. Because they are very

High friction tubes are a new concept that many climbers are now using.

new, the best design is perhaps yet to be developed, but this concept shows great promise and many climbers are now using these devices almost exclusively.

Pros:

- Provides some backup for the brake hand
- Some models are ultralightweight
- The most versatile type of belay device
- Can be used like a tube in guide mode
- Can be used to rappel on two ropes
- With the right rope and a locking biner, high friction tubes work like an assisted lock device

Cons:

- Performance is very rope/carabiner shape–specific—follow manufacturer recommendations
- Some plastic parts are not durable
- Each device needs particular training for proper use
- Hard to give a dynamic belay with most models

- Creates the illusion that there is no chance of human error

ASSISTED LOCK DEVICES

This type includes the Petzl Grigri, the Trango Cinch, and others. These devices are the gold standard for sport climbing belays and in many sport climbing areas it is unusual to see any other style of device. While assisted lock devices have made belaying easier and arguably safer, climbers have been dropped both in gyms and out-doors with these devices. No device is fool-proof.

Pros:

- Provides reliable backup for the brake hand in most situations
- Time-tested designs
- Makes it easy to hold a leader hanging on the rope
- Useful for advanced methods of belay and simul-climbing (see Chapter 9, Long Route Efficiency)

HIGH FRICTION TUBE WARNING

While high friction tubes are as versatile as simple tubes for belaying, they have the added advantage of potentially providing a form of backup to the brake hand, similar to a Grigri. The amount of backup, however, is dependent on rope diameter and surface as well as biner shape. With time, the rope and biner will behave differently with the device. A new, skinny rope may slide through the device without locking unless the brake hand is engaged, then stick solidly as the rope ages and develops a fuzzy surface. A new biner may lock the rope, but as the biner wears, creating a groove where the rope runs, the device may begin to slide.

Due to this inconsistency in braking power, it is safest to catch a fall with the brake hand similar to any tube but then use the assisted lock capability to help hold the leader while they hang or work out moves. *The bottom line with high friction tubes—as with any belay device—is this: keep your brake hand on the rope!*

Cons:

- Not designed for rappelling
- Can only hold one rope at a time
- Bulky
- Relatively heavy compared to other belay devices
- Hard to give a dynamic belay
- Creates the illusion that there is no chance for human error

CARABINERS

Any modern carabiner is capable of holding a climbing fall of the entire rope length, and even if the gate is opened, any biner made after 1998 is required by the UIAA to be strong enough to hold at least 7kN, or 1574 pounds of force—about the test rating of an average fingertip-size cam and strong enough to hold a typical leader fall. Conversely, any biner, even

It's more important to be able to quickly clip any carabiner than it is to buy any one type of biner.

a locking biner, if leveraged over an edge, can fail under forces as low as 2.5 kN, or 560 pounds of force—which is easily generated in even the shortest leader fall. In discussing the advanced perspective on biners, we'll split recommendations into the five primary biner types—wiregate, straight gate, bent gate, mini, and locker—and cover the safety and functionality considerations of each type.

One of the biggest misunderstandings in climbing is that biners should never be clipped to other biners, or "no metal to metal." If this were true, why is it okay to clip biners to bolt hangers or chain links? This common belief is a misinterpretation of a technique from the golden age of climbing before the invention of quickdraws. In those days, climbers would link chains of biners on pitons to create a quickdraw-like connection. The best practice of the day was that it was okay to link three biners together, but when linked in chains of four or more, a twisting action could cause the gates to open and one or more of the biners to unclip. In modern times, this bit of wisdom has been overblown to mean that biners should never be clipped to other biners. In fact, clipping biners to biners is safe, provided there are no more than three in a chain and provided that the orientation of the biners does not press the gate of any one biner against the rock in a way that could open its gate.

WIREGATE

The climbing application of wiregate biners, a technology borrowed from sailing, has created a biner with excellent characteristics—and a few issues.

Pros:

- Doesn't freeze in wintery conditions
- More durable spring mechanism than solid-stock biners with tiny springs
- Easy to clip
- Lightweight

Cons:

- Easiest biner to accidentally unclip
- Accidentally opens easily over crack edges if the crack edges press against the gate when weighted
- Racked wired nuts and other things clipped to the harness are more apt to fall out of the wiregate because the wires tend to hang up on the gate

STRAIGHT GATE

The original climbing carabiners had straight, solid gates, and there is still a place for straight gates in modern climbing.

Pros:

- Among the least likely to accidentally unclip—second only to a locker
- Holds a cluster of nuts most securely for racking
- Least likely to unclip from bolt hanger on bolt side of draw
- Keylock style (which has no nose hook) is the easiest to unclip from a bolt when cleaning a sport climb

Cons:

- Hard to clip on rope side of a draw, sling, or cam
- Freezes and binds up in wintery conditions
- Heavy
- Spring mechanism is small and fails more often than those on wiregates

BENT GATE

For decades the bent gate biner has been the best choice for its rope-clipping position for quickdraws used on sport climbs. Many experienced sport climbers still feel this is the easiest biner to clip.

Pros:

▪ Easy to clip

Cons:

▪ Freezes and binds up in wintery conditions

▪ Heavy

▪ Spring mechanism is small and fails more often than wiregates

MINIS

"Don't ever buy climbing gear unless it's the lightest possible."

Steph Davis

Recent designs of miniature, full-strength biners have gained popularity. For endeavors where carrying gear is part of the game, either on the rack or in the pack, the weight-saving potential of these biners is significant. It takes some change of method to use these well, but in combination with other light gear it is possible to shave several pounds off the normal climbing rack.

Pros:

▪ Lightweight—compared to full-size biners, saves approximately 50 percent in biner weight

Cons:

▪ Takes practice to clip efficiently

▪ Very difficult to use with gloves

▪ Hard for a climber to pull on, as needed, when aid climbing or cheating past hard moves

▪ Too small to clip more than one or two things to it (so of limited use in belays and aid climbing)

LOCKERS

One recent trend in climbing is the use of locking carabiners on strategic pieces on both trad and sport routes. The first, second, or even third draw on a sport climb is often one of those places where, should the rope come unclipped, the results would be catastrophic. For these purposes, the smaller, lightweight lockers are best. For belay biners, most climbers favor larger HMS-style biners. For belaying while cragging, fixed-position biners (featuring a spring wire or biner shape that fixes the biner on the harness's belay loop) are the bombproof choice because the design holds the biner in the optimal orientation and eliminates the chance of cross loading.

New designs in locking biners, like the Edelrid Pure Slider, use a sliding lock mechanism that can be operated quickly with one hand, potentially paving the way for lightweight biners with locking capabilities that are quick to clip. For now, the UIAA will not categorize a biner that can be unlocked and opened in a single motion as "locking." But for use on a quickdraw for key bolts, on tag lines, or in other places where extra security is needed but ease of clipping and unclipping is desired, the quick lock design is an ideal in-between for locking and nonlocking biners.

QUICKDRAWS

As with biners, what is ideal in a quickdraw depends on what you want to do with that quickdraw. For trad climbing, where the rack gets heavy, or for long approaches and long routes, lightweight draws made with thin webbing ($^3/_8$ to $^1/_2$ inch) and lightweight biners are the ticket. For sport climbs and projects, where you'll likely leave the quickdraws in place, draws made with fat webbing ($^1/_2$ to 1 inch) and full-size biners are the most robust and inspire the greatest confidence. Although the lightweight gear is plenty strong, there is something reassuring about clipping a meaty biner on a sausage-size draw.

Most sport climbers these days carry quickdraws of all the same length, clipping two together when they need a longer draw. Seven-inch draws are the most versatile and tend to be the best for avoiding insidious rope drag on blocky or irregular rock without having to waste energy selecting the right draw length. (If a few inches of extra fall length caused by the slightly longer draw is an issue, you're probably better off clipping a single locker directly to the bolt and shortening the fall as much as possible.)

STIFFY DRAW

Tall climbers who place bolts sometimes forget that other people can't reach as far as they can, so shorter climbers will do well to construct a "stiffy draw" for reaching bolts that are just out of reach. The top biner should be a specialty biner that is designed to stay open until clipped, such as the Mad Rock Trigger Wire or something similar. A longer quickdraw (10–12 inches) is then stiffened with a length of stiff plastic or wire taped securely to the draw with the upper biner held tightly in place.

Putting the stiffy draw to good use high on El Capitan

SLINGS

Sewn slings have almost universally replaced knotted webbing due to the obvious advantages of being both stronger and easier to handle, but there is still a place for knotted webbing for first ascents or alpine exploration where rigging rappel anchors is likely.

For sewn webbing, there are all kinds of options, but most expert climbers have settled on a couple of lengths and styles as most useful:

- "Shoulder-length" slings are typically 23-inch-diameter sewn open loops.
- "Double-length" slings are typically 47-inch-diameter sewn open loops.

For some rock types and for trad climbing, other lengths may be useful as well, but carrying more than a couple different quickdraw and sling lengths can cause inefficiency—not only are you expending time and energy finding the right piece to fit the crack but also finding the perfect sling for the piece. The sling's job is to prevent rope drag, keep the piece from lifting out or walking into a compromised position, and catch you nicely if you fall. A sling or quickdraw sized to the inch is rarely, if ever, necessary when protecting a climb.

Slings age. Testing suggests that Dyneema/Spectra loses about half its strength every year and should be retired after three years of use. Nylon webbing should be retired after five years of use.

Placing cams well in hard terrain requires composure and practice. Lots of practice.

CAMS

"I rarely use nuts anymore unless a cam won't fit—cams are just faster to place and faster to clean."

Tommy Caldwell

Cams are the cornerstone of the traditional climbing rack. For advanced considerations of cam usage, including specifics on four-cam units, TCUs, and offsets, consult Chapter 5, Traditional Gear Placement. Modern cams are all comparably useful, well designed, tested, and certified by UIAA. A phenomenon of climbing gear is that whatever gear you use most becomes the brand you prefer—and gear you are not familiar with seems awkward and harder to place.

However, it can be difficult to decide which brand of cam is best for you. From a purely practical and functional perspective for advanced climbing, these are the most important considerations for cam choice:

- Variability of design—Rock is variable (in texture, fractures, and features), so when using more than one set of cams, racking a second or third set from a brand different than the first allows you a slightly different crack fit—a huge advantage.
- Variability of cam lobe number—Due to the seeming security of placement, units with four cams are much more popular than those with three cams. However, a three-cam can fit well in many places where a four-cam will not fit. A set of each gives you choices.
- Price—From a practical use perspective, the difference between the least and the most expensive cam is not significant; and the less expensive cams are easier on the wallet to leave behind when necessary.
- Weight—Carrying lightweight gear makes climbing easier.

Offset cams, where the cams on one side of the unit are sized differently than cams on the other side, have gained popularity in certain rock types where flared cracks are common.

Regarding cam sling replacement: Although the metal part of cams will last for decades, the webbing needs to be replaced frequently. Many climbers do not replace webbing often enough—if your partner's cam webbing looks faded and old, ask them how old the webbing is, and *replace your own every five years.*

ROPES

"I prefer a 40- or 50-meter rope for alpine rock climbs."

Angela Hawse

Not long ago, there was a "standard" rope length of 60 meters and diameter of 10 millimeters. Today, there are many options, and ropes are a customized piece of equipment. Choosing the right rope for the job makes a huge difference in its function. Savvy alpine rock climbers like Angela may choose a shorter, 40- or 50-meter rope to lighten the pack on climbs with established shorter pitches; while some sport climbing routes, even entire areas, are only practical with an 80- or even 100-meter rope. For sport climbing and cragging, 70-meter ropes are now the most common. But unless the

The rope is one of the only components of the climbing system that is trusted without redundancy. Treat your rope well and replace it often.

extra length is truly utilized, 70-meter ropes add unnecessary weight and more rope management than needed.

Rope diameter is also worthy of custom consideration—and custom application. Modern belay devices behave differently on various diameter ropes, and the durability of a 9.8-mm rope is significantly greater than a 9-mm single rope and should be employed accordingly. Many climbers now keep in their quiver at least two different ropes: a fatter rope (greater than 9.5 mm) for projecting and general cragging, where the rope is heavily used; and a skinny rope (less than 9.5 mm)

for hard redpoints and long approaches or long routes where weight is critical.

Recent testing has shown that rope and other nylon equipment weakens dramatically when wet. Dry treatment helps somewhat, but even the best dry treatment wears off after a few hard days of use. This supports the argument for keeping multiple ropes available and selecting the rope based on the objective.

An ideal rope selection would include:

- A "performance" skinny rope (less than 9.5 mm by 60 m or 70 m) with dry treatment in good condition for alpine and longer rock climbs as well as hard redpoints

LOAD LIMITERS

Load limiters are usually nylon runners with extra stitching sewn strategically to blow out if weighted with a certain amount of force. They have been used for decades to help reduce the force of a leader fall on the protection. In 2014, a nearly inconceivable accident happened in Eldorado Canyon, Colorado. An experienced leader, working on a first ascent, fell, pulling out a couple of poor pieces, and somehow the action of the rope in the fall caused it to unclip wiregate biners on two lower, seemingly bomber pieces. The biners were found on the ground, clipped to neither the rope nor the slings of the protection. A load-limiting device, which releases in predictable increments to limit the peak load, had been used on the upper piece. It partly released before the piece failed.

Slow-motion video of load limiters releasing shows a violent, spring-like wave traveling through the rope. There has been no absolute conclusion to the unnerving accident in Eldorado, but most experts seem to agree that the load limiter on the top device contributed to the biners somehow unclipping entirely during the fall.

To prevent this, if using a load limiter, such as the Yates Screamer, always put locking biners on solid pieces below the load limiter.

- A "utilitarian" rope (9.5 mm or greater by 60 m or 70 m) for general cragging
- A tag line (6 mm by 60 m) for hauling and/or rappelling on longer climbs
- An extra-long performance rope (less than 9.5 mm by 80 m or 100 m) for world-class sport climbing areas and specialized cragging use.

CHALK ONE UP

Tiny chalkbags were popular at one time for hard sport climbs where every ounce matters, but the disadvantages—not being able to get your whole hand into the bag, getting your hand slightly stuck removing it from the bag, and carrying too little chalk—have convinced most climbers that a full-size chalkbag is the way to go. Look at photos of Chris Sharma, Adam Ondra, and Sasha DiGiulian on their hardest climbs; they're all wearing full-size chalkbags.

But do you really need to chalk up so often? For hard climbing, chalking up may be a waste of energy. If you habitually chalk to the point that you need it for every move, you will do well to wean yourself a bit from the white powder and learn to climb long sections without chalking up. On really hard climbing, it is simply not possible to chalk up and it requires time and energy to take a dip, even on easier terrain.

Chalk use is one of the biggest perceived impacts climbers have on the environment. The stuff itself is pretty benign, but the visual impact can be significant. For this reason, the conversation about using colored chalk, to better blend with the rock, comes up from time to time. It has been tried, and has revealed the following problems:

- Rock is impossible to color match perfectly, especially move to move. Pigmented chalk just paints the rock a different color.
- Pigmented chalks are harder to remove from the rock than white chalk, which comes off fairly easily in the rain or with a brush.
- The pigments lend a greasy feel, which changes the texture and friction of the holds more than does white chalk.

The conclusion has thus far been that it is better to use white chalk, while being considerate of land managers and public perception by avoiding unnecessary or excessive chalk use and paying particular attention to removing chalk from boulders and climbs that are close to trails and in visually sensitive areas.

Then there are tick marks. Tick marks cause two serious issues. First is the practical side: they can make a mess and not everyone wants to have every hold marked with a line as if it was in a gym. The second: tick marks slow your improvement as a climber. Here's why:

- When you make a tick mark you shortchange your own learning. The next time you do the move, instead of flowing with your intuition and muscle memory, and perhaps finding an easier way around the move, you simply grab the hold you used before.
- If you need tick marks to climb, you'll never be as good at onsighting.

Tick marks can be essential on hard redpoints, but using them all the time decreases the development of proprioception, the mind's ability to know what the body is doing and where it is in space.

There is certainly a place for tick marks and chalking with gusto, but the bottom line is this: if you save tick marks for the very hardest moves and when absolutely necessary, you'll leave less of a mark on the rock, have less of a possibly negative impact on other people's ascents—*and you'll become a better climber.*

CRASH PADS

Crash pads have made modern bouldering possible, and there are many good designs that serve the purpose. Depending on how you plan to use the pad and its carry system, pockets for lunch, a waist belt for long walks, and different sizes of pads must be considered. For advanced considerations, crash pads are a more-is-better proposition. If you have $300 to spend on padding, you're usually better off buying two less expensive pads than a single, pricey pad. Two pads are better than one in almost every case:

- For bouldering alone, where there is no spotter to move the pad, two pads increase the coverage significantly.
- It is difficult to estimate the precise trajectory of a fall, and more pads eliminate the need for the spotter to move the pad around in hopes of getting it in the right spot.

- Sometimes a second pad is needed to protect the spotter, not just the climber.
- Even if your partners also have pads, having yet another one is always a benefit.
- Extra pads give you the capability to fill in rough terrain and make dangerous landings reasonable.

See Chapter 12, Bouldering, for tips on spotting and using crash pads, but most experienced boulderers will agree that the game is the most fun with a huge stack of pads below your feet.

HELMETS

Helmets are finally becoming normal equipment for nearly all types of climbing. Aside from steep sport climbing, it is now common to see helmets on most climbers at any given crag. The lightweight and comfortable designs for a variety of head shapes and sizes make wearing a helmet an easy choice. There are, however, times where wearing a helmet is a hindrance and even occasions where a helmet can be dangerous. Consider these guidelines for helmet use.

Wear a helmet:
- Top-roping with any chance of the rope rubbing across the rock above and dislodging flakes or other rocks
- Leading with any possibility that a fall could flip you upside down on less than overhanging terrain
- Climbing below other climbers
- Belaying in the fall line of a leader
- Climbing in alpine terrain or on other big features with the potential for loose rock

Don't wear a helmet:
- Performing extreme redpoints on well-protected overhanging terrain
- Climbing off-width cracks where the helmet could get stuck
- Ascending awkward sections like flares or grooves where accommodating the helmet could cause you to fall

When in doubt, however, wear a helmet. With the rapidly growing popularity of climbing and increasing numbers of climbers on the rock, places we once felt were safe to climb without a helmet are now exposed to pulled ropes, rock fall, or dropped gear from other climbers.

If you're not accustomed to wearing a helmet, they can feel like a terrible annoyance. But after a short time, the helmet becomes largely unnoticeable. If all you ever want to do is clip bolts on overhanging rock, you probably don't need a helmet. For most everything else, wearing a helmet is the smart choice.

SHOES

"You'll climb better if your shoes are comfortable."

John Bachar

A couple of recent advances have helped comfortable shoes perform even better, and with all the different shoes on today's market, there is no reason to climb in an intensely painful pair of shoes. The thin, stiff midsoles used in the forefoot of modern models allow the climber to stand on thin edges while preserving the flexibility in

WHEN TO RESOLE ROCK SHOES

A little-known secret in climbing is that some professional climbers with shoe sponsors still have their shoes resoled. Why? Because a shoe that has already been perfectly shaped to your foot through wear, and then resoled with sticky rubber, is the cat's meow. The key is to have the shoe resoled before the sole wear begins to dig into the rand, the thinner rubber that wraps around the toe and heel.

This shoe is ready for a resole. The sole rubber has worn down to paper thin at the edge but has not yet begun to wear into the rand that wraps the side of the shoe. With the rand undamaged, the new sole can seal perfectly.

This shoe speaks for itself.

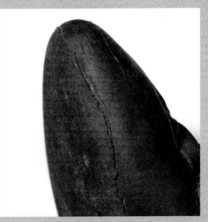

This shoe has been worn too long to be resoled with good results. It will require a rand repair, which usually changes the fit and profile of the shoe for the worse.

the rest of the shoe; this also preserves the shoe's stiffness throughout the life of the shoe and through multiple resoles. Mid-height models like La Sportiva's TC Pro, designed by Tommy Caldwell with a performance forefoot and ankle-protecting upper, have reinvigorated the old high-top design and further increased the comfort and versatility of climbing shoes.

It is usually best to stick to one or two pairs of shoes so you become intimately familiar with their feel, flex, and edge. But in some cases, it can help to have specialized shoes for certain kinds of climbing:

- Oversized slippers to allow more rubber to be pressed into 1-inch-wide desert cracks
- Radically downturned toe designs helpful for tricky, powerful footwork on steep rock
- The option of wearing different shoes on each foot for certain climbs, such as a jamming shoe on one foot and a tight edging shoe on the other
- High-top shoes for wider cracks and off-widths

Many years ago, Jonny Woodward, a climbing legend with footwork to make a ballerina blush, told me this: "Just wear the same shoe for everything so you know exactly how it performs." There's a lot of wisdom to his suggestion, and many expert climbers have come to this same conclusion and end up buying the same model year after year. Find a shoe that fits you, works well for the kind of climbing you like to do, and allows you to use your feet with confidence and conviction. When you find that perfect shoe, buy a couple of extra pairs, because climbing shoe companies frequently discontinue great designs in favor of marketing new models that don't necessarily perform better.

Opposite: Alex Honnold and Matt Segal topping out a spire in the Elbsandstein, Germany

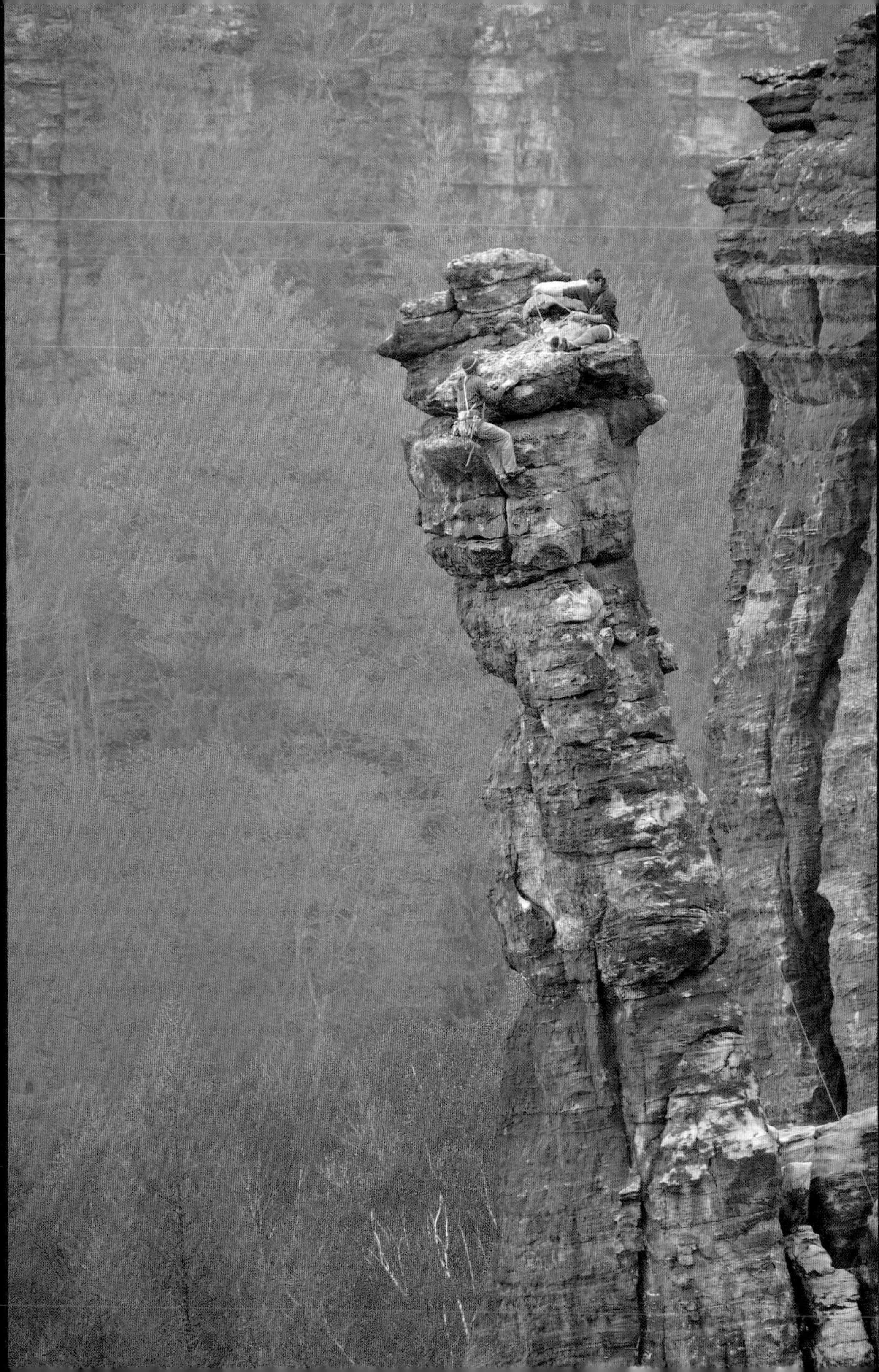

CHAPTER 4

Knots and Anchor Rigging

"Charley reminded me when I headed to the next rap anchor, 'Make sure you take the hammer and pound on the pins before trusting them.' At the next anchor I pulled out a pin [piton] with my fingers. If Charley hadn't said that I don't know if I would have caught it . . ."
Steph Davis, on her first trip to Patagonia with Charley Fowler

The methodology for tying into the rope and rigging anchors is a big part of learning to climb. Then, as we progress through the grades and gain experience, we become set in our ways, utilizing one or two knots for most of our climbing. This is a good thing. Keeping things simple is a smart approach to climbing knots and anchors. However, while this "I-always-do-it-like-this" approach may be safest for the majority of the scenarios you'll encounter while climbing, it can often limit speed, efficiency, and adaptability. It can even increase the hazard in some cases. The lesson is that advanced climbers never stop learning and improving their technique.

In this chapter we'll review the basic knots and anchor methods, but also cover alternative methods that can help even vastly experienced climbers become more versatile and efficient. For each technique, the photo of the knot or anchor rigging method is followed by the pros, cons, and considerations for each type. If you are unsure how to tie a particular knot or need to review the fundamentals of anchors, consult *Rock Climbing: Mastering Basic Skills,* or visit www.animatedknots.com for easy-to-follow animated knot tying instructions.

The section on knots in this chapter is designed for climbers who are already familiar with the basic climbing knots. The goal here is to help you become a more versatile climber by comparing and contrasting the knots available. Most of the traditional knots are shown in single photos, completed and in use. Two lesser-known but useful knots—the adjustable hitch and the Yosemite tree hitch—are shown by a sequence of photos describing the setup process.

The lion's share of knots used today are golden oldies that are still used and useful. One knot that has taken center stage among guides and should be adopted by climbers is the barrel knot for tying two ropes together. This replaces the flat overhand, a.k.a. Euro death knot, which has caused accidents and is no longer considered safe.

KNOTS FOR TIE-IN AND ATTACHMENT

These are the knots we use to tie the climbing harness into the ends of the rope, or to clip the rope into an anchor or other fixed point. These knots are one of the few points in the climbing system where there is no redundancy, so tie them each time with an unwavering focus and do not stop in the middle of tying the knot for any reason.

FIGURE EIGHT

This is universally the most common rope-to-harness tie-in knot. Although it used to be standard to use this knot with a safety knot in the leftover tail, tests have shown the figure eight will hold to nearly full strength even if the last pass is incomplete, so it has become standard to use this knot without the safety knot.

Pros:
- The most popular tie-in knot
- Easy for your partner to check visually for completion

Cons:
- Can be hard to untie after weighting by heavy leaders or following long falls

Figure eight

BOWLINE RETHREAD

A useful rope-to-harness tie-in knot that is popular in Europe and is now catching on in the United States.

Pros:
- Easy to untie after falling and heavily loading the knot

TO KNOW ABOUT KNOTS: A WARNING

Knots weaken rope, cord, and webbing! Some knots, like the figure eight that most of us use to tie in, will weaken the rope at the point of the knot by 20 to 30 percent. Others, like the girth and adjustable hitch, will reduce the strength of webbing by as much as 50 percent. Webbing is strong enough that in normal use a climbing fall will not generate enough force to break a knotted piece of webbing or rope; but it does mean you want to avoid using a girth hitch or similar knot in a non-redundant situation where it could receive a large shock load.

Bowline rethread

Clove hitch

■ Increases the rope and harness surface area, which reduces wear on the rope and harness

■ Doesn't untie itself as easily as a traditional bowline, a knot that has come untied and caused serious accidents

Cons:

■ Harder for your partner to check visually, because it passes twice through the harness and tends to hug close to the harness rather than hanging in the open like a figure eight

CLOVE HITCH

Hitch for clipping into an anchor or any fixed point. At one time, the figure eight on a bight was the standard anchor clip-in knot, but the clove hitch has become the most common method used by climbing teams.

Pros:

■ Uses very little rope

■ Adjustable

■ Versatile for many applications

Cons:

■ Hard to untie when weighted

■ Best when weighted strand is near biner stock

■ Double strand hogs biner real estate compared to bight knots

FIGURE EIGHT ON A BIGHT

Knot for clipping into an anchor or other fixed point. As long as there is no need for

Figure eight on a bight

Bunny ears figure eight

adjusting the knot, this is the gold standard for clipping in.

Pros:

- Easy to tie
- Usually easy to untie after weighting
- Efficient use of biner real estate

Cons:

- Time-consuming to adjust length
- Uses more rope than clove hitch

BUNNY EARS FIGURE EIGHT

Two-bight knot for clipping into a belay or other fixed point with two pieces. This knot greatly reduces the amount of gear needed in any situation where the rope will be clipped into two pieces.

Pros:

- Creates two-point clip-in with rope
- Allows adjustable-length loops
- Saves gear at belay

Cons:

- Hard to escape belay if used for belay clip-in
- Uses 3-plus feet of rope

BOWLINE ON A BIGHT

This knot serves two distinctly different purposes: for clipping into a belay or other fixed point with three pieces by using the resulting three bights, or for tying a mid-point of the rope around a fixed object (like a tree), through the harness, or through chains, without using biners.

Bowline on a bight as an anchor point

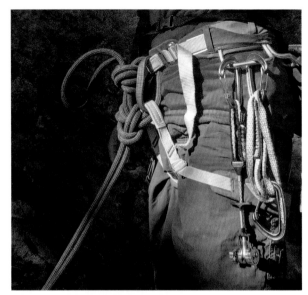

Bowline on a bight as a tie-in

Barrel knot

Double fisherman's

Pros:

- As an anchor point, it creates a three-point clip-in with the rope
- As a tie-in point, it requires no biners to tie into the middle of the rope
- Using the bight method of threading an anchor, it is possible to thread an anchor without using biners with this knot—provided you can let go with both hands to thread a bight through the rings.

Cons:

- Hard to escape belay if used for belay clip-in
- Uses 4-plus feet of rope

BARREL KNOT

The recommended knot for tying rappel ropes together. With all the advantages and none of the danger of a flat overhand (see sidebar), this is the new guide standard for tying rappel ropes together.

Pros:

- Creates flat side, which pulls over edges with less chance of getting stuck
- Fast to tie and untie
- Is secure for tying ropes of different diameters
- More secure than the flat overhand

Cons:

- Hard to untie after heavy loading
- Creates sharp bends in the rope, which could create wear spots if used to tie together fixed ropes

DOUBLE FISHERMAN'S

Knot for tying two rope ends together. Due to the locking nature of this knot, it is the best choice for tying cord ends together

---

FLAT OVERHAND, A.K.A. EURO DEATH KNOT

Warning: Due to the need to tie this knot perfectly (tightly and without twists) to prevent failure, it is no longer recommended! After becoming accepted worldwide, and passing tests for strength and security, new recommendations are that the flat overhand, a.k.a. Euro death knot, should not be used. An accident in Austria during a guide's exam where the knot failed was the impetus to remove this knot from accepted climbing technique. Instead, use the barrel knot (above), which has all the advantages of the flat overhand and is much more secure.

BAD

End-to-end figure eight

permanently, such as when threading a Big Bro or other protection that utilizes cord.

Pros:

▪ Locks tightly—good for semipermanent knots or fixed ropes

Cons:

▪ Hard to untie after heavy loading
▪ Does not have a flat side, so tends to get stuck on edges if used for tying rappel ropes together

END-TO-END FIGURE EIGHT

Knot for tying two rope ends together. This knot is often used in conjunction with a fisherman's knot in each tail for tying fixed ropes together where wind and time could loosen a single knot.

Pros:

▪ Easier to untie than double fisherman's after loading
▪ Good choice for top-roping with two ropes tied together

Cons:

▪ Does not have a flat side, so tends to get stuck on edges if used for tying rappel ropes together
▪ Time-consuming to tie

WATER KNOT

Knot for tying flat webbing ends together. This is the standard knot for tying webbing into slings if they are not sewn. Note that this knot has a propensity to work itself loose—always tie with at least 4 inches of tail, weight it heavily before using, and check it regularly.

Pros:

▪ Uses relatively little webbing length
▪ Low profile

Cons:

▪ Can slowly work its way loose over time
▪ Must be very tight to be secure

Water knot

A

B

C

Using an adjustable hitch to equalize two pieces: A. Clip one piece while preparing a sling on the second. B. Tie a slip knot with the sliding strand up and the stitching positioned near the bottom. C. Clip sliding loop into the top biner. D. Clip lower end of the loop to bottom piece and adjust the sliding hitch.

ADJUSTABLE HITCH

Hitch for adjusting a sewn sling to precise length. This hitch is ideal for creating a nearly equalized clip-in point between two pieces with minimal equipment.

Pros:

- Allows for precision adjustment for equalization with a single sling
- Easy to untie after loading
- Versatile in many applications
- Not widely used—impress your partner

Cons:

- Weakens the webbing as with any hitch
- Sewn part of webbing must be located outside of the hitch

D

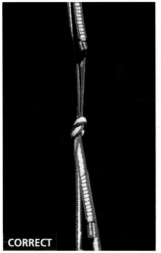
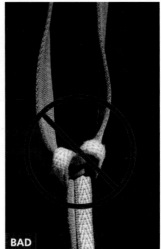
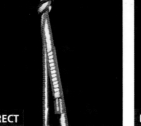

CORRECT　　　BAD　　　BAD

Girth hitch, correct

Do not use a girth hitch on two different sizes of webbing or to attach a sling to a wire.

GIRTH HITCH

Hitch for connecting two loops of webbing, or connecting webbing to a ring anchor or tree. It is also the most common way to connect a daisy chain to the harness, but in via ferrata–type use (where a long fall can be taken onto a short sling), girth hitches have been known to fail due to sling breakage when connecting webbing of two different diameters. When shock-loading is possible, do not use a girth hitch without backup.

Pros:
- Versatile
- Useful for rigging fixed anchors without leaving biners behind
- Cannot untie accidentally

Cons:
- Weakens the webbing as with any hitch
- Can be hard to untie after being weighted
- Can fail if webbings connected are different diameters

YOSEMITE TREE HITCH

Hitch for connecting rope to a tree using only one biner. This hitch was traditionally used in Yosemite with a single nonlocking biner because the rope tension prevents the biner from moving or accidentally unclipping; but a locking biner is best.

Pros:
- Easy way to connect the lead rope to a tree
- Can provide belay-quality security even with a single nonlocking biner
- Fast to set up

Cons:
- Biner must be clipped correctly or the hitch will fail
- Hard to escape the belay if needed

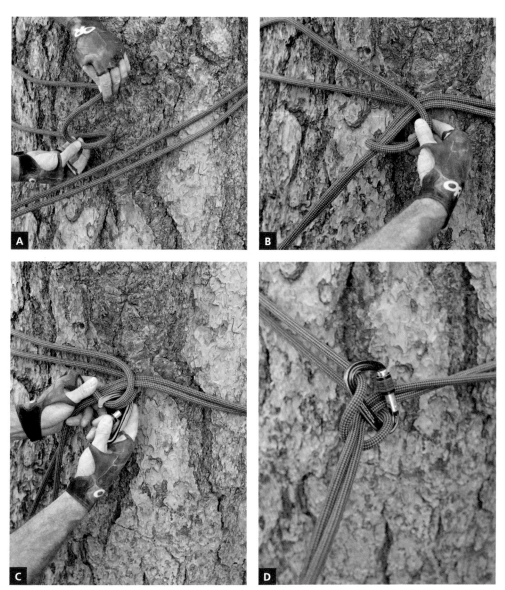

Setting up a Yosemite tree hitch: A. Wrap bight around tree and shape the end of the bight into two "ears." B. Wrap ears around rope strands running from the tree. C. Clip biner through ears. D. Adjust knot snugly against the tree.

KNOTS FOR ASCENSION AND LIFTING

These hitches allow you to take the basic climbing equipment and construct a system to ascend a fixed rope (let's say you are trying to follow a pitch and a rainstorm rolls in, making the rock too slippery to climb) or create a mechanical-advantage system to pull a heavy haul bag or a person upward (let's say your partner fell off while following an overhang and is unable to get back onto the rock). See Chapter 14, Improvised Rescue and Epic Avoidance, for applying these techniques.

GARTA HITCH

Hitch for improvised rope ascension, hauling, rescue, or other autoblocking uses. (See Chapter 14, Improvised Rescue and Epic Avoidance.) Due to the fickle nature of the interaction between the two biners and

Garta hitch

the rope, this hitch should not be used in situations where there is no backup.
Pros:
- Versatile
- Requires only two same-shaped biners

Cons:
- Dramatic shift of biners can cause hitch to fail in some scenarios
- Not as reliable as assisted lock or high friction tube belay device
- Not belay quality—must be used with some form of backup

AUTOBLOCK

Hitch for brake hand backup during rappel or lower, or for ascending the rope. Practice and become comfortable with this hitch— using it regularly makes lowering and rappelling infinitely safer.
Pros:
- Requires little gear
- Makes rappelling and lowering safer

Cons:
- Can behave differently depending on sling material and age, and rope diameter and surface condition

IMPROVISED AUTOBLOCK USING LONG QUICKDRAW

If longer slings are not available, it is possible to wrap a long, thin quickdraw around the rope, creating enough friction to act as an autoblock for improvised rope ascension.
Pros:
- Can save your tail in an unexpected sport climbing scenario

Cons:
- Will not work with shorter quickdraws

Autoblock

Improvised autoblock with long quickdraw

PRUSIK HITCH

Friction hitch for ascending a rope (in lieu of mechanical ascenders), such as during improvised self-rescue, when freeing a stuck rope, or after taking a big fall on steep terrain.

Pros:

- Easy to tie
- Locks tightly with different rope and cord combinations
- Multidirectional

Cons:

- Can be hard to release and slide after tightening

Prusik hitch

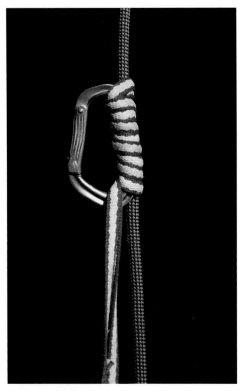

Bachman hitch

French prusik

BACHMAN HITCH

Friction hitch used for ascending a rope, with the biner forming a handle to help slide the hitch. In theory, this hitch works similarly to the prusik; but in practice the Bachman doesn't work well unless precisely the right cord is used. It works better with cord than with flat webbing.

Pros:

▓ Easy to release and slide after tightening

▓ Can be combined with a biner to create a handhold during rope ascending

Cons:

▓ Can be finicky about gripping slippery new webbing or rope

▓ Requires attention to arrange the sling threads in an optimal orientation to hold the rope securely

FRENCH PRUSIK

Perhaps the best hitch for ascending a rope or other similar improvised rescue needs.

Pros:

▓ Slides easily upward and locks securely under downward weight

- Can be modified (as shown here, with extra twists) to work well with a shoulder-length sling

Cons:

- Needs to be monitored—if it catches on something it can release easily.

KNOTS FOR BELAY AND RAPPEL

The following hitches and knots are often considered self-rescue knots, but they are also useful in case a belay/rappel device is dropped or anytime there is a need to release a knot under load.

MUNTER HITCH

This hitch can be used in place of a belay or rappel device. In Europe, the Munter is a commonly used belay technique, not just an improvised technique. Practice using the Munter on a few belays to become familiar with its use.

Pros:

- Can provide more friction with skinny ropes than a tube device
- Only needs a biner to work

Cons:

- Twists the rope
- When belaying, requires keeping the hand a few inches from the knot, as the knot will rotate under a fall, potentially pinching the brake hand if it is too close to the knot

SUPER MUNTER

Similar pros, cons, and purpose as a Munter, but provides added friction for heavy loads or on skinny ropes.

Munter hitch

Super Munter

Munter-mule

Slipped buntline

LOAD-RELEASABLE KNOTS

Full-strength knots that can be released when weighted are useful for improvised rescue as well as when releasing a heavy haul bag from an anchor.

MUNTER-MULE

This knot is the guide standard for releasable use in rescue scenarios.

SLIPPED BUNTLINE

Can be used for similar purposes as the Munter-mule, but requires less rope, making it better for clipping to a haul bag using a sling or other cases where there is not much cord or sling material to work with.

ANCHOR RIGGING

Your anchor rigging will evolve as you, the leader, become proficient at evaluating the quality of protection. For example, guides drill the cordelette with the single power point anchor method because it is easy to teach, works well with larger teams, and may help the anchor to hold even if the individual placements are less than perfect. But this concept invites the question: do you really want to set up an anchor with less than perfect placements?

The reason for cordelette use is sound—it provides approximate equalization and redundancy—but in practice there are often more efficient (and sometimes safer) ways to achieve equalization and redundancy. In climbing, we strive for redundant systems, meaning that if one element were to fail, another would do its job. With equalization, the idea is to share the load between pieces; but even with a cordelette, one piece is usually taking the lion's share of the load.

From my observations, elite climbers in teams of two rarely use a cordelette to build an anchor. The practice is time-consuming, limits the anchor to a small area, and requires the cordelette to be carried up pitch after pitch of hard climbing where every ounce makes life harder. Then there is this fundamental aspect of climbing physics: *Placement quality is far more important than any other aspect of anchor building.*

When building anchors, put 95 percent of your effort into finding bomber placements and 5 percent into your rigging method. Placements to avoid include cams in downward flaring placements or even parallel placements in glassy rock, nuts with poor surface contact, and gear in an expanding or loose feature. Consult Chapter 5, Traditional Gear Placement, for the intricacies of placing the strongest protection.

Several of the elite climbers I interviewed for this book mentioned that climbers would do well to expand their idea of the belay anchor. Rather than always striving to set up a textbook belay with one attachment point, consider including another attachment point and a piece high above the belay that can be used as part of

MISCONCEPTIONS OF ANCHOR RIGGING

Misconception #1: Cordelette with knotted power point creates equalization. Nope, not always. In one exact direction or vector, this method comes close to equalization; but the stretch in different lengths of cord, the way the knot distributes force, and the likely scenario of the knot being pulled slightly to the side all conspire to reduce equalization.

Misconception #2: Knowing the acronyms for anchor rigging (SERENE, ERNEST) is critical to placing bomber anchors. In truth, there is only one factor that really matters in anchor quality—and that is the security of the individual placements. A single bomber piece would be a better anchor choice than a textbook-looking three-piece anchor behind a loose block.

Misconception #3: Biner to biner is bad. In fact, if done properly and in chains of three or less, connected biners are safe. See Chapter 3, Climbing Gear, for an explanation of this misunderstanding. Using biner to biner can efficiently provide redundancy and near-equalization to improvised anchor rigging.

the belay and that will double as the first piece of the next pitch. Also, four pieces in the same crack—if the crack is expanding or in a loose rock feature—may be less reliable than two pieces placed in different cracks. Make a habit of utilizing different cracks when possible and expanding your rigging methods to accommodate a wider selection of anchors.

Cordalette with single power point

Additionally, once the leader has placed a couple of bomber pieces above the belay, the potential demands on the belay anchor are much less. If you use gear in the anchor that is needed on the next pitch, consider cleaning part of the anchor and passing the gear to the leader once they have established two or more bomber pieces on the pitch above. This is a common and safe method of maximizing your rack to the fullest—provided you and your partner both place excellent protection and are both comfortable with the strategy.

CORDELETTE WITH SINGLE POWER POINT

This is the guide standard for anchor rigging and the basic rigging method taught first by most instructors. Learn it, but don't limit yourself to it.

Pros:
- Single, redundant power point
- Easy for multiple climbers to clip into
- Creates a nearly equalized belay anchor
- Relatively easy to escape the belay if needed

Cons:
- Extremely time-consuming overall, when setup, takedown, and cord management over multiple pitches is considered
- Because it forms a single power point, can cause climbers to inadvertently place all gear in loose rock or poor-quality placements due to the need for keeping all pieces close together
- Requires additional gear and adds bulk and weight to the rack

CLOVE HITCHES IN SEQUENCE

A favorite anchor setup among experienced climbers. Be sure to clip the lower piece first, and then move higher to avoid a shock-loading extension should one of the pieces fail.

Pros:

- Uses the least gear of any anchor rigging method
- The fastest rigging method to set up and clean
- Provides equalization and redundancy and prevents extension when clipped correctly

Cons:

- Hard to escape the belay if needed
- Awkward for multiple climbers to clip the belay
- Can be nearly equalized, but often is not
- If clipped in the wrong order, such as with the top piece weighted first, shock-loading of the other pieces will occur if the first piece were to fail due to the sudden extension

PLACING GEAR IN THE OPTIMAL POSITION

By placing a couple of pieces close together and clipping the higher one with enough rope to create a power point using the lead line—an equalized, redundant, bomber anchor with a power point can be made with minimal gear.

Pros:

- Fast to set up and take down
- Uses minimal gear

Clove hitches in sequence: Clip lowest piece first.

Cons:

- Makes escaping the belay more difficult than methods that do not use the rope as part of the anchor rigging
- Uses rope that may be needed on the following pitch

Rope power point

2 PLUS 1 ANCHORS

The following anchor rigging methods require a subtle but significant change of thinking. Rather than building an anchor with three pieces all brought down into a single point, these methods work best as two-piece anchors with a third piece added above the anchor. This method simplifies the anchor rigging while expanding the options for gear placement. This works particularly well in loose or broken terrain, or in places with limited placement options, where adding a piece a body length or more from the anchor will greatly increase the security of the anchor. Use the two-piece part of the anchor as the master clip-in/belay point.

Power Point Plus 1

The power point plus 1 anchor method is often the best and most efficient way to rig a fast and bomber belay.

Pros:

- Creates a redundant, nearly equalized, no-extension belay using only a single sling and a couple of biners
- Fast to set up, take down, and adjust to different lengths

Power point plus 1

Cons:

- If climbing with a team of three, each climber will need to clip in the same way, using their rope to clip the third piece.
- Escaping the belay in a rescue scenario is more difficult because the rope is used in the anchor. (But remember, it is usually not practical to plan every anchor for a potential rescue and doing so uses valuable time and equipment that may boost safety better if used elsewhere.)

Magic X Plus 1

The magic or sliding X was a favorite method of rigging anchors; but the potential for shock-loading extension if one piece fails has caused it to fall out of favor. The fact remains, however, that this method provides true equalization where the other typical anchor riggings, including the cordelette method, do not—the other methods come close, but cord length, actual direction of pull, and the different tensions within the knot prevent true equalization.

If you are concerned about the strength of the pieces and feel that equalization is necessary, the magic X may be your best option. The knots allow for some sliding, so equalization will happen through a range of pull directions. The plus-1 arrangement adds the security of a third piece far from the primary anchor. The key to safe use of the magic X is to add stopper or limiter knots (as shown in photo to right) to the sling to prevent extension if one piece should fail.

Magic X (with stopper knots) plus 1

Pros:

- Creates true equalization between two pieces because the weight is shared, even if the direction of pull changes slightly
- Requires minimal gear

Cons:

- Can cause shock-loading extension if stopper knots are not used and one piece fails
- Stopper knots used to prevent shock-loading extension can be hard to untie after heavy weighting

WHERE THE FORCE HAPPENS

Much effort and attention is focused on building and rigging industrial-strength anchors, and for good reason; if your anchor were to fail the consequences would almost certainly be catastrophic. However, *in 99 percent of the scenarios we encounter while climbing, the anchor will actually receive far less force than the single pieces we fall on while leading.* Over and over, we build anchors that will hold a truck, but then set ourselves up on lead so that if a single cam or nut were to fail, we would take a horrible fall.

This does not suggest we should build weak anchors, but rather that there are many places on a climb besides the belay where anchor-quality placements are necessary. The point here is that, the majority of the time, the belay anchor is not the most important element of protection on the pitch. Unless the leader takes a fall onto the belay, which is rarely likely, even a fully hanging belay with both climbers on it will only generate a few hundred pounds of force. Compare this to the typical leader fall, which can easily subject the protection to well over a thousand pounds of force. Realizing this, experienced climbers will often use just two bomber pieces for a belay anchor, saving the gear to create mini-anchors at crucial points mid-pitch—the places where large forces are much more likely to happen.

ANCHOR SETUP USING PAS OR DAISY CHAIN

This method is similar to the plus-1 techniques discussed earlier, but incorporates a daisy chain or personal anchor system (PAS) for one tether to the anchor. The daisy chain was invented for aid climbing, and has been used for belay use, but the PAS designed by Metolius is far superior for belay use because of its full-strength loops. To eliminate the girth hitch weak point of a PAS or daisy, add a quickdraw or biner from your belay loop to a loop of the PAS or daisy—bypassing the girth hitch with the load. For body weight applications this is not necessary; but for anchors, bivys, or rigging funky rappels where shock load of the daisy is possible, the biner bypass is recommended.

BOLT ANCHORS

By far the most common use of bolted anchors is clipping and lowering off after ascending a climb of half a rope length or less. As long as there are two or more bolts in decent condition and the bolts are $^3/_8$ inch or bigger and placed in solid rock, there is usually no need to use slings, cordelettes, or locking biners to rig a textbook anchor. Simply clipping a draw to each bolt is adequate and perfectly safe. How you clip the bolts is important. Remember:

- Clip the rope so the gates of the biners are facing opposite directions.
- If the bolts are far enough apart that the two draws don't come together to a single point, consider using slings or enchained draws on each anchor bolt. This is not a safety factor, but anytime the rope

runs through multiple angle changes at the anchor it kinks the rope, making belaying and rope handling difficult.

- If the bolts are in poor condition, consider leaving a backup piece or biner on the last bolt to back up the anchor.
- For top-roping, don't make a habit of threading the rope through the fixed rings or hardware on the anchor—repeated lowering wears the metal of the rings and shortens the life span of the anchor. Use your own draws until you are ready to clean the pitch, and then lower through the rings just once for your last time down.

On multipitch climbs with bolt anchors where a leader fall may occur onto the anchor, be sure to clip the bolt anchors themselves rather than chain links or screw-link closures. The thicker-stocked chains and links are strong enough for climbing falls, but the thinner ones are far weaker than the bolt hangers. Modern bolt hangers are UIAA certified to hold 25 kN (5620 pounds of force) or more while the thinner, hardware store–grade chains and links found on many climbs may break under less than 1000 pounds of force. This is strong enough for lowering and rappelling, but for multipitch use—or anytime the bolt may hold a leader fall—it is best to bypass the chains and links and clip directly to the bolt hangers.

If the belay bolts are not in perfect condition, treat them as you would any other natural anchor and rig them with a redundant, semi-equalized method. If the bolts are at least $3/8$ inch in diameter and in perfect condition, equalizing is unnecessary. Equalizing can also create an awkwardly low power point and will often make the belay less comfortable and more time-consuming.

Opposite: *Sheyna Button punching it above thin protection in a granite finger crack*

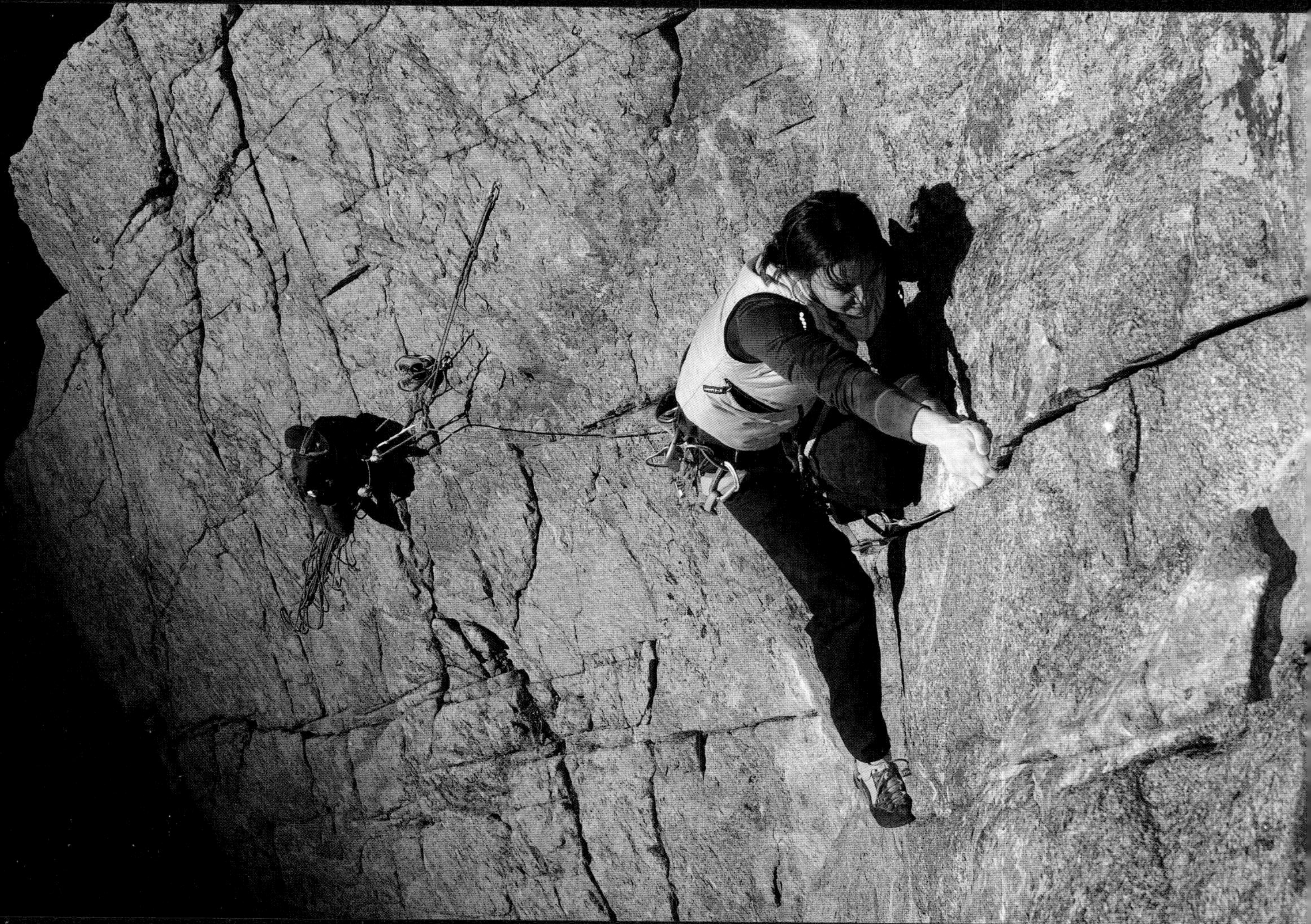

CHAPTER 5

Traditional Gear Placement

"You want to move above your gear with confidence, not uncertainty."

Sonnie Trotter

Traditional climbing equipment is incredible. Consider the engineering that goes into the design, the durability of the materials, the immense strength of the gear in a solid placement, and the versatility of use. Cams and nuts ranging from fingernail thin to monster off-width sizes, lightweight hardware, sticky rubber, and the online sharing of equipment information have helped advanced climbing standards by leaps and bounds. There is no doubt that progress in climbing technology has made most of today's hard trad climbs possible.

With these advances, however, there are dangers. There is now a tendency to assume the gear will work, where a few decades ago climbing gear was viewed with much more skepticism. In the 1980s it was a rare climber who would hurl themselves at a climb, taking repeated leader falls on natural protection. Today, such an effort is still challenging, but the average weekend in Yosemite, California, Mount Arapiles, Australia, or any popular trad climbing area around the globe will see more than a few meaty whippers onto natural protection.

This is a fantastic evolution of climbing. But for aspiring trad masters, the absolute confidence to go for it above your gear needs to be accompanied by a critical eye and acute understanding of the complex physics that happen to the gear, the system, and the climber's body in a leader fall. To develop this confidence safely, it is important to first see past some of the illusions of natural protection.

THE THREE ILLUSIONS OF TRAD GEAR

Before we dig into the idiosyncrasies of advanced gear placement, let's clear the slate and talk about how climbing gear can also create a dangerous illusion that it will hold. You go out to the crag armed with thousands of dollars worth of fascinating equipment. You surround your body with this gear like some kind of voodoo skirt to protect you against gravity. You stick some of the gear in a crack and go for it. It works, much of the time, but there are many, many stories of climbers placing what they call a "textbook cam" and having it pull out—because, well, it wasn't.

1. **The illusion of the favorite piece.** Climbers are a superstitious lot. Many climbers develop an affinity for what they call their "favorite piece." Perhaps it held their first leader fall, or it perfectly fits a common crack size at the area where they learned to lead, or it is the size of the crack that, given their druthers, they prefer to climb. There's nothing wrong with having a favorite piece and looking for spots in the crack where it will fit. But the reality is that the piece you like has little to no bearing on what piece will be best in any given spot or whether or not it will hold a fall. More than once, I've seen people fire in their favorite piece in a crux, and then fall, ripping out that favorite piece.

2. **The illusion of gear that isn't fallen on.** We use gear in the sense that we carry it, place it, and remove it, but 95 percent of the pieces we place while free climbing are never even weighted, let alone fallen on. So how can we be sure that what we think is "bomber" will really hold a hard fall? If it never gets tested, there is no direct learning. This process of placing gear over and over without feedback from falls creates a scenario where we can place less than optimal gear and get away with it for a really long time—until we don't. *Aspire to a skill level where 99 percent of the pieces*

Two pieces that had been judged "good enough" failed and ripped out in a leader fall, leaving a single biner hanging strangely on the rope.

you ever place would hold 99 percent of the falls you could possibly take. We'll cover how to do this in this section.

3. **The illusion of shiny new gear that is industry tested.** Because climbing gear was made for rock climbing and tested for strength, we are led to believe that the gear will

A BAD

B BAD

C BAD

D BAD

Bad and Good Placements:

A. This placement may hold if weighted perfectly without moving it, but it is too wide open and the slightest bump could open the cams entirely, making the piece worthless.

B. This placement is also unpredictable. The subtle interaction between the cams and the flared rock angle make it difficult to assess. Sometimes a cam like this will hold a huge load and other times it will blow out under less than body weight.

C. This placement does not have good contact on the outside cam. This piece may hold a leader fall, but there's a good chance it will fail.

D. This nut placement might or might not be any good. Because we can't see the surface contact between nut and rock, we can't be sure if it will hold a hefty downward pull.

E. This nut has substantial, obviously solid rock holding it in the case of a downward pull.

F. This cam has good contact as well as subtle rock protrusions under its cams, so there is more than the camming action holding it against a fall.

E GOOD

F GOOD

hold. These tests, however, are only for material strength and give no indication of the strength of a placement. The real-life testing comes during the falls you may take on the gear placements on *your* lead, not in the lab. In your exact situation while climbing, the gear has not been tested by the industry.

When you take a leader fall, there are many things at play: the length of the slings and draws that are clipped to each piece, the weight of your belayer, the belay device your rope is running through, the age and dynamic qualities of the rope you are using, the position of the belayer, and finally (and most importantly) the exact gear you placed and how it interacts with the rock. These factors all conspire to create complex physics unique to your situation. Every time you start up a lead you are creating a potential experiment, with you as the crash test dummy, in how untested, placed gear reacts to the mighty forces of a leader fall.

We climbers need the security of our placements to be no illusion. See examples on the page opposite of placements to avoid (A–D) and favor (E and F).

When searching for and then evaluating a piece, it is important to think beyond a simplistic view of the placement and train your eye to look for the combination of factors that make for a bomber placement. In fact, looking for textbook placements can often be a distraction from finding a piece that may be visually funky but physically strong. Examples include cams with their lobes in different ranges of constriction and nuts behind features where the nut sits loose but could never fall out in a downward pull. To detect these kinds of placements, it helps to think of trad gear in multiple dimensions.

THE FOUR DIMENSIONS OF THE BOMBER PIECE

"The thing I hate most is trying a hard move and not knowing if the piece below me is going to hold. So I try not to climb past a piece I'm suspicious of—I'd rather take 5, 10, 15 seconds extra to find a piece I'm comfortable with—that gives me the confidence to try hard."

Sonnie Trotter

When placing gear it is easy to become distracted by "small potatoes," things that don't matter in the moment—like the brand of your camming device, the type of trigger it has, your "feelings" for the piece, or your overall prior successes and failures as a climber. Don't get distracted: these have nothing to do with what makes a piece bomber. Focus instead on what causes each piece to be able to hold even the most scream-inducing whippers.

THE FIRST DIMENSION: THE CRACK ITSELF

Just as you're ready to fire in a piece, stop for a moment and look at the entirety of the crack in front of you, not just the first place that jumps out as a potential placement.

Check out the rock around the crack and make sure it's not a flake, that it runs through solid stone. Look up and down, into and along the crack. Careful scanning may show four or five different possibilities for protection. Quite often, the first placement you see isn't the best one, so take a few moments to really study the crack. Then reach down to your rack and pick the piece that fits precisely the spot you judge best. Challenge yourself to not slide the piece up and down the crack looking for a place where it will fit. Instead, learn to visualize first how the cams or nut will fit in the crack before you even reach for the gear, and then place the cam or nut exactly as you anticipated.

THE SECOND DIMENSION: WHAT REALLY HOLDS THE FALL

It's not the brand, not the gear review you read online, not the textbook position of the cam or nut. What holds a cam or nut in a fall is the interaction between the forces of the fall transferred into the rock through the material of the piece of gear. There is no gear made that will hold when placed behind an expanding or loose flake. There is no gear made that will hold a big fall in a downward flaring, glassy-surfaced crack. When trusting your life to your climbing gear, it is important to imagine the potential fall, its forces and direction of force, on the placed pro. This means you must rely on real time, common sense, and visualization of physics. Boil it down to the simplest question: *Would I trust my life to this placement?*

THE THIRD DIMENSION: MARGIN FOR ERROR

The best gear placements have a large buffer between holding and failure. A nut held in place by a small crystal, a cam placed just a millimeter above a section of rotten rock, or a bolt drilled in a block that's fractured on all sides: these pieces all have no margin for error and are potentially dangerous. You want to develop a habit of increasing that margin for error by finding placements that are good enough that you would trust your life to that single piece (even though we try not to rely on one piece). This means:

- Don't rely on nuts if you can't see clearly what is holding them in place. Whenever possible, place nuts where you can see clearly how they meet the rock.
- Don't rely on cams in downward flaring cracks. Whenever possible, place cams in places where the crack flares slightly upward.
- Don't accept placements that are just good enough. Learn to find the perfect placement!

Small cams require particular attention to the margin for error. With larger cams it is easier to see exactly how the cam surfaces are contacting the rock. With smaller cams it is hard to see into the tiny cracks where the pieces are used. To assess the placement, it helps to "feel" the rock with the cam, using the trigger in small exploratory movements to gauge if the crack is flaring inward and upward (good) or downward and outward (not so good).

With small cams, it is difficult to visualize the physics of the placement because you often can't see the interior surface of the crack or hole. But you can lightly pull the trigger, move the cam against the rock, and feel the position of the trigger to give you a sense of which direction the crack is flaring at the precise point where the cams contact the rock—then leave the cam at the optimal point.

THE FOURTH DIMENSION: THE DIRECTION OF PULL

Gravity is a daunting opponent, but it has one vulnerability—it's very predictable. When you fall off a climb, you tend to go straight down. The huge forces in a leader fall will pull the top piece straight down.

When a climb changes direction, there can be outward and even upward pull on certain pieces of protection, but this force is secondary and much less than the force on the top piece. If that top piece holds, you're golden.

Duh, you say. We all know we fall *down*. Well, here's the catch. What happens is that it can be tempting to bypass a piece that is really strong in a downward vector in favor of placing a piece that feels more "stuck" but is much weaker in the direction that matters most: down. Most of the time, it is far better to place a piece that will hold strongly downward and use other force-mitigating methods to keep side forces from lifting or skewing the piece to a position where it cannot hold a downward fall.

Ways to maintain downward direction of pull include:

- Short-clipping the piece below—clipping a lower piece close to the rock can prevent the rope from pulling outward on the pieces above it
- Placing a piece to hold the rope in place
- Tethering, or placing a second piece to hold the first piece in optimal orientation
- Clipping the piece extra-long to prevent rope movement from disturbing the placement
- Short-clipping a piece above a ledge
- Climbing past without pulling out on the piece

CAMS

Cams are the cornerstone of the modern climbing rack. The physics are also the most complicated of all types of climbing protection—so while they are easy to place, they are more difficult than a nut to assess for absolute holding power. Because of this, many climbers frequently and inadvertently place cams that will likely not hold a fall. Every year climbing accidents happen from cam failure. If there is one single piece of advice I'd like the reader to take away from this chapter, it is to *be more critical of cam placements and to get in the habit of only placing the best ones.*

THE THREE MYTHS OF CAMS

Cams are borderline magic—and that's the problem. It's easy to think that there is some mysterious force keeping them in the crack when it is really the opposition of the cams causing friction or jamming against the rock relative to the direction of pull. Although it is sometimes hard to visualize the physics that make a cam work, there is absolutely nothing magic about them. Because of their amazing capabilities (and hidden limitations) there are a few myths that have developed over the thirty-five years since spring-loaded camming devices were invented.

The Walking Cam

Many climbers are afraid that if you can wriggle the stem and the cam moves, or "walks" up the crack, the piece is poor. Consider any perfectly parallel crack. Put the right-size cam in the crack and start wriggling. Provided the crack stays the same size, it will walk all the way to the top (or out of sight into the crack), and be a solid

piece every inch of the way. There are two conditions that must both be present for walking to be a real safety issue:

- The cam must be in a place where it can walk into an opening where the cam will not hold a fall.
- Something must move, "wriggle," the cam to make it walk.

This cam could walk within the crack and become much less secure; however, it won't move on its own. If you can make sure it stays still, it will be perfectly bomber.

If only the first condition exists—the cam can walk into an insecure spot—but care is taken to prevent the cam from walking, there is no issue. The cam will stay where it is and hold a fall. To prevent movement, add a sling or quickdraw or simply climb by it carefully without moving it.

If only the second condition exists—rope angle or climber movement is causing the cam to walk—but the cam is only adjusting its position in a parallel crack that is essentially the same above the cam, there is no issue with walking. The cam will walk an inch or two but still hold the same under a downward fall.

A cam can walk into a position where it is difficult or impossible to remove—and every leader will eventually place a cam that walks into a position where it is hard to clean—but depending on the situation most of the time safety is a higher priority than easy removal of the cam. *The walking cam is only a safety issue if the cam moves into a spot where it will not hold a fall.*

The Overcam

It's scary to me how many beginner and intermediate leaders have explained that they placed a questionable cam at the outer limits of its range because they thought that the next size bigger would be "overcammed." Overcamming is an issue because the cam may be difficult to remove (and people hate to leave gear; but isn't your life worth it?) but not because it somehow makes the cam less secure or strong. The cam angle remains the same throughout the size range of the cam, and

This cam is touching all parts of one outer cam and the inner cams are in their tightest configuration—not textbook, but as bomber as a cam could possibly be.

in most cases, cams placed tightly are better than cams placed loosely. With practice it's possible to place tight cams that are easy to remove, but it's better to err on the side of too snug than too loose. Metolius developed a Range Finder indicator on the side of their cam, which demonstrates this concept perfectly:

- In the loosest fit, the red zone is against the rock. Metolius explains: "Placement is not secure. A larger cam should be used."

- In the middle range, the yellow zone is against the rock. Metolius explains: "Placement is secure, but may move to an insecure position. A larger cam is usually better."
- In the tightest fit, the green zone is against the rock. Metolius explains: "Placement is secure."

Contrary to popular belief, cams placed in their tightest configuration are often the best. Climb with any experienced trad climber and you'll see a lot of cams that are placed tightly yet easily removed by the second. To remove cams that are placed tightly, look ahead in this chapter to the section on cleaning cams.

The Flared Cam

This myth is related to both of the previous ones. Climbers often place cams in downward flaring parts of the crack when there are much better sites available. They do this because when placed in a downward flaring spot, the cams cannot generally walk, giving the impression of security. When pulled downward under the explosive force of a leader fall, however, even slightly downward flaring cam placements have been known to fail with surprising regularity. Many climbers place cams in a slightly downward flaring spot because they don't want to place a nearby piece that is "overcammed" or "might walk," when indeed, in the case of a fall, the downward flaring cam is usually the weaker choice.

If you must use a flared placement, advanced climbers look for subtleties on the walls of the crack—edges, dishes, bumps, or other places—where the cams can sit. Placing the cam lobes on a short section of parallel crack, instead of within a downward flare, can make the difference between a solid placement and one that, under the force of a fall, will pluck like a nose hair.

This cam is touching the rock in the green range of the Metolius Range Finder, indicating it is in a good range for the cam. However, the downward flare makes its holding power extremely unpredictable. A cam the next size up, placed in the long constriction, would probably be stronger.

A. A four-cam unit does not fit well in this flared crack. B. In the same spot, an offset cam, where the inner cams are smaller than the outer cams, fits perfectly. C. Super pinky! Tricams can fit in places where no other piece will fit and beef up the rack with minimal weight and space.

SPECIALIZED CAMS

Offset cams, TCUs, and tricams often fit where four-cam units cannot. The most versatile double trad rack will include a single set of four-cam units as well as a single set of specialized cams in the smaller sizes—the micro cams.

BIG BROS

The Big Bro has the lowest profile and is the lightest weight of wide crack protection.

The late Craig Luebben invented Big Bros for his engineering honors thesis at Colorado State University and named them after "Big Brother is watching you," from George Orwell's *1984*. For the Big Bro to work, the crack must have enough parallel rock, in the right places, to hold the ends of the Big Bro. The device requires practice to place efficiently and securely with one hand, but with practice the Big Bro is an indispensable wide crack tool. A rack of Big Bros takes up much less space and is lighter than

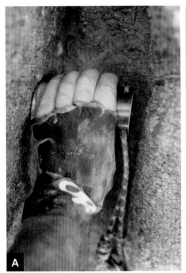

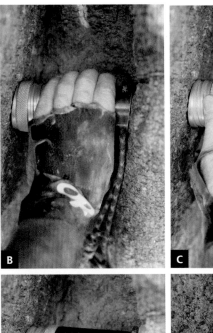

To place a Big Bro:

A. *Place the screw end of the Big Bro against the rock where it will align with a parallel spot on the opposite wall.*

B. *Press the release button on top of the Big Bro and allow the device to expand into position. Confirm parallel fit or adjust placement at this point.*

C. *Screw the collar down tight against the tube.*

D. *Pull hard on the cord to set the tube and reconfirm parallel seating of the ends against the rock. Clip the Big Bro with a quickdraw or long sling to prevent any lift.*

E. *A cam in the same spot does not fit deeply enough to be secure.*

a rack of similar-size cams. They will also fit in shallow cracks and pockets where big cams are too wide.

HOW TO MAKE A MARGINAL PLACEMENT GREAT

Finding good protection in sections that are tricky to protect is one of the joys and hallmarks of advanced climbing. Many times a less than ideal placement can be made reliable with a little work. This process takes patience, discipline, and a few tricks. The keys are to keep working on it until you find protection you can trust and to look beyond your first impression of the crack.

NESTING

Nesting together several pieces of micro gear can create a full-strength placement. Here's how. The placement shown in the photos on the next page had one obvious spot for a micro cam, but a bit of dirt in the bottom looked as if it might be hiding an additional placement useful for more pieces.

Doing the math, the one micro cam has a test strength of 5 kN, so even if the placement is perfect, 5 kN is as strong as it will be. The two smallest micro nuts test 2.5 kN each, not rated for free climbing, but in combination they are as strong as the micro cam. The bigger micro nut is rated for free climbing at 6 kN (the strongest piece of the four). In combination, the pieces add up to 16 kN, more than the test rating of a hand-size cam. Each piece, although small, adds to the surface area of the placement, contacts slightly different rock, and increases the strength of the combined placement. Of course, we can't be sure that each piece will go to its tested limit, but the lesson is that with persistence (and enough pieces on your rack), a seemingly borderline placement can often be made bomber.

TETHERING

A single nut that is in an easily knocked loose, but otherwise good, configuration can often be made solid by adding another piece as a directional. In this case, the directional cam is worthless for holding a fall, but by tethering the nut to the cam, the nut stays in place and will not move as the leader climbs onward. Tethering is an important consideration for cams.

Tethering protection

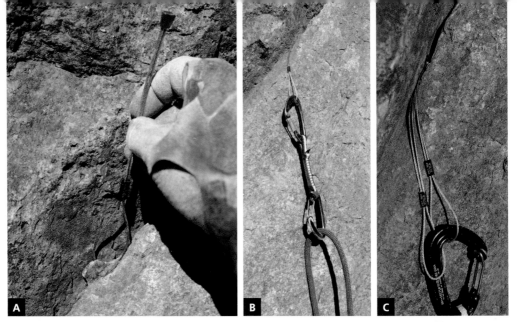

When nesting: A. If the crack is dirty, clean the crack with wire of micro nut. B. Place smallest micro that will fit the crack well, and clip it. C. Place second micro in horizontal configuration on top of first and clip it as well; horizontal configuration leaves more room for a third nut.

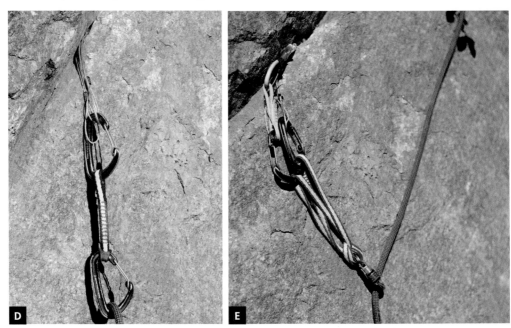

D. Place third and biggest nut on top of the other two. E. Place micro cam and equalize with the nuts. Then go for it.

THE INTERNET ON CLIMBING GEAR

A phenomenon of climbing is that many people think that the next person to lead a pitch will place exactly the same gear, in exactly the same order. With online forums, this phenomenon has become pervasive, and everyone who posts information online has become a guidebook writer, for better or worse.

With the enormous amount of beta available online, it is hard to separate the kernels of real wisdom from the endless spray of minutia, and to interpret other people's perspectives. Here are some translations for certain online information:

- "The climb is easy for the grade." This means the person who posted was climbing well at the time and enjoys letting others know how well they are climbing. Beware of sandbags.
- "This is hard for the grade." This means the poster struggled on the pitch and feels they should perform better at the grade.
- "You don't need any wide gear for the off-width." This means the poster is really good at climbing wide cracks.
- "The climb isn't as scary as its reputation." This means the poster was really scared before going up, but then climbed it more easily than they expected.

None of these comments have any bearing on the experience you will have on the same climb. Sometimes interpreting the internet posts can be more difficult than the climb itself. For a perfect example, read the Mountain Project thread on *The Naked*

Don't believe everything you find on the internet.

Edge in Eldorado Canyon. In the thread, several people talk about the key piece to a sketchy section being good because it held when they fell on it. Others talk about how that same key piece pulled out when fallen on. Reading the entire thread takes longer than the fastest ascent of the route. And if you've done the route yourself before reading the thread, there are many places where you stop to wonder, "Are they talking about the same climb?"

There is nothing wrong with using internet beta to arm yourself before a climb, but don't rely on it too much. What you read can guide you, but the actual climb is a mystery you must solve on your own.

A second issue of the internet is the frequent postings about failed gear. The vast majority of the time, climbing gear "failures" are user errors or misjudgments. Several times a year someone posts about how such-and-such piece failed when they thought it was a perfect placement. They blame the piece and the manufacturer and talk about how lucky they were to survive. Well, the last part is true, but when a piece of climbing gear placed by the leader pulls out, 99.99 percent of the time it's because the placement was inadequate due to loose rock, poor placement quality, or using a previously damaged piece of gear—not because the original piece of equipment was faulty. Climbing gear is required to undergo rigorous testing methods, and when a cam or nut fails, there is generally only one person to blame—the person who placed it.

GEAR STRATEGY

"With a double set, rack your gear on your harness, smallest in front and largest in back, with one set on each side so you can easily grab the correct piece with either hand."

Sonnie Trotter

The gear you carry, and how you carry it, can make a big difference in the outcome of a hard lead. As beginners we tend to carry extra gear "just in case," but as we gain experience and increase our capabilities this just-in-case gear becomes a burden and a limitation. The mental shift required is to proceed with the perspective that it is your decision-making at a given moment that creates safety—not the amount of gear you carry. Too much gear weighs you down, in more ways than one.

Consider these scenarios:

Climber A leaves the ground with a triple set of cams. Because the climber has plenty of just-in-case gear, they place with abandon, plugging gear with little thought to what they will need later. Also, because the climber is so heavily weighted and all the moves feel harder with the extra weight, they feel the need to place more frequently. High on the pitch, the leader runs low on thin-hands-size gear, tires out, and ends up hanging on the rope, lowering down, and backcleaning a thin-hands piece from lower on the pitch to use higher. The climber makes it to the belay safely, with a number of unused large and small cams remaining on her rack. Because she ran low on gear, it bolsters her impression that she needs to carry even more gear.

Climber B leaves the ground with a double set of cams, one set less than climber A. Climber B also runs low on thin-hands gear and ends up weighting the rope and lowering to backclean a thin-hands piece. He also reaches the belay safely with unused gear on his rack.

The free climbing rack (right) for El Cap's Zodiac next to the aid climbing rack (left) for the Zodiac. Take the right gear for you and your plans, but no more than that.

Climber C leaves the ground with a single full set of cams, but because the crack above appears to have a lot of thin hand jams, she carries a triple set of thin-hand–size cams, places nuts in a couple of places, and runs it out strategically where the fall is clean. She crushes the pitch without hanging and arrives at the belay safely with almost no gear left.

Obviously Climber C has the best strategy, and it appears that she had the knowledge needed to carry the right gear. However, in many cases this knowledge is gained not from having the correct guide-book information, but by practicing the philosophy of studying the pitch from the ground, doing your research, and carrying only the gear that is needed for a lead.

I've seen each of these scenarios unfold hundreds of times and the lesson is always this: *Carrying more gear does not translate into having the right gear when you need it.*

GEAR AND SEQUENCING

In the microcosm of trad leading, the places you stop to place and the precise locations where you insert the gear can make a big difference in the difficulty of a pitch. This balance between placing enough gear and

LEARNING TO CARRY JUST ENOUGH GEAR

The way to have the right gear when you need it is to practice carrying a rack that is customized on every pitch, for that particular pitch. A good way to practice this, and a method I experimented with frequently as a young trad climber, is to use short warm-up pitches as a challenge to select precisely the right gear. Stand on the ground and look up the pitch. Attempt to rack exactly the right gear on your harness, in the order you will place it. Take a few extra pieces, clipped a little out of reach on the back of your harness, and be perfectly willing to lower off of your last good piece if you don't get it right. Of course you'll predict incorrectly, but by practicing this you'll grow comfortable with anticipating the gear needs of a given pitch as well as solving the problem of not having the right gear, all while protecting the pitch perfectly safely.

Another way to wean yourself from the just-in-case monster rack is to invest in a lightweight 6- to 7-mm tag line. Then leave the extra gear on the ground and, using the tag line, pull it up if you need it, even if it means hanging on the rope to pull up the extra gear. The goal is to reach the anchor with almost nothing left on the rack. While this sounds preposterous to a climber who frequently reaches the anchor with a full set of cams dangling from their body, with practice it is incredible how often you can get it right if you look ahead, place nuts where they fit to save cams for later, and, for added efficiency, always place bomber gear so you're not wasting gear on sloppy placements.

A. A cam limits the climber to getting two fingers in the crack. B. A nut in the same spot allows the climber to get a secure fingerlock with all four fingers.

putting it in the optimal locations is part of the dance of trad climbing and part of the game that trad aficionados thoroughly enjoy. Gear placement considerations to make the climbing as easy as possible include:

- Carefully read the rock ahead and sequence your protection to avoid having to stop to place gear in the middle of the hardest moves.
- On pitches with a hard start followed by a good stance, leave part of the rack on the ground then stop to pull it up from the good stance.
- Remember that pulling up rope to clip, then falling before clipping, can result in a huge fall; it can be better to skip the placement and do one more move to reach better holds.

- Place a nut instead of a cam in cracks where you know you'll want to put your fingers for climbing.

CLEANING TRAD GEAR

Swapping leads up a big route at the limits of your team's ability is an exhilarating experience. And it is movement efficiency that spells the difference between a proud send to the summit and a pathetic grovel. Much energy can be conserved using careful strategy in how you follow pitches and clean gear. When following a pitch, consciously relax to the point where you are about to fall from every move—but not quite. You want to get into a Zen-like state that only a top-rope can inspire. The best mind-set for following a pitch on a long route is to be so relaxed that you are just

A WARNING AS YOU CLEAN

When a piece is clipped with a sling, do not put the sling around your neck before cleaning the piece. Many leaders ask their followers to do this to prevent dropping the gear (oh, the precious gear!), but it is a recipe for disaster. With rope stretch, a fall while the piece is still in the crack could strangle you. Seriously. If you're worried about losing the piece, leave it clipped to the rope until after it is cleaned from the route.

shy of falling asleep. Then, as you clean the gear, practice these strategies:

- Clean the gear from the best stances available. If the best stance is above the piece, unclip it before you move past so the rope doesn't lift the piece into a stuck position. Then reach down to clean it.
- If the climbing is strenuous, just pop the gear out of its placement and leave the piece(s) hanging from your rope for a few moves until you are at a secure stance where you can move the gear from rope to harness.

Contrary to popular belief, careful re-racking as you follow is usually a waste of time and energy. It is much more efficient to simply clip the gear onto your harness and throw slings over your shoulder in the fastest, easiest way possible. While at a good stance, removing a cam and clipping it with thought and finesse where you'll want it for the next lead is okay, but there is absolutely no advantage to hanging out on small holds to organize gear. Save gear organization for the belay, when you have both hands free, a partner to help, and perhaps even a ledge to work from.

STUCK GEAR REMOVAL

Many climbers are as proud of their gear rack as parents are of their children, and having to leave gear behind can send even a well-heeled leader into fits of mourning. Yet part of the onus for preventing stuck gear lies with the leader—the best trad leaders place bomber gear that is also easy for the second to remove. Here's how you can do it too:

- Don't heavily set your nuts, unless the direction of the rope pull could dislodge the piece or in cases where a placement is particularly shallow and the nut needs to be jammed in place to keep it from lifting out. Set most nuts lightly but securely, making sure to move past them without kicking them out. There is nothing wrong with setting some nuts with as much force as you can muster. But if you treat every piece like this, your partner will waste time and energy retrieving them.
- Do let your partner know how you put the gear in, to help them take it out. For example, "The red cam went in from below."

To free a stuck cam: Use fingers and/or a cleaning tool to further articulate any cam lobe that is not jammed—this will often allow the entire unit to move slightly, releasing the stuck cam lobes. Once loose, remove cam using the trigger.

For the second on the pitch, these little-known techniques ease and speed gear cleaning:

▓ Unless you need the piece to protect you (for example, when following a traverse), unclip the piece from the rope before you climb past it. Leaving gear clipped as you climb past can cause the piece to rotate upward, pulled by the rope, frequently jamming the cam or nut into a difficult-to-remove position.

▓ Before you move the piece at all, look at the crack and try to decipher how the piece went in, then reverse engineer the placement to remove it.

▓ When working to remove a stuck cam, don't rotate the stem and the trigger up and down or back and forth. This often jams the cam more completely. Instead, try to hold the stem relatively still as you nudge the cam into its loosest configuration.

▓ If a nut seems stuck after wriggling it lightly, leave it clipped to the rope and take the nut tool, with its keeper biner, off your harness and give the nut a hard, sharp stab—no need to clip the nut tool into something every time you use it. Put the nut tool back on your harness and remove the now loosened nut.

Old fixed gear tells a great story, but it is unpredictable in strength.

EVALUATING OLD FIXED GEAR

Regardless of the social maturity of climbers at times, climbing as a sport has been mature for several decades. Much of the fixed protection on crags and walls around the world that served well for so long has now deteriorated to the point where it is no longer trustworthy. The safest way to use fixed anchors and protection, aside from bomber modern bolts, is as a supplement to the protection you place and not a substitute for it. When using fixed gear, always look at the consequences if the piece or anchor were to fail and plan accordingly; a rusty bolt 5 feet above a perfect cam with lots of clean air below should

A. Soft iron pitons in Switzerland. Which ones to clip? All of them, with equalization.
B. A fixed bashie—you want a nearby backup for gear like this.

be assessed very differently than a similar rusty bolt 20 feet above a string of dubious micro nuts.

For gear of unknown or dubious strength, it is best to avoid pulling up rope to clip. If you clip it and then fall while the piece is still above you, and the piece fails, you will take a much longer fall than you would have if the piece was clipped such that no extra rope was pulled up to make the clip. As you move past such a piece, consider clipping it shorter to shorten the potential fall onto it.

Bolts

Even most sport climbing areas are now old enough to have many suspect bolts, and without sustained investment in rebolting efforts, many climbs will fall into obscurity and be forgotten (if they haven't already) simply because people stop climbing them when the bolts become unsafe. See Chapter 7, Sport Climbing, for further discussion on bolt aging and evaluation. Contributing to the American Safe Climbing Association and to local rebolting organizations and climbing groups is an excellent investment in our sport.

Pitons

Pitons are good for the person who places them but afterward they quickly become mystery pieces. Fixed pitons are still found in areas around the world. They may be surprisingly strong for decades or fall out under their own weight after a single winter of freeze-thaw cycles. Many savvy climbers now skip fixed pitons

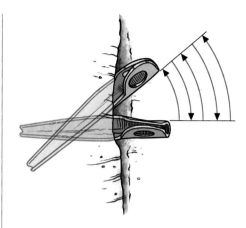

Piton Removal: To remove a piton so it leaves a nut or cam placement instead of a blown-out pin scar, hammer up and back only to the midpoint— don't hammer the piton too far down.

entirely when possible, preferring to use the gear they place rather than waste gear and energy clipping old fixed gear of unknown reliability. Note that soft iron pitons, like those used on the limestone alps of Europe, as well as pitons in horizontal features, tend to be the strongest for the longest.

If you remove a piton, make sure to hammer it conservatively, (see above illustration), to leave a useful nut placement rather than a beat-out pin scar.

Fixed Nuts and Cams

I was attempting to climb what was for me a test piece in Yosemite. I made it through the crux, terribly pumped, and clipped a fixed nut. At the (perceived) limits of my strength

I gave up, and weighted the nut. It pulled out under body weight only, and I took an upside-down 20-foot fall that I am certain I would have avoided had the piece not been there—I would have instead placed my own piece or continued climbing.

Many pieces that are stuck and therefore "fixed" may be as strong as the day they were placed. But just because a piece seems stuck doesn't mean it will hold a fall. Freeze-thaw cycles can move nuts into unreliable places in the crack and it is not at all unusual to find cams stuck in flares that would quite likely pop given a sharp 500-pound pull in the downward direction. Even bomber, stuck cams quickly become unreliable as their nylon leash ages in the sun. Evaluate found fixed gear exactly as you would evaluate your own placed gear, and consider skipping the piece entirely if it doesn't help you create a predictable and reliable web of safety.

Opposite: *Karina Kemper belaying Jochen Haase on the big runouts and dreamy stone of the Wendenstocke in Switzerland*

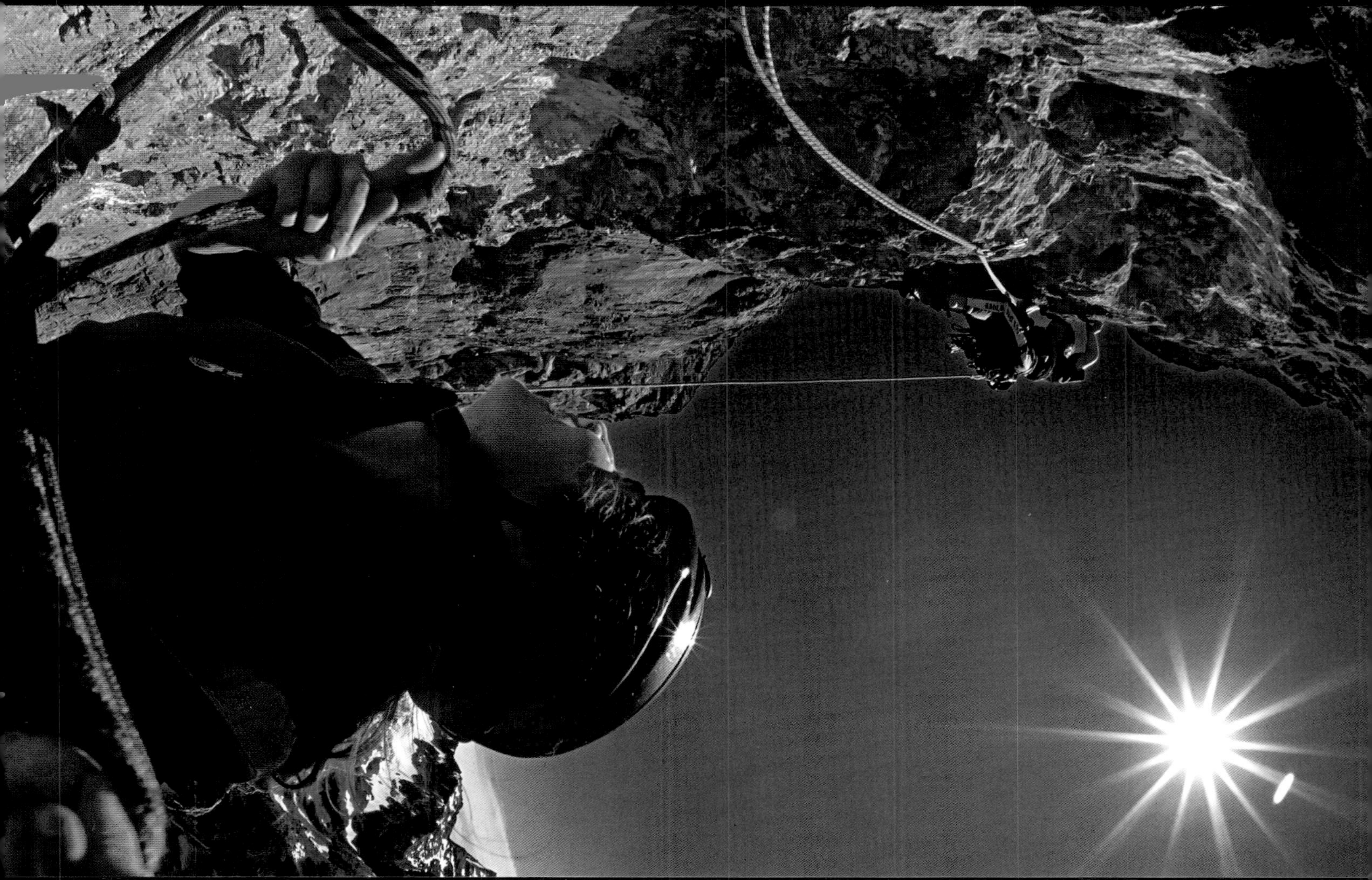

CHAPTER 6

Belaying for Mastery

"One of the biggest issues of this generation is inattention to belaying."
Lynn Hill

Of all the roles we play in outdoor sports the role of belayer is among the most important and least appreciated. Sure, when the leader falls, they are extremely happy for the belayer's successful catch. But in the history of climbing and in the culture of our sport, the stature of the belayer is not what it should be. Where are the records for the greatest catches in climbing history? How about blog posts devoted to the lightning-fast reflexes of a belayer who kept the leader off the ground in a fall? One of my most vivid moments in climbing was falling off with a huge loop of rope in my hand while clipping the fourth bolt of a sport climb in Canada. My belayer reeled in rope like a demon and jumped down a crack between a snowbank and the rock to shorten my fall further. I stopped with my tailbone mere inches from the ground: my belayer's quick reaction literally saving me and my nether regions.

Belaying is a little like driving a car: it appears easy once you know how; but it is hard to do it consistently well thousands of times in a row without making a mistake or causing a problem for someone else. There are a lot of average belayers out there, and by average I mean not so great. I'm not going out on a limb when I say that most climbers are far better at, and more attentive to, climbing than they are belaying, and this needs to change. So you can do pull-ups on a hold the size of a toothbrush? Terrific. Surely you can give your partner a great belay.

An ace belayer adjusts their belay style to the leader's situation and needs:

- You keep no slack in the rope when the leader needs to be caught quickly.
- The rope is slack when it needs to be slack.
- You feed the rope so quickly that the leader doesn't feel your belay.
- You can give a dynamic belay while using a static device.
- You give a much smaller climber a soft catch.
- You reel in slack and move quickly to shorten a dangerous leader fall.
- You don't get distracted by conversation while belaying.

The belayer's job is not only to hold the rope and catch a falling leader, but also to help the leader discern bigger-picture details harder to see from the sharp end. The excellent belayer notices the leader's rope management and where the rope runs. Did the rope get caught around a flake? Is a piece about to cause the leader significant rope drag or has she clipped a piece out of sequence from the others? How much rope is left? What is the weather doing? Does the leader need moral support? Are other climbing teams above or below? A good belayer notices all of these things while keeping the leader's safety as their ultimate priority.

THE ACTIVE BELAY

The belayer's methodology should vary depending on the situation the leader is facing. The demeanor of an active belayer can range from extremely relaxed, kicking back in a lawn chair, to wide-eyed intensity, ready to explode into action: most belays require a bit of both. The bottom line is that you want to be actively in tune with the leader, aware of and reacting to their risks, near misses, successes, and body language. You are a partner. An active belay begins with paying attention. Belay glasses can help; they increase the focus on the leader as well as help reduce the distractions of other climbers.

Let's break the active belay into phases; a single belay will often have cycles of each.

The belayer-as-the-leader's-biggest-hazard phase: This is when the leader is

Active belay with ground anchor: the "inches matter" phase

just leaving the ground and has yet to place a piece. At this point, if the belayer was to step back and trip over something, a fall could pull the leader off the rock. It doesn't even have to be so dramatic to be dangerous. If the belayer decides to sit down, or adjust their position, just moving can pull on the leader. To avoid this, feed out more than enough slack to get the leader to their first piece of gear. Monitor the rope to make sure it doesn't catch on anything, and either spot the leader or stay out of the way depending on the scenario. As soon as the leader has placed that first piece, haul in the rope to a close belay and let her know she has your full attention; something like, "Okay, I've got you close."

The inches-matter phase: Once the leader has clipped the first piece, but while they are still close to the ground, belay with the attitude that every inch matters. If the leader has just clipped a piece above them, pull in rope as they move up, monitoring every move they make and adjusting the rope accordingly. If they fall, pull rope in, sag down, and stop their fall as quickly as possible. This also holds true for anytime the leader reaches a ledge and proceeds to climb above it. In fact, with the extra rope out, rope stretch can add to the fall length, so extra attention must be given to a leader climbing above a ledge: should they fall, you don't want them to hit it. Because it can be hard to see the precise trajectory of a potential leader fall from the ground, the leader should also tell the belayer if they want a particularly close or tight belay by calling down, "Keep it close here, I'm step-ping above a ledge."

The feed-out-rope-like-you-just-found-a snake-in-your-pocket clipping phase: When you see the leader getting ready to place and clip a piece, their body language changes. They are establishing a position from where they feel solid enough to clip. You can often see them relaxing on a hold, adjusting their feet, and then reaching for the rack or a quickdraw. At that point, get prepped to feed out rope with lightning speed. If the leader is looking at bad consequences if they fall while clip-ping, don't feed rope until they reach for it. But if they are well above the ground

Clipping is hard; anticipate the leader's clips to avoid making it harder.

Active belay, leaving extra slack

element to the belay. Leaving slack in the rope is a valid and important technique, but it is also overused and often used incorrectly. Just about every time I go to a busy sport crag, I see people with 6 feet of slack in the rope while the leader is just above the first bolt.

Getting-ready-for-the-mega-whipper phase: Again, it's about being in tune with the leader. When you see the leader looking pumped—they reach for that piece of gear, find that it doesn't fit, return it to their

Active belay; keep leader in sight when possible.

and falling a few extra feet is no big deal, start feeding rope before they need it. An average clip uses at least 5 or 6 feet of rope, and a desperate leader will pull up that 6 feet in less than a second, so the belayer must be ready.

The leave-extra-slack-in-the-rope phase: On a redpoint burn of a steep sport climb where a longer fall doesn't matter, leave 2 or 3 feet of rope ahead of the belay device at all times (the Euro belay) to ensure that the leader has enough rope to make the clips, throw dynos, and move without feeling the belayer; the extra rope will also soften the fall for the leader on overhanging rock, as it adds a dynamic

harness, and then keep on climbing in hard terrain—you'd better get ready for air time.

As the fall length increases, a couple of things happen. On the bright side, the belayer has more time to participate in the event: reeling in slack, running down the hill to take up even more slack, and simply readying for the impact are all possible actions, and sometimes all are required. On the dark side, the chance of serious injury increases dramatically with the length of fall. Thirty-two feet per second squared is nothing to scoff at. When the leader hits the end of the rope after a 10-foot fall, they're already moving at 15 miles per hour. By the time a falling leader has gone 30 feet, they'll be doing about 30 miles per hour. By 90 feet they're ripping along at 50 miles per hour. Imagine having the rope you're belaying tied to the rider of a motorcycle at various speeds and you get a feeling for the timing and force of what it's like to catch a big fall. You'd better be ready.

The leader-is-out-of-sight phase: Consider extending the belay or moving it entirely to be able to see the leader, but there are times when it is impossible or simply impractical to watch the leader. The game changes when the leader disappears around the corner or over the overhang above. The leader must realize that the belayer cannot anticipate the leader's situation; they can merely react by feel to hold a fall. The belayer must use the rope as a feeler to read the leader's movements, translating into action the sudden pulls of clipping a piece, the long pauses while deciphering tricky moves or fiddling with

Extended from the anchor to watch the leader

gear, and, of course, the strong force of a sudden fall.

When a leader is out of sight, if the rope hasn't moved for a while, consider pulling ever so lightly to see if the leader is downclimbing and judge whether you might have to take up rope. This may not often happen on straightforward routes, but on chaotic or difficult terrain the leader may have to downclimb out of a crux section or a dead end and, if the rope piles on a ledge or tangles over a flake without the belayer realizing it, the situation can quietly become quite dangerous as neither party realizes the rope is stacking up rather than being managed by the belayer. Ideally, the leader will yell down and tell the belayer they are downclimbing, but near a rushing river, in windy weather, or due to the unpredictable acoustics that happen on big cliffs, the belayer may not be able to hear the leader and will need to read the leader's situation through tactile feedback alone.

BELAYING A SMALLER LEADER

The influence of weight differences between leader and belayer may be the least understood of climbing physics. Talk to any diminutive hardwoman or hardman about what it's like to be caught by a bigger belayer with a Grigri or other assisted lock device, and you'll hear stories of sprained ankles and violent blows resulting from even the shortest falls. It is not easy to give a soft catch to a smaller leader, and belays with a high friction tube or an assisted locking device in particular require specific techniques and a strategic setup to give a soft catch. If there is more than about 20 pounds difference between the leader and belayer, it is necessary to adjust the belay method.

What to do? First, consider which phase of the active belay you are in, as noted in the previous section. If the climber is above the ground or a ledge, it is better to catch them quickly even if it results in a more static, abrupt catch. If there is room for them to fall, however, use the following methods to avoid giving them that hard knock. Nobody likes to be slapped.

Best practices for belaying a smaller leader:

- Don't belay a smaller leader while sitting down with an assisted lock device or high friction tube. This eliminates any chance of a more active, dynamic belay.
- As the leader reaches the safe zone, such as after placing a few bomber pieces or clipping a few bolts, step away from the first piece. Adding this angle to the rope essentially gives the smaller leader a mechanical advantage over a bigger belayer. As the force of the fall hits the belayer, the belayer will be pulled in toward the first piece, creating a cushion. Stepping away from the cliff or sideways from the first piece so that the belayer is first pulled toward the cliff creates this mechanical cushion.
- Don't use an assisted locking device or high friction tube in autoblock mode on a hanging belay where there is no chance of moving with the force of a fall. If all you have is a high friction tube in this situation, add an additional carabiner under the device, which will eliminate the assisted locking action and cause the device to behave more like a traditional tube device.

BELAYING A LARGER LEADER

The best practices for catching a larger leader are almost the exact opposite of the previous section on catching a smaller leader. I have seen a larger leader knock a smaller belayer unconscious in a climbing gym fall, as well as countless near misses when a leader pulled the belayer so far off the ground that the leader came close to decking, even hitting the

TO CATCH A FACTOR 2 FALL

A couple of studies in Europe, some video footage, and anecdotal evidence suggests that the force of a factor 2 fall, when redirected from a belay device on the waist through a carabiner on the anchor to the leader, will cause such enormous force that the belayer will likely be injured or be unable to catch the fall. To avoid this, place gear closely together above the belay. But if this is not possible and the climbing is hard, consider this technique: Belay through a Munter hitch clipped directly to the belay (see photo: A). This can be done in combination with a traditional belay device (B). Pull enough rope through the device so the leader can reach the first good piece or two above the belay, then tie a backup knot below the device (C) and belay off a Munter on the anchor. When the leader has arrived at gear above the belay, pull any remaining slack through the device and remove the Munter to belay the rest of the pitch from the device on your waist.

Belaying directly off the anchor at the start of the pitch to best catch a factor 2 fall

ground in some cases, but thankfully without injury. As the leader clips more pieces, and the rope runs over rock higher on the pitch, the forces on the belayer are dramatically reduced; but while low on the pitch, much of the falling force of a larger leader is passed directly to the belayer.

Best practices for the smaller belayer:

- Anchor down. Climbing gyms usually have bottom anchors drilled into the floor or weighted bags that can be clipped. If you are significantly smaller than your leader, use these anchors. If outdoors, set bottom anchors: even a scruffy tree or bush can give the smaller belayer enough of an anchor—just be sure that the tree or bush won't be damaged in the process.
- Protect yourself. Set bottom anchors for smaller belayers anytime there is a crux near the ground, if the trajectory of a fall will slam the belayer into the rock, or if the leader is significantly heavier than the belayer.
- Belay directly under the first bolt if possible, so a fall will pull you straight up rather than in at an angle to the wall. If you are a smaller belayer, do not stand more than a body length or so from the cliff unless anchored—a fall will propel you into the rock with surprising force.
- Belay with your feet oriented toward the rock so that if you are pulled into the wall you will have your feet between you and the rock.
- Once the leader is clipped into bolts above, consider unclipping the first bolt (if it can be reached from the ground) to give yourself a cleaner trajectory in the case of a fall.

BELAY GLASSES

As a belayer, there is no better way to concentrate your focus on the leader and know exactly what they are doing at all times than by wearing belay glasses. They also prevent belay neck beautifully. Here are a few simple safety considerations for their use:

- Belay glasses should only be used by experienced belayers; they distract from learning belay basics properly.
- Belayers shouldn't use belay glasses in terrain where they may need to execute quick footwork to dodge rock fall or avoid being pulled into obstacles such as tree branches and rock spikes.
- Wait until the leader is several body lengths above the ground and has clipped a couple of pieces of protection before putting on the glasses.

Belay glasses: climbing will never be as cool as surfing.

- Be aware that the glasses block the view of the rope in front of you; take care to monitor the extra slack in front of the belay device.

BELAY MISTAKES

"Don't talk to people who are belaying a leader, even in the gym."

Steph Davis

As Lynn Hill notes in the chapter opener: lack of belaying skill is a serious problem. Unfortunately, most belayers I see at the crag these days give an inattentive belay rather than an active one. Sure, there are lots of great belayers out there, but most climbers tend to think they are better at belaying than they really are and that it's all just a piece of cake.

Common belay mistakes include:

- Giving a large loop of rope while the climber is close to the ground
- Not adjusting the belay for different lead scenarios
- Talking while belaying and paying more attention to others than to the leader
- Heavy belayers catching small leaders with sharp, static catches that slap the leader into the rock
- Small belayers not using bottom anchors when belaying larger leaders
- Being poorly positioned: too far from the base of the cliff, in line with rock fall, or where the belayer's trajectory will slam them into a protrusion or other hazard
- Not using a bottom anchor in situations where the entire team could tumble

down the hill or cliff at the bottom of the technical terrain
- Keeping too tight a rein on the leader; a few ounces of pull from the belayer feels like a million pounds on the sharp end.

THE GRITSTONE BELAY

"If you use advanced belay technique, you can make really dangerous things a lot safer."

Alex Honnold

The gritstone belay—a method perfected by British climbers for the notorious danger climbs on the short but pristine gritstone cliffs where bolting is not allowed—has demonstrated just how much a belayer can do to save a falling leader. Thankfully not all climbing areas require gritstone belay prowess, but understanding the gritstone belay technique makes for a more capable and aware belayer. The gritstone belay is an example of advanced belay technique and includes:

- Generous use of crash pads, both against the rock and on the ground, to help cushion both the leader and the belayer against the fall forces
- A belayer's preparation to reel in slack through the belay device as well as sprint away from the cliff as the climber falls, shortening the leader's fall as much as possible
- Placing a directional piece at the bottom of the climb so the rope will pull straight down even as the belayer runs away from the cliff

A high awareness by the belayer of the expectations and potential forces they will be dealing with should the leader fall

A variation on the gritstone belay is useful for catching a leader falling onto extremely thin gear like the smallest cams and RPs. To catch a leader falling on the thinnest gear:

▓ Do not use an assisted lock device or a high friction tube in assisted lock mode; this gives you more responsive flexibility.

▓ Use a traditional tube device that will slip a little with the force of the fall.

▓ Wear gloves to protect your hands and, when the leader falls, step back and reel in slack, but then as the force of the fall hits the device step forward and allow some rope to slide through the device.

▓ If the leader is climbing on thin gear right off the ground or off a ledge where a soft catch is not safe to execute because of the extra braking distance that results from a slow rather than abrupt stop, have a conversation before the leader starts to climb to find out what kind of catch they are expecting (asking the leader what kind of catch they would like is always a good idea, anyway).

The idea here is to pull in rope quickly and begin applying the brake as early in the fall as possible, but then to stop the climber's fall slowly rather than catching them abruptly. Think of it like stopping a car on an icy road where a driver should give the car more time and distance to stop and apply the brakes slowly. This method also works extremely well on the soft sandstone of the desert Southwest where hard falls have caused cams to fail, tearing through the softer inner walls of the crack, on multiple occasions.

ADVANCED COMMUNICATION

"There's a lot of communication that's said without words in belaying—watching the body language of the leader, seeing what gear the leader places, and noticing the consequences of a fall."

Sonnie Trotter

Advanced belay communication consists of two seemingly opposite approaches: specific, ongoing verbal communication that begins before the leader even leaves the ground and silent communication.

Silent communication is useful when hearing is limited or impossible due to the acoustics of the cliff. It also reduces the chance of verbal miscommunication, which has resulted in numerous accidents. Perhaps the best time to practice silent communication is when finishing a crag pitch and preparing to lower. Perhaps you want to cheer, and that's great, but *there is no need to yell "off belay" or anything else to your belayer*. To say something simply because you've reached the top can be confusing. Instead, clip in, thread the anchors, and then yell, "Take!" In fact, many climbers, as they begin to lower, prefer to hold their own weight with the rope on the other side of the anchor, and lower themselves to the point where they can make visual contact with the belayer before committing to the lower. This simple step would have

prevented a great many accidents where the belayer mistakenly thought the climber yelled something that the belayer interpreted to mean "off belay." Also, nearby teams yelling "off belay" has caused the belayer to take their leader off belay, with tragic consequences.

With the popularity of climbing, it is best for a belayer not to respond to "off belay" or textbook belay signals in busy cragging scenarios unless those signals are accompanied by visual confirmation and appropriate rope movement. Some climbers use two-way radios to communicate, but this is not practical in hard climbing where every unnecessary ounce is left behind.

Silent communication, as Sonnie points out, can also be important during the lead. When the leader is placing the tiniest gear, the belayer should adjust and prepare to give a soft catch. When the leader is placing gear or clipping from a desperate stance, the belayer should be ready to throw the rope out with blistering speed to keep from causing the leader to fight with the rope to make the clip. The belayer is part of the success or failure of the lead, and every move the leader makes is a form of communication in silent signals—if the belayer can read the language of the climb.

The other extreme, the ongoing verbal communication, goes far beyond the basic "on belay" and "off belay" commands we learn our first day rock climbing. There are also variations on even the basic commands: if your partner is new to you, double-checking basic commands before

the climb is helpful. To help the belayer learn the language of each pitch, make sure to give the belayer every bit of information that could be relevant for them to give you the best possible belay. This means the leader should explain the likely outcome of the pitch and continue to communicate at every opportunity:

- Especially on a redpoint, tell the belayer where you are likely to fall and where the difficult clips or gear placements will be.
- Especially on an onsight, explain your strategy.
- When resting, alert the belayer that you'll let them know when you are going again.
- If you are on a long climb and you realize there may be some simul-climbing to extend a lead, explain the possibility to the belayer while you are still within earshot.
- Tell the belayer your plan for the crux; e.g., "I'll climb up to place this piece first before returning for a rest," or "I'm expecting a runout or a long fall."
- If you see a place where it would be best to fall a little farther, like above the lip of an overhang, explain the situation to the belayer and have them feed out a few extra feet of rope so you'll fall cleanly into space below the overhang.
- On long pitches there is usually a point, like moving around a corner or out of sight, where it becomes likely that verbal communication will become difficult. At that time, the leader should explain their thinking. For example, "Be ready

Opposite: *A great belay is a crucial part of a high-end climbing performance.*

Climbing partners enjoying teamwork, an attentive belay, and perfect rock

strategy of using verbal, visual, and tactile communication as an integral part of the leader/belayer team is mandatory for smooth teamwork and for maximizing the safety potential of the belay.

MOVING THE BELAY

"People should be more flexible about the belay. Move it up 20 feet to a good ledge, out of the way of rock fall, whatever is best."
Alex Honnold

The belay anchor can be a double-edged sword. A solid anchor is paramount to safe climbing, but if the anchor pins the team in a bad spot it becomes a liability. Relocating a belay anchor is desirable if it increases safety, efficiency, and the comfort and enjoyment of the climb. There are a number of reasons why the belay should be moved, including the ability to:

▦ Move out of the line of potential rock fall.
▦ Belay from a comfortable ledge.
▦ Set up the next lead to minimize rope drag.
▦ Locate the belay as high as possible in anticipation of a long pitch above.
▦ Accommodate other teams on the same climb.
▦ Get back on route or in sequence with the guidebook belay locations.
▦ Build an anchor with different-size gear— for example, changing an anchor built with hand-size cams before a long hand crack pitch to free those cams for use in protecting the lead.

to simul-climb," or "I can see the belay about 50 feet higher, but you probably won't be able to hear me so just start climbing when the rope runs out."

This kind of communication is in some ways more important than the basic commands. With experience, it is easy to tell the difference between the movement of the rope when a leader is climbing and when they have stopped climbing and have switched to belaying. But the overall

The need to be flexible with the belay is another reason to set simple, efficient anchors that don't demand cordelettes and complicated rigging; it is much easier to dismantle and rebuild an anchor if it is rigged with a single sling and a couple of biners. The best strategy for moving anchors is to anticipate the need for the new location before even building the first anchor. If the leader runs out of rope in an awkward spot and has to set up the belay there, when it is obvious that moving the belay later will set up the next pitch perfectly, then the leader should plan ahead and strategically rig the first anchor in anticipation of efficiently moving it once the second arrives at the belay.

BELAYING THE SECOND

"When belaying a top-rope or a second, be aggressive about a tight belay until the climber is at least 12 feet off the ground."
Steph Davis

The strategy for belaying a second is not so different from belaying a leader—in both cases, the belayer constantly considers and anticipates the consequences of a fall. In my first years of climbing, I was belaying a much larger second who fell! with his foot stuck in the crack. Even though he fell only a couple of feet, the force that resulted from the combined effect of rope stretch and me being pulled up toward a redirected anchor was enough to break a bone in his ankle. Had I belayed off a Munter hitch on the anchor, eliminating the distance I was pulled up to the anchor (tubes with guide mode had not yet been invented), I could likely have prevented the injury.

As Steph says, it's vital to keep a tight belay on the second at the beginning of a long pitch. Far too often I have seen teams where the second climber (even on top-rope) falls and hits the ground because the rope is not tight. The tension of the rope and the method of belay are critical to the safety of the falling climber.

Best practices for belaying a second include:

- If it is possible that the climber will want to lower down a few feet to reclimb a difficult section after a fall and you're using a device in guide mode, be prepared with a slider biner and autoblock to turn off guide mode (see Lowering

Belaying the second off the anchor

with Tube Device in Guide Mode later in this chapter).

- If the second climber is much larger than the belayer, know that the belayer should rig the belay so the anchor supports much of the climber's weight. This involves using—directly off the anchor—a tube device in guide mode, a Munter hitch, or an assisted locking device.
- On the longest pitches or top-ropes, pull the rope tight then have the climber weight the rope to remove some stretch *before* they begin climbing. At the start of a long pitch, body weight alone can cause 6 to 8 feet of rope stretch and some thin ropes will stretch even more.

BELAYING DIRECTLY OFF THE ANCHOR VS. REDIRECTING

With the invention of tubes with guide mode autoblocking belay capabilities, it has become standard to belay the second with the device clipped directly to the anchor. Belaying directly off the anchor has several advantages:

- It provides reliable backup for the brake hand.
- It can reduce total force on an anchor (unless the belay is already a hanging belay)—a redirected belay adds about 50 percent to the total force on an anchor because both the climber and belayer end up pulling on the belay if the second falls. (With bomber placements in solid rock this should not be an issue.)
- If the climber is bigger than the belayer, it can shorten the fall length of the climber.

- It's much easier to escape the belay, if necessary.

If there is any chance of wanting to lower the climber, and the climbers are close to equal in size or the climber is smaller than the belayer, redirection is often the better choice. In a redirected belay, the belay is off the harness but the rope is redirected through the anchor before going to the climber. Redirecting through the anchor has several advantages:

- Pulling the rope through a redirected belay is much easier than pulling it through a tube in guide mode. Accounting for rope drag and weight as well as the way in which the rope runs over the edge of a belay ledge to the anchor, belaying directly off the anchor can be strenuous. On a hard climb, making the belays as restful as possible is essential.
- Redirecting makes it easier to lower the climber or feed out slack when needed—a common occurrence when working hard terrain.
- You're better able to feel the rope movement of the climber (if they are climbing down a couple of moves, adjusting for a traverse, etc.).
- Using a high friction tube or assisted locking device provides a backup for the brake hand.

A redirected belay adds to the complexity of escaping the belay, should the need arise (see Chapter 14, Improvised Rescue and Epic Avoidance). However, the need to escape the belay while belaying a second is incredibly rare: in forty years of climbing and listening to tales of climbing epics and

LOWERING WITH TUBE DEVICE IN GUIDE MODE

To switch from pulling in rope to lowering in guide mode is awkward and can be dangerous if not done correctly. There are two scenarios when this is necessary: when the climber can unweight the rope and when they cannot. Both of these methods effectively turn off the autoblocking capability of the device, so before changing the device from belaying in rope to lowering mode, wrap the rope around your leg or add a friction hitch to back up your brake hand as you begin the lower. *This braking action change is sudden; when using this method the first time, belayers have been taken by surprise, dropping the climber.*

A. When the climber cannot unweight the rope, follow these steps: 1. Redirect brake hand side of the rope through a biner on the anchor. 2. Girth hitch a sling through the small hole at the bottom of the device. 3. Redirect sling through the anchor to harness and pull, maintaining a hand on the brake side of the rope. B. When the climber is able to unweight the rope: Add a carabiner as shown to turn off locking action of the device. Lower as needed, then remove the extra biner to belay. NOTE: For visual simplicity, belayer tie-in is not shown.

Warning: These techniques turn off the locking mechanism.

rescues I have yet to hear of a single incident that necessitated this technique. I'm sure it's happened. But if you balance the low probability of needing to escape the belay while belaying a second against the high probability of needing to lower the second so they can try a crux section again (as well as consider the brake hand backup provided by assisted lock devices and high friction tubes), the redirected belay remains a reliable and efficient technique that has a place in every climber's bag of tricks.

For belaying two climbers at the same time, or if the climber is significantly heavier than the belayer, guide mode is the way to go. For hard climbing where the second may want to lower down a hard section to try it again, a redirected belay off the harness is often the better choice. Of note, guide mode was invented so guides could belay two climbers on two ropes simultaneously, not because a redirected belay is unsafe.

As with many climbing techniques, the best approach is to be comfortable with both methods and use the right one for the right situation.

TOP-ROPE SOLO BELAY WITH A PCD

Many climbers now use progress capture devices (PCDs) to top-rope climb alone. These devices were not designed for this use, but many variations of setup are used to make them work—some of which are safer than others. Whatever method you use, remember, you are attached to a rope, but you are still solo climbing. Don't count on anyone helping you out of a jam. Considerations for this method include:

- Some people trust just a single PCD, but this is not recommended. A simple grain of sand in the action, or inadvertently pushing the locking lever open, will render the device useless.
- Carry a rappel device, a separate ascender, a couple of extra slings, and—depending on the terrain—a few pieces of gear to help you get out of trouble if needed.
- Use a secondary backup system that utilizes a different device than the primary system so the same action cannot lock both devices open.
- Be sure the secondary system does not interfere with the function of the primary system.
- Avoid any kind of shock-loading of the device—its teeth can sever the rope sheath even under relatively short falls.
- The system should slide easily on its own so as to provide a continuous close belay as you move, without your needing to manually move the device along the rope.
- Manually and visually check each device to make sure it is in lock mode before climbing.
- Use an improvised chest harness to hold the upper primary device as high as possible. Some climbers use a small shock cord around the neck in place of a chest harness; but be sure this cord is weak enough that if it catches on something in a fall it will break rather than strangle you.
- A shock cord or other stretchy material is the best way to attach the device to the

A properly set up top-rope solo system using progress capture devices

Weight the bottom of the rope so the devices can slide without your having to manually pull the rope through.

chest harness so the device can be pulled snug while still allowing unrestricted movement. The cord holds no weight but keeps the primary device as high as possible and ready to hold your fall.

▪ Carry a roll of tape to cover the rope where it runs over edges and carefully run the rope to avoid the sharpest edges. Remember, while climbing with a traditional belay, the rope moves, so if you fall at different points on the pitch, the sharp edges will wear different spots on the rope. With a fixed rope, the wear points will remain the same each time the climber falls, dramatically increasing the damage to a single point on the rope.

▪ Carry enough extra clothing—a jacket, hat, gloves—to handle any potential change in conditions. You'll have no partner to help you out if a sudden snowstorm rolls in, and soloing while hypothermic is poor form.

▪ Wear a helmet—the rope above you can dislodge rocks.

▪ Give right-of-way to ground-up climbing teams at all times and be extremely considerate of other climbers.

THE POLITICS OF THE BELAY

At the average busy crag, the air is thick with ongoing beta spraydowns explaining the details of every move, expounding on how many of each sized whatzit to carry, and professing comparisons of this route to that. In the culture of rock climbing, it is seen as perfectly acceptable to receive advice about which holds to grab with which hands, where to place our feet, what gear to take on a climb, and even what clothes to wear. *Yet weirdly, receiving suggestions about improving belay technique is all-too-often viewed as a personal insult.*

It wasn't always this way. Just a couple of decades ago, it was considered poor form to give someone sequence beta when they didn't ask for it because the information ruined the onsight experience, yet the methodology of the best belay technique was a common discussion. The legend of Layton Kor, one of the best climbers of the 1960s, is accompanied by folklore of his belayers who had to catch his falls. Layton was a big man who was one of the first climbers to push free climbing of routes hard enough to fall from, and with the hip belay of the day, catching Layton was a demanding task—and his belayers are part of his legacy. Belaying was commonly taught at belay towers, where a weight was dropped onto the rope, giving the new belayer a very real impact force experience without putting someone's life on the line.

Fast-forward 50 years. It is not uncommon to see 5.13 sport climbs with waiting lines, and the world's best are pushing the limits well into 5.15. Yet the average belaying technique today may be worse than it's ever been. Honest conversations about belay methods need to become as comfortable as the conversations about which hand grabs the sloper or the crimp. We need to develop our belay skills alongside our climbing skills. And we need to take belay critique constructively as well as be perfectly willing to explain better belay habits to others.

A great way to help spread the word on the importance of the belay is to make a point of being grateful for a good belay. Thank your belayer when he gives you a good catch, feeds the rope quickly through a section of difficult clips, and belays you on a proud send. Thank him for being attentive and for keeping it close above a ledge. If you are following a long pitch, and the belayer keeps the rope tight for the first few moves, tell her you appreciate it.

Then when it's your turn and you are doing the belaying, tell the leader the kind of things that you'd like to hear on the sharp end. Say things like, "I'll keep you close above that ledge"; or if the fall is clean say, "If you fall I'll give you a soft catch." This attentive and appropriately communicative approach can do wonders to spread the word about the true, high value of top-notch belay skills.

Opposite: Steph Johnson putting the "sport" in sport climbing in France's Verdon Gorge

CHAPTER 7

Sport Climbing

"Changing how you climb is all about subtleties: subtleties of body position and alignment, and the coordination of push/pull forces between the holds."

Lynn Hill

Virtually all of today's strongest climbers have paid their sport climbing dues. Even the trad masters often spend more days sport climbing than they do climbing cracks. And it's largely thanks to pushing their limits using bolts for protection that these trad daddies and trad mommas can also execute such incredible feats on natural gear. While once there was a Great Wall of China–like barrier between trad and sport, today the game has changed and the old battle lines have faded. Even free climbing El Capitan, arguably the world's most iconic trad climbing objective, has become a sport climbing–like project in the sense that every aspect is practiced and learned to the smallest detail to perform an athletic feat of incredible difficulty. From an advanced climbing perspective, sport climbing is just that: *the sport of climbing.*

The blurring of the lines between sport and trad have made the lessons of sport climbing applicable to both naturally protected and bolted climbs. If you top-rope a trad climb repeatedly—until you have learned every detail of the moves and the protection—and then you lead it: for all practical purposes you are sport climbing—albeit with natural protection. Go onsight a multipitch bolted route high in the Swiss Alps, surrounded by swirling fog and facing huge runouts and tricky routefinding, and for all practical purposes you are trad climbing—albeit with bolted protection.

Sport climbing is largely about attitude—turning the amp up to 11, pulling out the stops both mentally and physically, and redlining your inner monkey for as long as you can hang on. Clipping solid protection and punching it through improbable terrain makes for one of the safest, most enjoyable styles of climbing. Just writing about it makes me want to go climbing.

At some point, however, even bolted sport climbing gets just as serious as any other kind of climbing, and the consequences of a mistake in your safety basics like the belay, the tie-in knot, or threading the anchor can be as lethal as a Himalayan avalanche. Avoid blowing the basics, however, and practicing sport climbing on bolted routes is the best way to become a really good climber.

Bolted sport climbing has in many ways become what climbing is to most people. Developing the strength and skill to send ever-harder sport climbs quickly develops into an addicting progression. Lacking some of the objective risks of naturally protected trad climbing, as well as the abrupt hitting-the-ground-whenever-you-fall aspect of bouldering, bolted sport climbing allows you to try your absolute best with a healthy safety margin, until you explode off the rock.

Keeping all this in mind, in this chapter we're going to build off of the classical definition of bolt-protected sport climbing to reveal some of the finer points of improving the gymnastics and psychology of climbing a long pitch of demanding moves, no matter what kind of protection is used.

If the info in this chapter is familiar to you and you've mastered sport climbing, but would like to apply your skills to naturally protected lines, take heart: you're probably set up to be a great trad climber. What you need is to spend time learning the skills that are unique to trad climbing, like rope management and placing protection. If this is you, the next chapter (Chapter 8, Traditional Lead Climbing) contains the information you'll need to build your skill set and move into trad climbing at a high level.

USING MOMENTUM

"I think a lot about flow in climbing. Moving fast and dynamic is more efficient."

Tommy Caldwell

The rock isn't going anywhere, so it's easy to develop a rrreeeaaallly sssllllooooww style of climbing. The gentler terrain we learn on as beginners is conducive to standing around wondering what to do. Then, as we get better at using our feet, we can stand around even longer on even smaller holds. We then learn to climb higher grades in part by developing patience and static strength for holding on while we solve problems, clip bolts, place gear, and gather courage for the next move. Inadvertently, this process reinforces a slow and static style that inhibits movement and momentum and, as we move into more demanding terrain, holds us back from climbing at our very best.

As climbers have pushed into upper 5.14 and 5.15—and on routes demanding power-endurance as well as on long climbs linking multiple pitches of 5.12 to 5.14 in a day—a newer, faster, and more dynamic style has emerged. Sure, not everyone aspires to climb 5.15 or to free climb El Cap, but *the movement and momentum-oriented approach to climbing is simply better.*

Of course there will be those technical or dangerous places where it takes discipline and patience to unlock a difficult crux sequence, and as a beginner or intermediate climber it is important to take the time to develop balance and accuracy without being hurried. But once you are climbing hard enough to get pumped, Tommy is right: dynamic, flowing movement *is* more efficient.

For some time I was terrible at climbing on steep rock, and I have many fond

Momentum, both mental and physical, is critical to sport climbing performance.

memories of learning to move with momentum. Take it from me, developing a fast and dynamic style is one of those athletic improvement scenarios where you need to accept getting worse for a little while in order to get better. Here are some powerful ways to develop your skill at climbing with momentum:

- Pick bolted climbs with safe falls about one number grade below your onsight limit.
- If you're on a climb you are familiar with, don't stutter or hesitate in the places you're accustomed to slowing down. Perform the moves with momentum and speed.

- Once you're far enough off the ground that a fall will be comfortable for both you and your belayer, push it: climb fast, even if it causes you to make some mistakes.
- Spend more time on the true rests—the idea is to move fast when it counts and where it's strenuous *not* to skip the rests.
- Look for bigger moves, places where you can span your body between really good holds and use your momentum to keep from getting stuck in an overextended position.
- Experiment with small dynos and dead-points. A big dyno can drain your power quickly, but channeling momentum is almost always more efficient than using tenuous, static moves.
- At the top, notice your energy and power level; more often than not you'll find you arrive at the top with more strength remaining than if you had taken your own sweet time on every move.

BREATHING

"I've really been working to use breathing to support movement. To get maximum extension, I breathe in with the move—this expands my lungs and helps elevate my torso, which helps extend my reach. To get maximum power, I breathe out with the move and make a grunt or 'karate-style' noise to help recruit greater core strength."
Lynn Hill

If Lynn Hill is still working to integrate breathing into her climbing, imagine the work the rest of us have yet to do. The reason even the best and most experienced climbers in the world must concentrate to breathe properly is that it is really difficult to breathe properly while climbing. Yet holding your breath on tenuous moves depletes your muscles of oxygen. Breathing too hard at rests prevents you from monitoring your oxygenation accurately. And breathing erratically during core strength moves handicaps your cardiovascular function.

The best way to learn to breathe while doing strenuous or uncomfortable movement is to practice yoga. With its focus on combining breath with motion and strong body movement, even a few sessions with a good yoga instructor will give you the basic concepts of yoga breathing. To develop your skill at breathing effectively when climbing:

- Consciously breathe, even during the most difficult or easiest moves.
- Become hyperaware of your breathing and how it relates to the moves you are executing.
- Learn to monitor your power reserves and energy output.
- Use your breath rate to time your rests—when breathing slows, it's time to move on.
- Execute the most difficult moves at the optimal point in the breathing cycle.
- With the practice of yoga, become a better athlete in the most basic sense.

This is just the beginning of using breath to drive climbing performance. If you are interested in developing your breathing technique like a world-class athlete, see more on breathing in Chapter 13, Performance.

READING SEQUENCES

"Climbing well is about flowing and not second guessing yourself—trusting your intuition. Your brain will figure it out—if you let it."

Lynn Hill

There are two kinds of hard moves—those that are difficult to execute and those that are difficult to figure out. In the redpoint culture the only thing that matters is executing the moves *after* you've had all the time in the world to figure them out. As a result, redpoint climbers can end up being really poor at figuring out sequences quickly. In the onsight culture, however, the focus is on rapid calculation of movement sequences. This leaves onsight climbers often really poor at reading moves that are hard to execute or a little beyond their limit.

Of course the best climbers can onsight hard and redpoint hard, but even these gifted climbers will admit that to excel, a different mind-set and practice for each is essential. To improve your skills at reading sequences:

- Keep in mind the innovator's definition of insanity: doing the same things over and over but expecting different results.

Learning what sequence works for you is often more important than what other people do.

Try the move differently each time until a solution begins to reveal itself.

- There's nothing wrong with learning from others. Study the chalk and rubber marks from previous climbers. It is often possible to deduce which hand other climbers grabbed a hold with because of thumbprints or chalk concentrations or which footholds other climbers used by the black marks left from rock shoes. Of course, just because it's marked by others, doesn't mean it will work for you.
- If hangdogging, and you're stuck on one move, winch up to try the move ahead to learn how you'll want to exit the move in question, or even skip the move entirely and come back to it. Don't quit just because a move seems impossible at first.
- If onsighting, experiment with the least energy-consuming options before trying the burlier alternatives.
- Before you prejudge that a hold is out of reach, try hanging on the rope and spanning between the holds—you'll be surprised how far you can really reach.
- Go bouldering—there's no better way to learn to read and execute hard moves.

Like so many things, our greatest strengths are often closely related to our greatest weaknesses. Reading sequences is no different. If we are used to practicing each move every possible way before deciding on a sequence while hangdogging, we'll never get better at reading sequences quickly. If we always obsess over doing a move correctly the first time while onsighting, we'll never get better at doing really hard moves. The best way to learn to execute *hard* sequences is by redpointing beyond your limit, but to learn to read hard sequences *quickly* you must also practice the onsight. So do both! Every climbing trip you take, spend some days pushing your onsight limit and other days pushing your redpoint limit. Most of us prefer one style over the other. But to be the best climber you can be it is essential to do both.

CHOOSING A PROJECT

"Find climbs that fit your personality and style."

Steph Davis

At some point on the path to becoming a better climber just about everyone decides to take on a project. When you do, set yourself up for success. Shop routes and rock carefully to choose a project climb that best suits you and your style. Pick a climb a full step above your current skills. If you've never really projected a route before, try something at least a couple of letter grades above your personal best; you'll be amazed what learning a route will allow you to accomplish. If you're an experienced sport climber with a lot of projects under your belt, but you're feeling stuck on a plateau, you'll probably want to pick a route that is a single letter grade above your personal best. But there is much more to it than the number.

I spent a day with world-class climber Bobbi Bensman while she was doing what she called "route shopping." Having sent a

Everyone and every climb is different. When pushing into a new level, find a climb that is right for you.

pile of hard 5.13 routes in Rifle, Colorado, she wanted to raise the bar. I belayed her and climbed easier pitches while she spent the day playing around on the moves of just about every 5.14 in the area, an impressive feat on its own. In the end, she chose one that she liked most and went on to eventually send it after a lot of hard work and dedication.

There was a good reason I climbed easier routes that day with Bobbi. For much of my early climbing experience, I just had a go on whatever climb happened to be in front of me. Turns out, this indiscriminate approach, while good for learning different styles and a whole lot

of fun in its own right, is not conducive to pushing climbers to the hardest climbs they can possibly do. As a result, for many years my redpoint limit was about the same as my onsight limit.

Eventually I learned that always climbing tons of different routes helps you learn, but it's taking on the "right" climb that will push you to a new level. Choose a project that:

- Inspires you. Finding a climb that inspires you is more important than anything else to help you break into the next level.

- Gives you courage. The next grade up sounds daunting; but grades are subjective and finding a climb that suits you at a grade harder than you've ever done helps get you over that hump.

- Builds morale. Weaknesses need working, but finding a climb that lets you flex your strengths is just the ticket to make you strut.

Finding the right climb:

- When you're project shopping, be exceedingly careful not to pick a climb with moves that feel likely to cause injury.
- Don't be disappointed if a chosen climb turns out to be the wrong one. Just try others until the fit is right.
- Thoroughly working your weaknesses at your home area increases the odds you'll find a project route at another climbing area that suits "your style."

FALLING

"You want to get used to spending time in the air."

Tommy Caldwell

Don't kid yourself. If the rope system didn't work, you wouldn't be climbing—at least not climbing hard. Every day around the world, hundreds, if not thousands, of falls are safely taken by rock climbers outdoors and in the gym. A study of indoor climbers by Dr. Volker Schöffl in Germany revealed that out of half a million visits to a climbing gym, 30 acute injuries occurred, or .02 injuries per 1000 climbing hours—lower than the rate of injury among skiers and surfers. Interestingly, over half the injured were intermediate-level climbers, 17 percent

beginners, 20 percent experts, and 10 percent professionals; and most of the accidents were due to belay mistakes.

Of course outdoor climbing has other elements that increase the risk, but even in Yosemite, one of the more adventurous of the world's popular rock climbing areas, the fatality rate between 1970 and 1990 was estimated by a National Park Service study to be 2.5 out of 25,000 to 50,000 climber days, with only a quarter of the fatalities due to falls (of note, 40 percent were due to simple mistakes with gear and 80 percent of the fatalities were categorized as preventable). The point here is that on a well-bolted climb on solid rock with an attentive belayer using their device properly, with double-checked harness knots and a knot in both ends of the climbing rope—the system keeps you remarkably safe.

The key to falling safely is to recognize those places where falling is especially safe—and go for it there—and those places where it is dangerous—and learn to climb in a way where you do not fall at these points. Finding these zones where you are free to try hard to the point of falling is an important part of breaking out of your difficulty plateau.

That said, there are times and places where you should avoid falling:

- When clipping the first, second, third, and sometimes even fourth bolt off the deck with an armload of slack in your hand
- Where the rock angle shifts from shallow to steep and a fall would whip you onto the slab
- Above a ledge

If the gear didn't work, you wouldn't be there, so go for it!

- When traversing out of a corner where a fall would cause you to swing into the corner and the rock
- Anytime your fall would endanger the belayer

It is ideal to try to the point of falling:

- On long sections of gently overhanging terrain with reasonably spaced bolts or bomber protection
- After clipping the first few bolts of a steep pitch
- When you have an experienced belayer who is paying attention
- When your belayer is well versed at providing a soft catch for someone your size

For many climbers, learning to try to the point of failure is one of the most challenging parts of climbing hard, and breaking through the fear of falling is one of the best ways to achieve incredible success. In the twenty-five years I've spent helping solid intermediate climbers work into advanced or elite levels, the best way to learn to go for it at the right time includes these steps, in this order, with the situations described in the previous bullet list as ideal places to try until you fall. Once you are where you can safely fall:

- Let your belayer know your intentions—it's not good form to jump off suddenly—and the heads up also opens up the conversation as to what makes a great belay.
- Try a couple of practice "falls" where you jump off. This can be in the gym or at a well-bolted sport crag. (In the gym, only take practice falls near the top of the wall—most gyms are not tall enough for really uninhibited falling otherwise.) Climb a couple of feet above your last bolt. Then jump.
- Take a couple of falls while really trying. Tell your belayer you are going to go for it until you fall (which also serves as a promise to yourself to go for it). Then, even if you're really just giving up instead of falling, don't yell, "Take!" and reach down to grab the previous bolt. Instead, yell, "Falling!" and jump off.
- Jumping and falling are good first steps, but it only gets you partway there. To

really break free of the fear of falling you have to push until true failure. Generally, the best way to tell if you really pushed to failure is to notice the direction you were looking when you fell. If you were looking up, you probably tried your best and pushed it right to the limit. If you were looking down, you probably gave up a moment before you fell.

"There's this phenomenon of physiology where your brain thinks you can't hang on any longer, yet you can. If you really look at the next hold, focus on it and convince yourself you can grab it, you can usually succeed and keep going."

Lynn Hill

Of course, you can't count on falling only in the safest places. But with experience, it is possible to adjust how you fall to make potentially dangerous falls much safer. To increase the safety margin on leader falls:

- Wear a helmet: catching the rope behind your foot can result in being flipped upside down on even short falls. Wearing a helmet has the added benefit of giving you one less excuse for not going for it.
- Practice good foot position relative to the rope to prevent the scenario described above where you could be flipped upside down.
- Explain to your belayer how you want to be belayed. See Chapter 6, Belaying for Mastery, for recommendations.
- On less than vertical rock, a little running motion, actively pushing away from the rock and running down it (rather

than hugging the rock in desperation to stay on), keeps your body from being abraded as you drag down the rock.
- As tempting as it may be, don't grab the carabiners or quickdraws as you fall—it won't do you any good, only harm, and occasionally someone spears their hand or arm on the nose of a biner while trying to grab it. This goes for top-roping as well.
- If you think you may take a dangerous fall, look down and make a flight plan to avoid obstacles and help set up your trajectory for the best results. When the fall is clean, try hard until the last moment; but when the fall gets messy, take that last split second to plan your plummet: push off, lean left or right, run a few steps, whatever it takes.
- Yell, "Falling!"—especially important if you are out of sight on a long natural pitch. Don't be a silent martyr. Telling your belayer helps them react properly to catch your fall.
- Practice falling. As Tommy says, get used to it. You'll be safer when it happens.

REDPOINT VS. ONSIGHT

"The strategy is totally different for different goals. Cragging hard and sending your hardest route are not the same thing. I can't just go casually cragging, do a ton of onsighting, and also redpoint at my limit. If I want to climb at my limit, it dictates my every decision for the days or weeks I'm working on it."

Sonnie Trotter

It was a drizzly day in Germany's Franken-jura, the climbing area where the term "redpoint" originated. I was standing below a soaring arête of pocketed limestone with a faint red dot painted on the rock in front of me. Kurt Albert, a German climbing icon, painted small red dots—the *rotpunkt*—at the base of routes that had been free climbed. I was tied in, clipped to the first bolt, and had stepped down to get my wits about me. My belayer, a German mountain guide, noticed I was getting psyched up to throw down, looked at me incredulously, and said, "Are you going to try to onsight?"

I was flabbergasted. I'd never considered trying a pitch for the first time with any attitude other than the onsight. But the guy had a point. Was I going to learn the route and give myself the best chance of sending it that day? Or was I going to get all fired up with the third eye popping out of my forehead and go for the onsight? That day I went for the onsight and it worked out, but on other days on other climbs I have pulled finger tendon pulleys, shoulders, and ham-strings trying to onsight climbs that were realistically above my onsight level.

The point is that there is a very good reason to approach the two ideals differ-ently from the very beginning. For many climbers, the difference is profound—usually a number grade or more. If your best onsight is 5.12a and you're tying in for a 5.13a, you'd be wise to approach it as a project and hang at the first sign of a potentially damaging move or a section you feel you didn't figure out well enough. If your best onsight is 5.12c, however, and you're on a 5.13a that is flowing reasonably well, let 'er rip. You might just pull down a personal best. It's a delicate game—with potentially injurious results—and for that reason it is often smartest to make a very clear decision about the kind of climb you are setting up to do. It is also a good reason to choose a project well beyond your best onsight level and save the onsight climbing for climbs within a letter grade or two. Regardless of where you draw the line—once you fall, the best you can do is a red-point, so proceed accordingly.

THE REDPOINT

"First, analyze the heck out of it. You need a really patient belayer. Figure out as much as you can. I see people spend up to three hours working on a pitch. After that first time, each burn is to the death—try as hard as you possibly can; getting that fire in the eye is really important."
Tommy Caldwell

When most people talk about climbing, they're talking about redpoint sport climbing—executing the climb without falling or weighting the rope, after first practicing the climb to figure out the sequences and moves. Crafty redpoint

Opposite: *Onsight climbing in a new area on a different kind of rock than you are used to is important to becoming a great climber.*

climbers are so good at the finer points of the game that on the redpoint they make the hardest routes seem almost easy. The redpoint process can be broken down into three phases: learning the moves, breaking it down, and putting it all together to send.

Learning the Moves

"When I come down from a climb, I have a blueprint in my head. It requires training mental capacity to memorize these micro details."

Sonnie Trotter

Once you have picked out a project, spend time on it. Don't just go from bolt to bolt, top out, then lower off. Instead, check out sections in detail as you go. If a climb is vertical, you may be able to lower back down after clipping the anchor to study the sections or practice the moves on top-rope, but on overhanging or traversing lines it can be impossible to top-rope, so take the time on the way up to study the smallest details of each move. To learn as you go:

- Try a move multiple ways, and go beyond the first one that works—this is how you find easier ways.
- Minimize tick marks, since you might just be tick marking the wrong holds; learning the climb by muscle memory and intuition is far better.
- Ideally work the climb with someone else—their beta (and motivation) may help you.
- Practice the rests—just like the cruxes; with practice you'll become better at resting too.

- Find places where you can bypass strenuous moves, especially the easier strenuous moves. Hey! It's all relative.
- Be really nice to your belayer—give them chocolate, make them sandwiches, serve them hot tea or coffee on cold days, and generally appreciate their patience and support.

Breaking It Down

"Get out of the onsight mentality and just get on hard things and work on them until you can do it. Be willing to try things that are too hard."

Steph Davis

A long pitch of demanding moves is a daunting objective. At first, even the world's best climbers have to look at their projects in sections. With practice, they begin to link sections. Watch a good redpointer at work, and you'll see that they will often not even talk about a complete redpoint, but instead get fired up about trying to link a couple of sections or doing the whole pitch with fewer hangs. To break down a hard pitch:

- Find the natural rests or breaks, then give it your all between each one.
- If there is a distinct crux where you always fall, after falling lower down a few feet to climb through those moves leading into the crux. In this way you'll program your body to climb through the crux rather than fall from it.
- Be willing to pull on bolts to skip lower cruxes you've already worked out in order to have maximum power to put into the higher sections.

- Celebrate small victories—if you get through a hard section that you've never linked, you should be thrilled. Enjoy the feeling.

Don't be surprised if, while working your project, you have days where you seem to lose ground. Your natural biorhythms are incredibly powerful and some days you will climb much better and stronger than others. On the bad days, practice the easier sections, or just go climb some easy pitches and enjoy yourself.

The Send: Putting It All Together

"People disconnect from their bodies and get stuck in their heads, which doesn't allow them to feel the right sensations. You gotta check in with your body."

Lynn Hill

Success in redpoint climbing is a unique moment among sports. Strangely, on the day of the redpoint, a climb that has been slapping you down for weeks can seem almost easy. The key is to keep this in mind throughout the project: surprisingly often there is a way to make hard climbs feel easy. One of the reasons for this is that the redpoint often comes together when you move past the disconnect Lynn describes above, and feel the right sensations.

The subtle sensors for redpoint success include:

- Grasping every hold with just enough power to hold on—but no more
- Recruiting the minimum power needed to execute each move
- Maintaining constant pressure on the feet

Putting together a long, hard redpoint requires a diverse skill set and a good memory.

169

Putting it all together for the send is one of those fleeting, but powerful experiences in life.

- Monitoring pump and power reserves
- Optimizing the rests with both body position and duration

The accidental send: The redpoint typically unfolds in one of two ways. The first comes unexpectedly. It often goes something like this: you were just planning to try to link the first part of the route and then work on the upper moves to learn them a little better. Because you were over-psyched for the full send, you completely relax on the first crux. Getting through it feels good, and you decide to keep going. Before you know it you're fighting the pump but closing in on the anchors. On the last moves, when you are finally fully committed to the climb, an interesting phenomenon happens: you attain the *power of investment*.

When you experience this power of investment several things happen:

- You fight to hang on until the end.
- You have no mental noise to distract your focus or sensation.
- You are able to hold on far past the point where you thought your muscles would fail.

The result is that you trick yourself into climbing as you should always strive to perform. If you are one of those climbers who has pulled off your three hardest sends each time as accidental redpoints, know this: if you can learn to do this strategically and intentionally, you'll climb even harder and become an even more awesome climber.

The wholehearted effort: This leads to the second way that the day of the redpoint often unfolds, and this is how the world's best climbers pull off the hardest climbs as well as how you will raise your own performance to a new level. To do this, you must intentionally achieve the power of investment before you even leave the ground. In fact, it is best to harness this power on your very first redpoint attempt. *Don't practice halfhearted efforts!* Halfhearted efforts develop muscle and mental patterns that lead to failure just as surely as wholehearted efforts develop muscle and mental patterns that lead to success. Practice wholehearted effort and set it into your mental and muscle memory. It's okay to take it easy to warm up on a hard route, or to get the draws hung; but once you're trying for the redpoint, as the Canadian climbers say, give 'er!

The wholehearted effort is a common trait of the superstars. It is often surprising to watch a truly world-class climber do battle with a hard redpoint. More often than not they don't make it look easy. Rather, they make the same kind of miscalculations we all do, *but they continue to try their best even after making mistakes.* Sure, these superstars are always working to eliminate the lapses and climb their best, but the point is that they are always fully invested in the effort: moving beyond the mistake, staying in the moment, and keeping the flow.

To develop the habit of the wholehearted effort you must practice the mind-set and become physically comfortable with the feeling of going for it. (See Chapter 13, Performance, for techniques to develop a wholehearted style of climbing.) There may be certain moves that put your body into

Inspiration is important for giving a wholehearted effort, and rock is an inspiring playground—feel it.

injury-prone positions if done incorrectly, and finding yourself in an injurious position is a good reason to stop, or even better, change how you're doing the move. It is easy to fall into the trap of giving up anytime a move doesn't feel right—a habit you don't want to develop if you want to climb hard. By the time you're going for the redpoint, you should have worked out a way to do the hardest moves without hurting yourself during the learning phase of the project; so stop thinking about injury or failure and just climb.

While both the accidental send and the wholehearted effort can lead to success, the latter is by far the best way to achieve repeatable, high-level performance. Even if you often fall in the midst of a wholehearted effort, that's good stuff. In the long run, practicing the wholehearted approach will make you far and away a better climber.

THE ONSIGHT

"My best onsights were when I was training to free the Nose*—practicing to relax even when I felt really tired in the face of extremely difficult moves."*

Lynn Hill

I watched Yuji Hirayama do the onsight first ascent of a salt-encrusted cave route on a sea cliff in Japan. He first scoped the climb with binoculars for over an hour, called the climber who bolted it to get their permission to try it, and then went on to onsight the 5.13 first ascent. It was one of the most impressive climbing feats I've ever seen, not for absolute difficulty but for the mastery required to climb something so difficult without tick marks or chalk on the holds, and zero information about the climb. Truly a world-class onsight.

Opposite: *Yuji Hirayama, 5.13c onsight first ascent*

For many climbers, the onsight is the ultimate climbing experience. Sure, the redpoint process usually puts bigger numbers on the board, but practicing a climb removes a valuable part of the overall climbing experience: *adventure.*

With the proliferation of tick marks, vast amounts of information available from other climbers and the internet, and a climbing culture that loves to share beta, the true onsight is an endangered species. In its most fundamental form, onsight means executing a climb on the first try with no prior information. Sure, you can claim an onsight of a climb that is covered with tick marks, after reading several pages of online forums and perusing guidebook information, and nobody will question your style. But if you want to enjoy one of climbing's ultimate experiences, one that many climbers have never had, make a point of trying a pitch every once in a while with zero information—provided it looks safe enough.

"Information changes the whole experience. Without beta you have to listen to your body more."

Angie Payne

Most of the time, however, we go into an onsight with some information. The grade alone gives us an idea of approximately how hard we can expect the moves to be. If you find yourself entering a gymnastic sequence that seems harder than the grade should indicate, this tells you there is a good chance there is an easier way to do the moves.

Knowing who did the first ascent of a route, and when, can be one of the most important pieces of information. If it was put up by someone with a reputation for sandbagging, then you know there is a good chance it will be hard for the grade. In general, older climbs tend to be a little harder for the grade than newer climbs.

One of the best ways to perform hard onsights with consistency is to always do a number of similar climbs, ideally at the same crag, before chalking up for the climb you most want to onsight. This will serve the dual purpose of familiarizing yourself with the rock as well as with the grading culture of the area.

"For a hard onsight attempt, review the route before you start—find those target handholds and best footwork options before you even leave the ground."

Sonnie Trotter

Language of the Route

Once you're ready to go for it, remember to look ahead every chance you get. As Sonnie suggests, take the time to study the climb visually to decipher as much as possible before even donning your shoes. Then use rests and stances to scope out the terrain above. Onsight climbing is about reading the language of the route as you go, and gathering information is critical. To learn the language as quickly as possible:

- Explore all the possible clipping holds before clipping a bolt.
- Climb through any strenuous positions quickly.

- Use footholds with absolute conviction.
- When necessary, downclimb to a rest in order to figure out the best way rather than forcing a move if it feels too strenuous.
- Stay on good rests longer than you think you need to. Resting on route is key!
- Try to keep climbing well even if your brain is screaming at you that you are about to fail.
- Watch for clues of moves other climbers have made, including black spots from shoe rubber, thumbprints that indicate which hand should grab a hold, and oversized tick marks in crux sections where somebody got frustrated and took their aggressions out on the rock.
- Look beyond the tick marks—many times climbers who rely on tick marks don't find the best holds, particularly footholds, because they simply see only the hold marked.
- Do the moves your way, no matter what anyone else does. Use your own strengths.

Resting

"Try to recover by breathing and shifting body positions—using different muscles to allow the fatigued muscles a chance to recover; hold on using your larger muscles if you can."

Lynn Hill

Many climbs can be broken down into mini-pitches separated by rests. Sometimes the rests are obvious, but many are slight and subtle; yet if you miss a critical rest on

Resting is a delicate balance—rest too long and you'll tire out and lose momentum, too short and you won't recover.

a pumpy route you might as well kiss your forearms goodbye.

Power-endurance has never been my strong suit, so I've gotten really good at finding rests. This means not only the rests where I can fully take weight off my arms, but also those places where I can give the critical body part even a brief reprieve or shake out. These subtle resting techniques include:

- Finding hand jams on face climbs to rest the fingers
- Finding face holds on crack sections to rest the jamming muscles
- Being willing to sacrifice the right arm to rest the left before a left arm–critical sequence
- Hooking an arm or leg over knobs or flakes
- Finding kneebars, off-width-style arm bars, or shoulder scums in angular or blocky terrain where two opposing faces can be treated like a crack (crack technique pays dividends on faces too)

Once you find a rest, it is hard to know how long to stay there. Dawdle too long on a tenuous rest and you begin to lose strength; don't rest long enough and you will pump off later.

"It's tricky—when you feel like you're losing power instead of recovering strength, you've rested too long."

Lynn Hill

How long to rest? Good measures for resting effectiveness are breathing rate and heart rate. If possible, stay on the rest until your heartbeat and breathing slow significantly. This means you have regained as much oxygenation of your muscles as you're likely to get. Sometimes you must rest in places where you can regain a small but crucial amount of power, but the body tension required to hold the rest will not allow you to recover breathing and heart rate. So it goes.

Not all resting in climbing means taking a real break. Finding moments of rest within the movement itself is an effective way to preserve and regain power in the midst of hard terrain. This means:

- Pause, chalk up, and breathe during thumb catches or palming moves where a new group of muscles is being used.
- Climb high enough to clip the bolt with a straight arm when possible.
- While hanging quickdraws, it is often most restful to clip the draw to the bolt with one hand, then switch hands and clip the rope with the other.
- When most of the weight is on your feet, look for places where adding a thumb, elbow, knee, head, hip, or any other body part to the sequence will allow you to take weight off your fingers.

"Use the rest not only to recover but to assess the terrain above."

Lynn Hill

SPORT CLIMBING SAFETY

Clipping bolts makes for relatively simple safety management compared with other

It's a good idea to keep a few pieces of trad gear in your pack while sport climbing. This can be used to rig a belay in an exposed place, to back up a manky bolt, to protect getting to the first bolt, as shown here, or to shorten runouts.

kinds of climbing, but getting it right is just as important for sport climbing as it is for the gnarliest big wall or crustiest crack climb. There are three primary points where accidents happen in sport climbing, and three easy ways to prevent them:

First, check your and your partner's knots and harness buckles! Anecdotal evidence strongly suggests that an unfinished knot is the most common, dangerous mistake made by extremely experienced climbers. Even Lynn Hill took an 80-foot ground fall after not finishing her knot, but thankfully emerged relatively unharmed. It's easy to tie in properly ten times, but can you do it right a thousand times in a row with all the potential distractions that accompany a thousand pitches? A great habit to develop to prevent a potentially fatal accident is to never stop in the middle of tying a knot or buckling your harness: finish the knot. If you do find yourself stopping, untie the knot and start over from the beginning. And always double-check your knot and your partner's before you begin climbing.

Second, make sure there are knots in both ends of the rope! Getting accidentally lowered off the end of the rope is one of the most common sport climbing accidents at all ability and experience levels. Practice tying the knot in the bottom end of the rope even on short pitches; make a habit of it so you never forget on the long ones.

Third, don't yell "off belay" at the top of a climb when you plan to lower off. After all, you don't want the belayer to take you off belay; you want them to lower you back to the ground. To avoid confusion, particularly if you're out of sight and can't monitor the belayer visually, it's best to say nothing at all upon reaching the top. Just thread the anchors (see Cleaning the Pitch, later in this chapter, for threading methods) and prepare to lower.

CLIPPING

While there is much conversation about clipping the rope in the right orientation relative to the carabiner, there are very few cases of ropes coming unclipped from the biner in a sport climbing scenario. But it is possible and it has happened, so learn how to avoid backclipping the rope to your biners. Some climbers are so adamant about making sure every draw is clipped with the optimal orientation that a lot of energy is wasted on a climb changing clips—energy needed for other things. The best practice is to develop a habit of clipping correctly and being sure the most critical bolts are clipped the right way. But once several bolts are between you and a bad fall, stop worrying about how the biners are clipped and just throw the rope into the biner and keep climbing.

For the majority of clips on hard climbs, getting the rope into the biner efficiently is far more important than which way the draw is oriented, and learning the fastest way to clip is a valuable skill. The hand motion required to make a fast clip differs depending on where the draw is relative to your body, as well as which way the biners are facing. When possible, rather than using a series of motions to make the clip, use a single pinching action that grabs the biner and drops the rope through the gate in one swift motion. The best way to learn to clip with lightning speed is to watch footage of climbing phenom Adam Ondra slapping the rope into the biners—then go channel your own inner Ondra.

Stick clips: Some climbs are bolted in such a way that stick clips are mandatory to do the pitch safely. Using a manufactured stick clip is easy. A growing fad among climbers who abhor the idea of climbing into unknown terrain without a top-rope is to carry a stick clip all the way up the climb and use it to clip each bolt while hanging from the last. For climbers who love the adventure in climbing, this stick-clip aid climbing removes the best part of climbing. To each their own, of course, but one

CORRECT

In a fall, the rope above the biner will pass outside of the biner.

WRONG

In a fall, the rope will pass across the gate, potentially unclipping from the biner.

issue with this method is that many of the world's best sport climbing areas have bolts too widely spaced, or climbs too steep, for this method to work. If you never practice leading into the unknown you will never learn to do so.

CLEANING THE PITCH

The most dangerous parts of climbing are the transitions, and switching from climbing mode to lowering and cleaning mode is no exception. There are two danger points in the lowering process. The first is when, as you are clipped into the anchor, you untie the rope and thread the anchor to transition to lowering off. The second is when you unclip the lowest quickdraw and the rope transitions from being tethered to the wall to being completely free of the quickdraws on the pitch.

Consult *Rock Climbing: Mastering Basic Skills* for a review of best practices for

IMPROVISED STICK CLIP

Use a small stick that can be easily broken to the right length to hold the biner gate open. For wiregate or keylock-style biners, the short stick works best if it has a small fork to catch on the gate. Break the short stick to a length that spans between the open gate and the biner nose. Place the long stick between the upper biner and quickdraw as shown. Keep tension on the rope to hold the upper biner in place while clipping. The small stick drops free as the biner nose is pulled into the bolt hanger.

 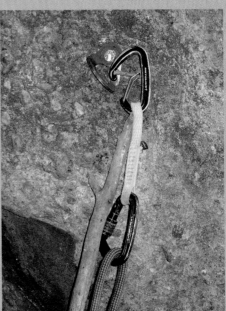

Improvised stick clip

threading an anchor. The current best practice for most scenarios is the bight method, shown in the following sequence in a situation where the climber had only one sling left to thread the anchor. Using this method does not require the leader to attach themself to the anchor with redundancy because they are protected by the belay on the lead rope throughout the process just as they were while climbing; the leader is never completely untied from the rope. Using the bight method in conjunction with

Threading an anchor with a single sling: A. Clip in with your remaining sling or draw. B. Pull up several feet of rope and thread bight through rings. C. Tie a figure eight or overhand on a bight in the end of the bight and clip to your harness using a single locker or two non-locking biners with gates reversed and opposed. D. Untie from lead knot and pull through anchor. Proceed to lower.

the bowline on a bight, it is even possible to thread an anchor without clipping it at all—provided there is a no-hands stance to stand on while threading and tying the knot. This method uses approximately 10 feet of rope, so use the standard re-tie method instead if you need every inch of the rope to make it down.

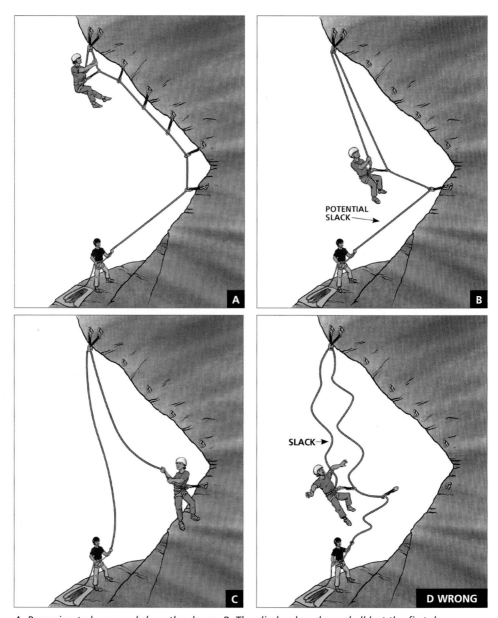

A. Preparing to lower and clean the draws. B. The climber has cleaned all but the first draw. C. The climber clips to the first bolt with a quickdraw before unclipping the rope, while the belayer pulls in all the slack. Once the slack is pulled in, the climber unclips and lowers or downclimbs safely. D. Don't do this! Unclipping the first draw without first removing the slack caused by the angle change in the rope can cause a dangerous fall.

COMMUNICATION

Communication errors are one of the primary culprits behind sport climbing accidents. Foremost of these is the mistake of taking the leader off belay when they are threading the anchor, then not putting them back on belay before they lean back on the rope to lower. To avoid this issue:

- The climber must never say "off belay" while sport climbing, unless they plan to rappel or are on a multipitch climb.
- If in doubt, the belayer should not take the leader off belay. It is much better to be mistakenly left *on* belay than it is to be mistakenly taken *off* belay! Unless the leader specifically states that they plan to rappel, which is rare in sport climbing where lowering off is the norm, the belayer should keep the leader on belay from the time they leave the ground until they return to the ground.

Other communication can help ensure smooth teamwork and improve performance, especially important on a hard climb: The leader:

- Says, "Clipping!" just before wanting slack for a difwficult clip.
- Informs the belayer before taking a long rest, then again before leaving the rest.
- Yells, "Take!" when they want the belayer to hold them, but waits for a moment to allow the belayer to pull the rope tight before weighting it.
- After hanging, informs the belayer before they unweight the rope to continue climbing. This prevents dropping the belayer onto their butt with the unexpected unweighting of the rope.

- Clips directly into the bolt if resting on the rope for a long period to take the weight off the belayer. By saying "I'm in direct" or "Slack," the leader lets the belayer know when they can relax and give a bit of slack.
- Says, "Watch me here" or something similar when entering a section where a fall is likely.
- Tells the belayer when a tight belay or a particularly loose belay is preferred.

The belayer:

- Says, "I'm with you" as the leader steps off the ground or enters a crux section.
- Voices their strategy, such as, "I'll give you a tight catch"—if the leader is above a ledge—or, "I'll give you a soft catch"—if the leader is on vertical terrain.

BOLT SAFETY AND AGING

First generation sport climbing bolts have now been in the rock for close to thirty years—the life span of most of the bolts placed in those days. The quality of the rock, how the bolts were placed, the gauge of the bolts and hangers, and the specific metals used in them affect their strength, but one thing is certain: many of the thousands of bolts placed in the late 1980s and early 1990s are reaching an age where they are no longer reliably strong enough to hold leader falls.

Unless it's so new it's shiny, there is no way to be certain of a bolt's strength. Corrosion usually occurs primarily underneath the bolt hanger and is not readily visible. If it's wiggling, that's a problem. Some other indicators that a bolt may be dangerously weak:

Be careful to make clips with the rope running the right way out of the biner when you're close to the ground. But clipping can be hard; after you have several bolts between you and the ground, stop worrying about it and just clip and climb.

A. A biner on a fixed draw worn by repeated swinging falls in a bolt hanger. B. A sharp edge on a fixed draw that is obscured by the rope when clipped in. C. The same biner with the rope removed, showing the razor-sharp edge.

- Rust is visible between the bolt head and the hanger.
- It's an old-style design.
- It's smaller than 3/8 inch in diameter.
- Any bolt (other than glue-in titanium or a brand-new expansion bolt) in a sea cliff or wet limestone environment. Recent research has shown that a wet limestone cliff creates the same corrosive chemical environment as the notoriously corrosive sea cliffs.

Because a climb is bolted doesn't mean it's safe. In fact, in many old climbing areas the bolted climbs are now more dangerous than the average traditionally protected climb, because people are tempted to use the uncertain bolts. Be willing to leave gear and retreat from any climb with bolts that show aging; avoid trusting your life to a single bolt if at all possible. Here's another reason it's good practice for sport climbers to always carry a few pieces of trad gear in the pack: it may let you back up a critical bolt that appears less than bombproof.

FIXED DRAW BINER WEAR

With the growing popularity of climbing (more people, more wear and tear on the equipment), an additional hazard is becoming more prevalent and that is the wearing of carabiners on fixed draws. The hanger holding the fixed draw can wear the top biner to a dangerous point, but it's the rope-end biner that is of particular concern because repeated rope action can wear a sharp, cutting edge into the biner, which can sever, and has severed, climbing ropes. This has caused multiple serious accidents. To make matters worse, once you clip your rope into the draw, it is hard to see that the biner is dangerously worn because your climbing rope obscures the sharp edge. From the climber's point of view below the clip, the dangerous biner will appear perfectly fine. The nylon draws will decay as well, but this is not as serious of an issue as a sharp biner edge that could cut the rope. If you're in doubt about the integrity of a fixed draw, use your own instead.

BOLTED FIRST ASCENTS

Ahh. The first ascent. Going where no monkey has ever gone before (okay, in some tropical climbing areas, maybe monkeys have already been there first). Discovering, visualizing, and establishing a quality climb is a rewarding experience. There is enough technique to the art of the first ascent to fill an entire book. But if you're an advanced climber and have your eye on some new lines, before you start drilling holes consider these first-ascent fundamentals:

- Climb other lines in the area to develop a feel for the style, bolt spacing, and the accepted distance between routes.
- Consult a local climber to learn about the area's ethics and traditions.
- Check the local climbing management plan to see what bolting guidelines are recommended or required in the area.
- Install bolts according to the manufacturer recommendations for the hardware you intend to use.
- Be sure hangers and bolts are made of the same metal to minimize oxidation.
- Place enough bolts. Dangerously runout sport climbing has never been well received. If you want to create a sketchfest, do it on natural gear. If you're going to place bolts, make it safe enough for someone to onsight.
- Don't place too many bolts. Uninterrupted climbing is fun; clipping bolts on every move is not. Of course there are times when close bolt placements are needed to keep a falling leader from hitting the ground, a ledge, or from swinging into a spike, but the best newroute developers tend to put a body

Opposite: *Sport Climbing Danger Zones. Bolted sport climbs have predictable danger zones that a wise climber will assess on every pitch, similar to how a trad climber monitors potential hazards. Here, caution areas (and potential accidents, mistakes, and consequences that tend to occur in each zone) are listed referencing this photo of a sport route on a crag in Frankenjura, Germany. Most of the dangers can be avoided by standard safe climbing and belay tactics, but it is important to be consciously aware of each danger on every pitch you climb.*

AT ANCHOR
- Mistake while threading anchor
- Communication error

WHILE HIGH OFF THE GROUND
- Belayer fumbles brake hand or locks device open
- Rope cut on worn, sharp fixed biner
- A small climber receives a hard catch from a bigger belayer

WHILE AT APPROXIMATELY SECOND THROUGH FOURTH BOLT
- Fall while pulling up rope to clip
- Accidental unclipping or biner/ bolt failure causing long enough fall to hit the ground
- Hard catch causing hard swing into ledge or ramp

AT FIRST BOLT
- Fall before or during clip
- Belayer leaves too much slack in rope

BEFORE CLIMBER REACHES FIRST BOLT
- Knot tied incorrectly or incompletely
- Harness not buckled
- Belay device rigged wrong
- Belayer stumbles or sits down without enough slack in rope, pulling climber off the wall
- Fall from ledge at the start of the climb

length or more between bolts when the fall is clean.

- Place bolts where they are easy to clip by a climber of any height. Thousands of great climbs are marred by bolt placements that are difficult to clip. *When possible, place the bolt so you can clip it easily while hanging from the clipping hold with a straight arm.* If a bolt must be placed high to prevent a bad fall, try to place it so someone 5'0" can still clip it safely.

The spacing and location of the bolts can make the difference between an oft-repeated classic and a cobweb-covered obscurity. If you are an aspiring first ascentionist, visit a world-class sport climbing area to study well-done routes *before* firing up the drill. Your climbs will be so much better as a result.

Opposite: *Patience Gribble enjoying the beauty of a world-class trad climbing venue in the Bugaboos, British Columbia*

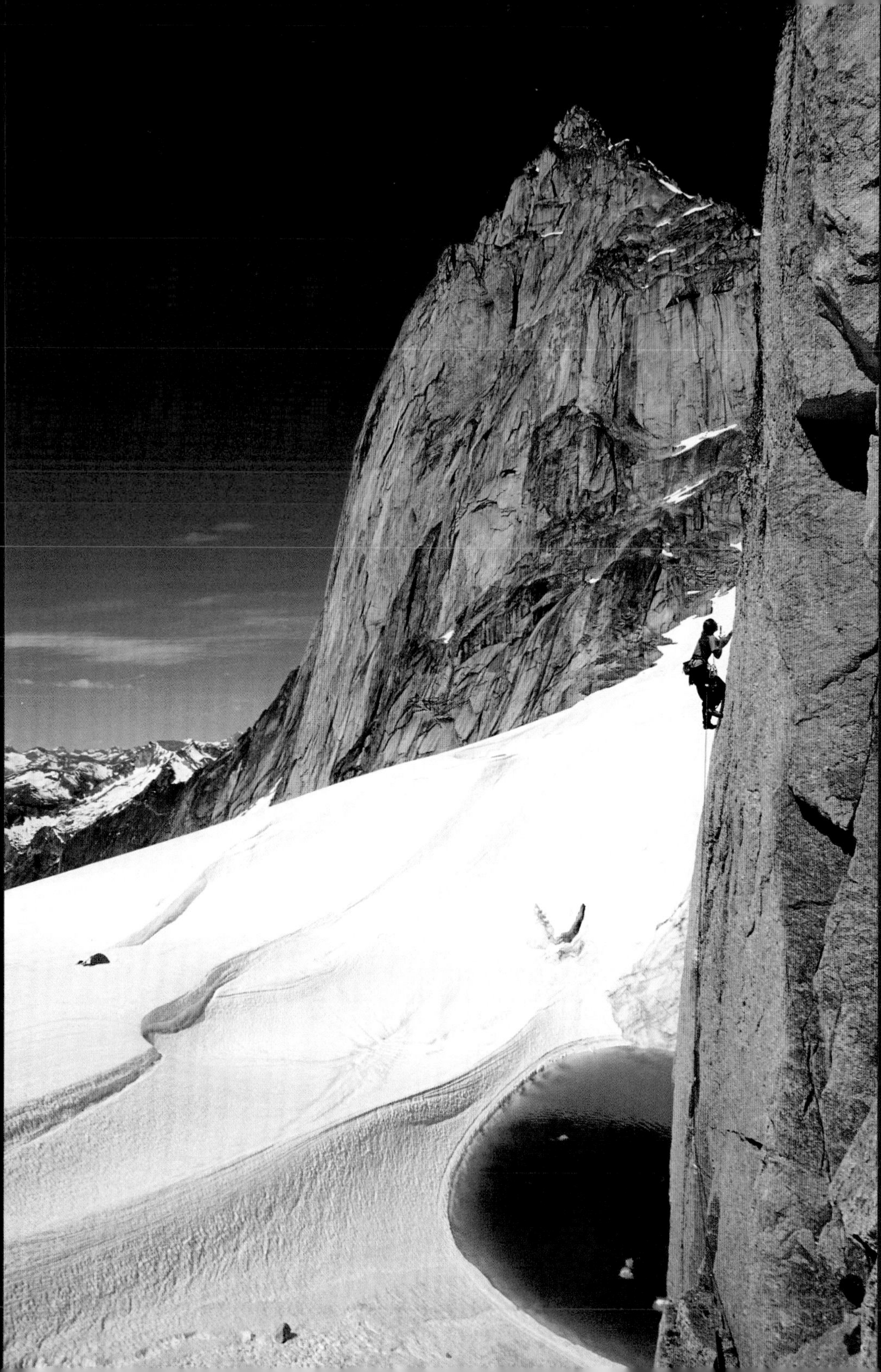

CHAPTER 8

Traditional Lead Climbing

"I make the same decisions everyone else makes. If it's sketchy to you, it's probably sketchy to me."

Alex Honnold

Traditional climbing is the latest rage, and it's about time. The objectives are the most awe-inspiring rock features on the planet, the gear is fun and sometimes challenging to use, and the satisfaction and aesthetics of doing a climb that isn't bristling with fixed protection are undeniable. Trad was the original climbing game, but for the last couple of decades it has largely been overshadowed by the prodigious feats and ready accessibility of bolt-protected sport climbing and bouldering. In the twenty-teens, however, the joy of trad climbing was firmly placed back in the world spotlight by the proliferation of inspiring climbing footage across the big screen and social media, topped most notably by Tommy Caldwell and Kevin Jorgeson's ascent of El Cap's *Dawn Wall* and the international attention their climb received.

This book is for climbers who want to try harder and climb harder. For sport climbers this may mean climbing stiffer sport climbs—we covered how to do that in the last chapter, Chapter 7, Sport Climbing. It may also mean breaking into traditional lead climbing, opening the doors for long routes and big walls. Perhaps you are sport climbing well but have plateaued out. You want to break into trad lead climbing, long routes, and even big wall free climbing. What is holding you back?

Getting into advanced trad climbing can be a daunting objective. But the great news is that if you follow the appropriate learning curve, the harder you climb, the safer trad climbing becomes. Steep rock, solid protection, and clean fall potential are what hard trad climbs are all about. Keep it that way, and with the right climbs and partner you can push yourself just as far with natural gear as you can with bolts.

In Chapter 5, Traditional Gear Placement, we covered the specifics of placing the protection so that 99 percent of your gear will hold 99 percent of the falls you will ever take. This chapter is about the rest of the trad climbing system: rope management, runout strategy, routefinding, and optimizing the day for success. This chapter also dives into aspects of the different subspecialties of trad climbing, including improvised aid, following traverses, and headpointing.

ROPE MANAGEMENT

Complications in rope management aren't usually an issue on sport routes, but in trad climbing, rope drag can turn a pleasant day of climbing into a nightmare of a slog. Drag is dangerous: for the leader, who must yank and drag to get enough rope for the clip, and for the belayer, who can no longer "feel" the leader on the end of the rope or feed or take in rope helpfully. Managing the rope to reduce resistance, and preventing it from getting stuck in flakes or dragging over loose rock, is an important part of learning to trad climb.

Like many things in life, the causes of rope drag are usually obvious in hindsight. Our goal is to set these things up to run smoothly beforehand; however, it is not so easy. In our first efforts to prevent drag, we put longer slings where the climb makes dramatic changes in line or angle. The problem is, extension isn't enough. The difference in total length between a standard draw and a shoulder-length sling is little more than a foot. If a rope runs sharply through a piece just before a 6-foot overhang, a 12-inch sling and a 24-inch sling will cause the same amount of drag. Simply clipping some pieces with slings is not enough to adequately reduce rope drag. When managing the rope around large overhangs, corners, and other large terrain features, or where the route changes trajectory dramatically, the use of slings is not enough.

How, then, do we get the rope to run as straight as possible in these cases? The answer is to add these concepts to your rope drag prevention strategy:

- Rope drag must be evaluated in three dimensions. It is easy to grasp the idea that a piece clipped to the left or right of the straight-running path of the rope should be clipped longer than the rest, but you need to consider also pieces that are placed farther *in* or *out* relative to the path of the rope.
- The absolute location of the set pieces makes a bigger difference in rope drag than the length of the sling to which they are clipped. A cam at the lip of a 10-foot roof can be clipped with a single biner and the rope runs free. But a cam placed in the corner, where the back of the roof meets the wall, needs a 10-foot extension to prevent rope drag at the end of the pitch. Of course, a 10-foot extension is rarely practical, so placing at the lip if possible is the best answer. The same is true of zigzags. If the protection is only placed in the middle of the zigzags rather than at the left and right extremes, it is often possible to use only short extensions or clip the cams directly; the rope will run straight up the middle even if the moves take you to the left and right.
- Anticipate backcleaning or backextension opportunities to straighten the rope. Rather than just looking back

Look ahead for places you can clip both short and long: A. The short clip protects the difficult move past the piece. B. After placing another piece above, the climber reaches back and unclips the quickdraw. C. This leaves the long sling to reduce the rope drag. In this case, the quickdraw alone would have created impossible rope drag and using only the extended slings would have set the leader up for a potential fall onto her partners.

for places where you can remove the culprits that are putting sharp bends in the rope (a good first step), look ahead as you lead for placements where backcleaning after the move will reduce drag. An added benefit to anticipation is that it often allows you to do hard moves with a piece clipped short to protect the move, knowing that once past it you can either remove that pro or leave it and extend the sling on it.

The desirability of reducing rope drag creates a scenario where it can be safer to place *less* protection in carefully selected places. Let's say the first half of a pitch is fairly hard, then it zigzags up a section of complex but easier terrain before finishing with a crux headwall and a moderate but tenuous runout slab to the top. If you place

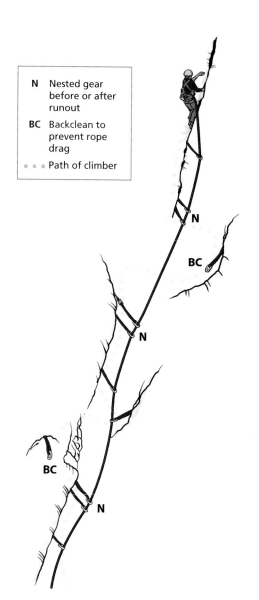

Rope management in complex terrain

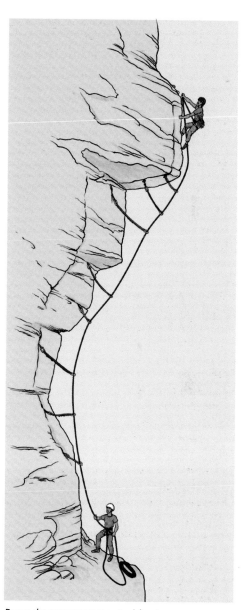

Rope drag management, side view

gear close together throughout such a pitch, by the time you reach the runout finish at the top, where you cannot place gear close together, you will be committed to tenuous climbing with rope drag pulling down on you (believe me, this is one of the worst sensations in climbing).

If you are careful on the early part of the same pitch—backcleaning strategically, using slings in the optimal places, and running it out when the climbing is secure on the moderate terrain in the middle (see more on runout strategy in the next section)—you may be able to do both the crux and the tenuous runout slab without rope drag threatening to pull you backward and send you soaring.

The goal is to eliminate rope drag completely whenever possible so that, when it is unpreventable, you can still pull the rope. A route that makes dramatic turns, goes around big corners, traverses multiple times, or goes over unavoidable features will create some rope drag despite your best efforts. This rope drag can be irritating but can usually be pulled along; however, place a couple of pieces in the wrong places, or forget to extend a piece or two before traversing around a corner, and you may find yourself unable to climb farther, necessitating an early belay or downclimbing to free the rope. The key to learning advanced rope management is to look back on every pitch you lead with an eye for how you could have reduced rope drag even further.

But in all your monkey business to reduce rope drag, remember this: *Be willing to risk rope drag in the future to stay safe in the moment*. You don't want to bypass good protection because you are worried about rope drag, and then take a bad fall because you skipped good protection.

RUNOUT STRATEGY

"The ability to run it out safely is so important—doing it safely without using so much gear. Become aware of your body so you know when to protect it."
                                Tommy Caldwell

If you aspire to climbing anything except heavily bolted climbs or perfect cracks, such as those in Utah's Indian Creek and select other places, you will encounter runouts in your climbing. Some climbers feed on the thrill of the runout, others hate any kind of runout, but we all run it out to one degree or another.

Runout is relative. For one leader, climbing more than one body length between gear makes those moves feel runout. For another, going 20 feet between placements on the same terrain may not feel runout at all. What is runout is also relative to the type of climbing. It may be possible to climb 30 feet above a bomber cam in a perfect hand crack without feeling dangerously runout; but the same grade of friction slab can feel nightmarishly runout with only 10 feet between protection.

My mountain guide father once told me, *"You can challenge your ability to place good protection, or you can challenge the climbing—but not both at the same time."* Many times you will encounter both

Using intermittent, small runouts separated by nests of closely spaced gear is a wise strategy on adventurous trad climbs.

scenarios—protection that is challenging and climbing that is challenging—on the same pitch, and the goal is to do everything you can to avoid having to deal with both at the same time. This is the essence of the runout strategy.

There are two kinds of runouts. The first is a *forced runout*, where the leader has no choice but to run it out. They either have no protection options at all or they have no gear to fit the crack. The second is the *strategic runout*, where the leader runs it out purposely and strategically, for example where the climbing is secure in order to reserve enough pieces to thoroughly protect the coming difficult or insecure sections. The strategic runout is much better than the forced runout: you want to be a master of your runouts rather than a victim of them.

The old saying in climbing—*"When in doubt, run it out!"*—is only half wise. Imprudent, obviously, because falling off a long runout could kill you. But also wise, because overprotecting—when gear is precious and needed for dicey sections anticipated ahead, or the weather is threatening and you need to climb fast—may not be the better option. There are times you'll want to "embrace the runout"—and set yourself up for the safest runout possible.

THE SAFE RUNOUT

The best and safest runout strategy integrates three key elements.

First, don't restrict yourself to the textbook image of placing one piece every body length. In some places it can be best:

- To place gear as high as possible before difficult sections, even if that means placing one piece at waist level to protect you while you place another as high as you can possibly reach

- Not to place at all, but instead to first make another move upward so that you can place from a better stance and establish the next piece as high as possible
- To place a nest of pieces from a single stance, creating a miniature belay anchor mid-lead in order to be absolutely sure you have bomber protection, before casting off on a section with uncertain gear
- To run it out between placements on easy terrain with clean fall potential so you preserve your limited equipment for difficult sections. This is often a better option than using all your gear before the crux, which limits your placements just where you're most likely to fall.

"I run it out on easy terrain to save gear for the crux sections, then I place more gear in the cruxes."

Steph Davis

Second, develop an acute sense of fall potential at all times:

- A 50-foot fall in steep terrain can be much safer than an 8-foot fall onto a ledge—place your gear accordingly.
- Always consider two falls—the fall onto the first piece below you, as well as the fall if a piece or two were to fail. This secondary fall has been the cause of many fatal accidents. One bad piece above bomber gear is not usually a big deal; a string of bad or unpredictable gear is a recipe for disaster. (Of note, cam failure in glassy-smooth rock is the frequent cause of this accident.)

- Factor the belay into the fall equation—if you fall from the first half of the pitch and the belayer can see you and react instantly, the fall will be much shorter than falling from the same length runout, out of sight, near the end of a long pitch.

"I hardly ever trust my life to a single piece of gear."

Alex Honnold

Third, be willing to do whatever it takes, including downclimbing or weighting the rope, to solve problems with your gear and make it right before pushing on; you want confidence in your system. This means:

- If you find that you are at the base of a finger crack with no finger-size pieces left on your rack, downclimb or lower to backclean pieces placed below, or have your belayer take finger-size pieces out of the belay and send them up to you on the tag line.
- If you realize you botched the rope management and are developing rope drag before a challenging section, go down and fix it.
- If you place a mediocre piece, and feel that a better one is possible, use extra energy and time to remove the bad one and place the good one—this has the added benefit of making you better at recognizing the good placement in the first place.
- Know that great climbers make gear mistakes too, but they learn to quickly adjust and fix the problem.

Opposite: *Alex Honnold, runout and onsight on hard terrain*

Downclimbing to backclean near the ground is helpful when it is clear that the first piece is no longer doing any good.

After removing the first piece, the rope runs perfectly straight into the meat of the pitch.

RUNOUT SKILLS

Conceptualizing and putting into action a strong runout strategy when climbing requires several underlying skills:

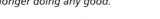 Practice and become proficient at downclimbing. Sport routes provide a great opportunity; try downclimbing moderate, well-bolted sport climbs during a warm-up process. It is amazing how well you can downclimb with very little practice and it will make you a much better—and safer—trad climber.

You'll also learn to monitor when down-climbing is a viable option—and when it's impossible.

- Practice backcleaning safely. Don't remove too much of your safety net through backcleaning. But by establishing mini-anchors partway up the pitch, or strategically leaving the very best placements, you can safely back-clean and reduce the amount of other gear you leave behind.

- Place bomber protection 99 percent of the time. If you place only the best gear in the right places, you will actually be safer while placing less gear overall.

- Develop a calm head. A serene attitude helps you to accurately assess risk at all times and helps prevent the stupid mistakes that can be caused by excessive stress.

- Develop a big-picture "court sense" that constantly balances the requirements of the climbing above with rope management and the gear you've left below.

THE FOUR KINDS OF FAILURE (AND WHY THE FIRST ONE DOESN'T MATTER)

"Don't just say, 'I'm just being scared, I should just go for it.' Instead, place good gear and create safety and confidence."

Steph Davis

Working alongside the philosophy of runout strategy are the dramatically different kinds of failure that can occur while trad climbing. To distinguish between these failures it is critical to develop a constant, down-to-earth evaluation of real risk vs. perceived risk.

Real risk is when you are facing bodily harm if something goes wrong.

Perceived risk is when your mind is freaking, but your body is perfectly safe.

The category of risk is inseparable from the consequences of failure, which can be broken into four types.

#1 SPORTS FAILURE

This is when you failed to play the game according to the arbitrary rules of the sport; basically, you hung on the rope or pulled on a piece of gear. Yep, you failed to free climb the pitch; but you can always come back and try again, and even if you don't come back you can still have a great adventure or gymnastic performance without successfully climbing the pitch as a free climb. This is the most trivial of the four kinds of failure, though climbing culture can easily mistake it as the most important.

The consequence? A bruised ego. Take-away? Climb for yourself, not the peanut gallery.

#2 PROFICIENCY FAILURE

This is "getting away with it," and it happens far more often than any of us would like to admit. Proficiency failure is when you fail to climb a pitch as safely as possible given what you have to work with. Anyone who has been trad climbing for more than a few months has had the experience of getting away with a dicey situation that could easily have been avoided. It is possible to

Some kinds of mistakes, like grabbing the wrong hold, are just fine to make. Others? Disaster. Don't confuse the two.

technically "send" a pitch without falling, but in the process you risk so much that you failed to execute the pitch proficiently. I see this kind of failure far too often when climbing at popular trad climbing areas.

The consequence? Encourages sloppiness. Takeaway? Critique yourself in a positive way every time you climb and become a better climber.

#3 LEARNING FAILURE

This is when you not only experience a proficiency failure but fail to learn from it. If you climb a pitch that could be done perfectly safely, but you botch a bunch of the placements, kick out the last one as you move past it, flail to the anchors looking at a death fall, and then celebrate wildly because you just sent your hardest climb, you are failing to learn a critical part of becoming a competent trad leader. We've all had moments like this, but if you view such an ascent as entirely a success you are cheating yourself of a vital part of the learning curve. Look back at every single pitch you've lead, both the ones you've sent and the ones that kicked your butt, and evaluate honestly what you did right and what you did wrong.

The consequence? Encourages taking unnecessary risks. Takeaway? Learning is more important than sending.

#4 SAFETY FAILURE

At best, safety failure results in the dreaded close call, near miss, or minor injury. At worst, safety failure results in serious injury or death. Frequently, the safety failure is a result of habitual learning failures compounded by habitual proficiency failures. For example, frequently place poor pieces of gear and eventually you'll fall on one of them and it will drop you. Continually run it out and your chances of taking a long fall go way up. Frequently shortcut basic safety

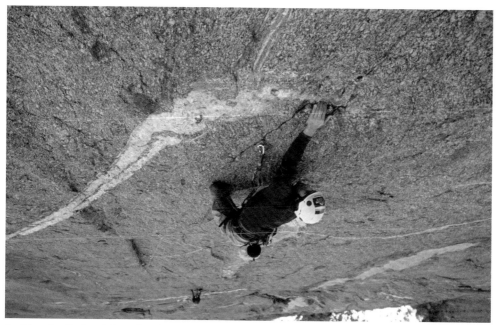

Pushing the limits of the safety buffer with thin gear, long runouts, and hard climbing

protocols, like double-checking knots and harness tie-ins or foregoing use of auto-block rappel backups, and your chance of a catastrophic safety failure increases exponentially.

The consequence? Potential disaster. Takeaway? Monitor safety at all times, no matter what else is happening.

DISASTER PREVENTION

"Anything that can happen will. Put a second biner (or locker) on important pieces. Alternate gate direction from piece to piece if the rope runs weird."

Steph Davis

Elite climbers who are frequently pushing the envelope have developed ways to dramatically reduce the chance of all four types of failure. These climbers spend several days a week, all year round, playing the vertical game; and most of the climbers I've met who climb this heavily are also the most conscientious about going to great lengths to prevent a climbing disaster. When you play the game every day, you quickly realize that the less often you roll the dice, and the more you plan and control, the better.

The major ways to prevent disaster, like double-checking your knot, are well known and culturally, pretty well practiced.

It's with the smaller, less obvious keys to climbing safely that many climbers have room to improve.

MAINTAIN A HEALTHY SAFETY BUFFER

The best way to execute the boldest, most difficult, and inspiring ascent you can imagine and to do it in good form is to preface the effort with a bombproof web of safety. Peak performances while trad climbing often require setting up a line of gear so powerfully solid that you can treat the gear as if it were indeed a bomber bolt.

"When placing gear, lock the door and throw away the key."

Sonnie Trotter

This means, as Sonnie implies, you put all the effort necessary into finding protection that is so good that you can mentally put the gear out of your mind and carry on as if you were sport climbing—at least until you need another piece. Many intermediate-level trad climbers trying to move into higher levels have yet to experience this freedom from concern about the gear failing. But in order to climb hard safely it is essential to place gear that is so solid that you can unquestionably trust it with your life.

Aside from on-lead performance, the healthy safety buffer should surround your entire team at all stages of the climbing process. Specifically:

- Rope up for the 3rd class sections on the approach or descent anytime it is safer to do so. There are certainly 3rd class approaches that may be safely climbed without a rope, and sometimes terrain with loose rock or complete lack of protection can be more safely traversed unroped than tied together. But you want unroped climbing to be a conscious decision, not the default.
- Place a simple ground anchor for you and your partner anytime the bottom belay is above rugged terrain at the base of the route—the potential fall from the bottom of a climb is often not obvious at first, particularly when standing below a large cliff that dwarfs the features below.
- Place gear close together above every belay. These pieces should be as bomber as the belay anchor if at all possible. Unfortunately, it is common for confident climbers to run it out off the belay, not entirely realizing the catastrophic potential of such a move.
- Stack the odds in your favor while maintaining efficiency. As static as climbing can seem at times, it is a movement sport. If you spend too much time trying to make every safety decision pass a six sigma quality control equivalent, you'll create an efficiency hazard by spending too much time in dangerous places. Get 'er done and get on with it!

WATCH FOR LOOSE ROCK

"Loose rock. That's what separates the men from the boys."

Earl Wiggins

Both sport and trad climbs sometimes require moving across sections of rock that

DON'T SACRIFICE CRITICAL SAFETY IN THE PRESENT
DUE TO FEAR OF THE FUTURE

I was crossing a ledge to the base of a big wall free climb deep in the Wind Rivers of Wyoming and was so concerned about the upcoming ascent that I stepped on a loose block and very nearly took a 50-foot fall into the talus. This is an extreme example, but it is easy to make this and similar mistakes in many climbing scenarios. These mistakes include:

- Climbing easy but runout moves nonchalantly because your mind is preoccupied by an upcoming crux. Focus on the moment, even on the easy terrain—not only will you be safer, but you'll also climb better overall.

- Being stingy with gear on lead because you habitually worry about having enough gear to build an anchor. If you make it to the anchor, you're golden! If you need more gear to build a full anchor you can always lower back down and backclean, or pull up gear on a loop or tag line as the second follows.

- Being sloppy with anchors and protection or taking foolish shortcuts because you're hurrying to meet some arbitrary deadline. Give yourself extra time to do the climb right, and explain to your husband, wife, or co-workers that you'll usually come in early from a climbing outing, but on occasion you might be a little late.

On a huge climb, maintain the basic safety systems throughout the climb no matter how tired, cold, wet, or exhausted you become.

Developing awareness of loose rock is critical for every climber.

are not entirely solid and, in Earl Wiggins's world of onsight adventure trad climbing in the 1970s and '80s, being able to climb hard on previously untouched and sometimes loose rock was a mandatory skill. Today, climbs are much more travelled and tend to be cleaner; but as a result climbers have generally grown more cavalier about loose rock. You're much more likely to make the mistake of pulling hard on a loose block that is covered with chalk than you are to pull hard on that same block if you're the first person to touch it.

If you see a suspect hold—one with a crack all the way around it, detached from the wall on one side, hollow sounding, or that is part of any suspicious-looking features, approach the hold with the air of an inspector, not a climber. Determining how solid or loose a hold may be is an art more than a science, but the bottom line is that identifying the hold as potentially loose is more than half the battle. I've seen numerous leader falls due to loose rock, and I've experienced my own, and in almost every case the leader did not recognize the hold as being potentially loose. Providing the belayer, rope, and other people are out of the fall line, it can be safer to remove a loose rock than to leave it in place.

There are ways to test for rock quality on the microscale, but there are also big flakes teetering on ledges that will appear solid enough to build an anchor on but would tip off the ledge under just a few pounds of force. *Constant visual and tactile assessment of the rock structure surrounding you and the risk asssociated with loose rock for you and your belayer at all times is of critical importance in many climbing scenarios.* With a focus on finding solid rock, however, good protection and reliable holds can often be found in many sections of less than ideal stone.

BECAUSE IT WORKED ONCE DOESN'T MEAN IT WILL WORK NEXT TIME

The inherent positive feedback we so enjoy about climbing is also seductive and dangerous. When we succeed on a climb without obvious close calls, the experience leads us to believe that we must have done it right—when, many times, we were relying on a system that, if tested, would have failed.

Most protection placed is never subjected to the actual force of a big fall, so it is easy to assume you are placing solid protection when it is possible instead that a significant fraction of your placements would pull out if tested by a fall. To consider yourself a "solid climber," you must place bomber protection 99 percent of the time when solid protection is available and execute the climbing system in a manner that doesn't just work once, but works thousands of times in a row. Sure, there are times when you might choose to lay it on the line for a dangerous lead or a climb that is above your ability level. But that is very different than regularly exposing yourself to danger on climbs that can be done perfectly safely.

There are several things that will dramatically help you see through this dangerous feedback cycle of climbing:

- Be critical of every one of your climbs—define success by sustaining safety, not whether or not you hung on the rope or made it to the top.
- Practice easy aid climbing—there is no better way to get immediate, real feedback on the behavior of climbing protection in the rock. The first time a cam or nut you thought was "good enough" pops under body weight, you'll become a far better trad climber.
- If an experienced partner follows one of your leads, ask them what they thought of your gear placements; take advantage of learning opportunities when roping up with skilled climbers.
- Treat every climb as if it is the one that matters most. Every pitch, regardless of the grade, is a new chance to execute the vertical game safely while having loads of fun.

Test rock quality before using it: A good habit to develop on everything but obviously perfect rock is to hit the holds with the palm of your hand as you grab them and listen for hollow or rattling sounds and feel for vibrations. For small crimps, rapping on them with your knuckle will often reveal vibration or confirm stability. These two simple methods will save you from the majority of loose rock issues. From there, several techniques can reveal even more of the rock's internal structure and the resultant strength of the holds:

- When you first touch a suspect hold, try not to pull on it, and instead establish more weight on your feet.

- Then, use your other hand to rap on the hold, next to the hand you are holding it with, and feel the vibration that passes through the rock. With practice, this method reveals far more than a visual check or simply hitting it with the palm of the hand you intend to grab it with.
- Do everything you can to avoid pulling outward on suspect holds—they are usually strongest in a downward direction.
- On popular climbs with suspect rock, challenge yourself to climb with minimal pressure on the holds. The idea is to use them more gently than most other climbers who did the climb before you.

Test the rock with not just your hands—use your feet: Some of the same methods used by the hands are also applicable to the feet, but rock shoes and leg strength bring up additional considerations and limitations.

- Tap lightly on holds with your toes, or harder with your heels, while listening and feeling for vibration.
- Weight a hold slightly, then twist with part of your shoe against the wall and part of the shoe on the hold. It's a great way to either pry the edge off a dubious flake or to make sure it will hold your weight before committing to it.
- When you see a potentially loose hold, look around for other options before touching it. Use precise footwork on small, solid features nearby rather than immediately standing on big, loose features. It is usually safest to avoid loose rock entirely.

WHEN IN DOUBT, PLACE MORE GEAR

This may seem obvious, but frequently newcomers to advanced terrain will take significant risks when protected by just one piece or a series of dubious placements. Advanced climbers know to add more, even if it means using almost the entire rack in a short section of climbing if that's what's needed.

Look for every opportunity to add to your web of safety without reducing your efficiency. Placing two pieces next to one another from a good stance is often more efficient than fighting upward in an attempt to spread the gear out, and it is much safer than just placing the one piece.

A little-known secret in hard climbing is this: placing more gear can allow you to climb without holding on so tightly, increasing your efficiency and safety at the same time.

ROUTEFINDING

There are three tricky parts about routefinding while climbing. First, it is easy to get distracted by the micro-routefinding (where to put your hands and feet and where to place the pro) so that you make mistakes in macro-routefinding, that is, finding the desired route up the cliff. Second, it is difficult to see much of the wall when the farthest you can get from the wall is an arm's length. Third, even when you can see it, the obvious line is not always the right one.

To avoid the distraction of micro-routefinding, switch gears between the close-in and the big view every chance you get. When the climbing is hard, stay focused on the immediate moves, but as soon as you reach easier terrain, a rest, or a ledge where it is possible to take a look around, do so. On big climbs this can mean leaving the line of ascent to look around, placing a piece of gear or two if need be to protect your recon, then removing it as you move back onto the line. Traversing out of the line of ascent can help—even if you are certain of where the route goes at that point—because it can offer a view of the upper part of the route that you will not get from the climbing line.

On a big route, the best way to work around the issue of being too close to the wall while climbing is to do as much route-finding as possible during the approach:

- Use the approach to study the line of ascent and descent from the various vantage points provided along the way. Consider leaving the trail if a slight detour promises viewpoints of your objective.
- From a distance, snap a photo of the climb and of the descent with your phone or camera so you will have a reference photo you can zoom in on while on the route.
- Before starting the climb, take note of places where it would be easy to get off-route.
- Develop a habit of evaluating not only the chosen route but also alternatives—in case other parties beat you to the main route, for example—as well as any features that could help with an emergency descent, such as ledges leading into a walk-off gully or alternative descent anchors.

Big-picture thinking: Look for places to move out of the line of ascent to look ahead for the route, even if it requires placing a piece of gear to allow you to inspect the terrain above safely.

Because once you're in the belly of the beast the obvious line is not always the right line, it is important to consider other factors in addition to the route description or guidebook photo to stay on route while climbing. Guidebook authors make mistakes, cracks lead nowhere, first ascentionist descriptions can be obtuse, and chalk from other lost parties can lead you astray. To help you stay on route, ask these questions:

▥ Who did the first ascent? The personality and reputation of the first ascentionist can reveal a lot.

▥ When was the first ascent? The first route up the cliff, for example, done in

In the middle of a long route, it's wise to take a minute at each belay to consult the topo.

1975, will have certain characteristics and follow a very different kind of line from the twentieth route up the same cliff done in 2005.

▥ How experienced are you with the area, the routes, the rock? If it is your first time, plan for extra time to get it right and beware of making assumptions.

▥ Ask yourself: Does the terrain you're on live up to the climb's reputation for quality and popularity? If you're trying a climb that is supposed to be excellent and popular, and you find you're climbing lichen-covered cracks full of dirt, there is a good chance you're off-route.

Online information is a blessing and a curse. It can help immensely with staying on route; but it can also complicate your decision making, be just plain wrong, create a false sense of security, or lead you further astray than you would have ever gone without that information. This is why common sense must remain at the core of your routefinding—only go there if it is right for you, not because someone else said that was the way to go.

HEADPOINTING

Climbs have been practiced on top-rope before the lead throughout the history of free climbing. But it wasn't until the 1980s that the term "headpointing" was coined to describe a lead ascent after top-rope rehearsal. Headpointing originated on the gritstone crags of the UK, where no bolts are allowed and short but high-quality lines with minimal or no protection on excellent rock naturally inspire rehearsal before leading.

Like many concepts in climbing, the definition of "headpoint" is not black and white. A one time top-rope before the lead may technically be a headpoint; but the lead isn't truly considered a headpoint unless an unprotected or dangerous section has been practiced multiple times on top-rope before the lead.

The fundamental aspects of the headpoint include:

▨ Practicing hard and insecure moves on top-rope to the point where not only can you do them, but you can do them with almost zero chance of falling
▨ Involving the belayer intimately (see more below)
▨ Using crash pads to cover rocks and swing impact zones to protect the climber, and even to pad the belayer's potential trajectory
▨ Studying the gear placements, if there are any, to be sure of the most solid possible placements
▨ Removing tick marks after the ascent

Perhaps the most useful technique to be borrowed from the headpoint culture is not from the climber, but from the belayer. Belaying a true headpoint is nearly as intimidating as executing the lead. The headpoint belay consists of:

▨ Being ready to reel in slack and run away from the base of the wall to shorten the leader's fall
▨ Placing a piece below the wall as a directional to run the rope through, so as you run away from the wall the rope pulls straight down rather than outward

▨ Critically assessing the fall forces on the belayer to be sure you can hold the fall without injury
▨ Considering complex double- or triple-rope methods to maximize the safety provided by the scant protection

Many climbers have little interest in true headpoints, preferring to stay on climbs with good protection. But there is wisdom to be gained from the headpoint tactic that can help give even the most safety-conscious climber a more diverse skill set. Big wall free climbers use elements of the headpoint in order to work out difficult sections with tricky protection. Cragging areas like Colorado's Eldorado Canyon, The Gunks in New York, and Devil's Lake in Wisconsin, Mount Arapiles in Australia, and, of course, the gritstone of England's Peak District are notorious for climbs that are hard to onsight but reasonable with a little headpoint attitude and technique.

With the resurgent interest in trad climbing, many climbers are using headpoint tactics simply to tick high number grades. If you are pushing your grade using this method, be aware that practicing everything on top-rope before leading can become a crutch and limit you in the future as well as create an illusion that, because you ticked a hard pitch, you are now ready for other hard trad climbs. It also removes the sense of adventure that is so much a part of trad climbing. Save the headpoint strategy for times where it is needed to improve the safety margin and you'll be a much better climber.

FOLLOWING TRAVERSES

If you're following an experienced leader, traverses should be relatively well set up to protect you while following the traverse. In places, a good leader will reach back to place protection that they don't really need in order to make your traverse safer while following. Even with the best leader, however, the harsh reality is that there are times when the second must do a reverse runout where the next piece on the traverse is far enough away to cause a sizeable fall.

The best approach to following a traverse is to consider it as a sort of hybrid lead/follow

Some traverses are obvious to protect while others are subtle. As a leader, develop a sense of what it will be like for your second to follow your leads at all times.

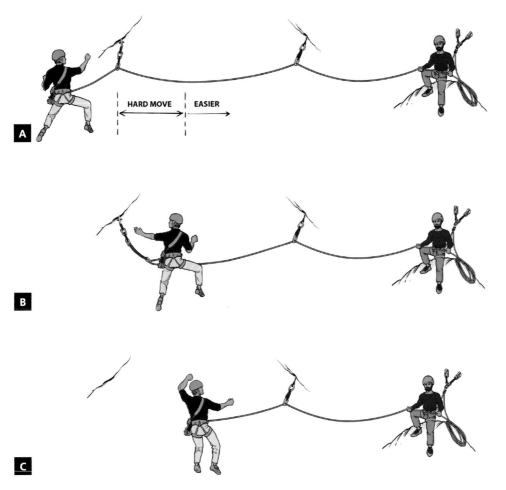

HARD MOVE | EASIER

Following traverses: A. Approaching a piece of protection before a difficult move. B. Leave protection in place with long sling added to facilitate movement. C. Reach back and clean protection.

experience that has elements of both roles. It is like following because you are taking out the gear as you go, but it is also like leading because your gear management has a direct influence on your exposure to risk.

To mitigate risk while following traverses:
- Look ahead and anticipate the difficult sections as well as the runouts.
- When possible, climb past a piece so it provides protection as long as possible,

and then reach back and clean it from a good hold or stance.

- If you are uncertain of the moves past a piece, clip a long sling to the piece and work out the moves with the sling clipped. Then, once you have the moves figured out, reach back and clean the piece.
- If necessary, reach ahead and place another piece to protect yourself.
- If you see the leader heading into a traverse, don't be shy to ask them to place some gear for you too.

TRAD FIRST ASCENTS

For those who have experienced it, the traditional first ascent can be one of the most rewarding of all climbing experiences. However, in most climbing areas the obvious lines have been long established and what remains are the distant, obscure, dangerous, extremely difficult, or simply chossy and lousy routes. To find a high-quality first ascent today, comfortable hiking shoes and often a plane ticket to a faraway land are standard equipment.

There is no textbook way to establish a first ascent, but there are a few certainties you can count on when you establish your first new route:

- You will think your route is the best climb ever.
- Other people will think your climb should get a different grade than you do.
- In hindsight, you'll often realize your route wasn't the best route ever.

The climbers who consistently put up the best first ascents take time to learn an area and get in tune with its ethics, style, and risk level. When you do a climb for the first time, you are shaping the experience others will have in doing the route. A first ascent that you headpoint may be appropriate in some cases, but to headpoint a route and then list it with other climbs that are okay to climb onsight is a huge disservice to the climbing community. Unless you aspire to being known for establishing lousy routes, be honest with both yourself and the climbing community regarding how a climb was done.

Some lines are left unclimbed because of copious amounts of lichen, dirt, or plants in the crack. If you are sniffing around for a first ascent, remember that the plants were there first. In some areas, the plants that grow on cliffs are unique to the vertical world and removing them can deal a serious blow to the survival of the species. Also, on many public lands, removing plants for the sake of sport, or for any other reason, is illegal.

Do your homework before installing bolts. Most climbing management plans recommend or require bolts like the Power-Bolt or Rawl 5-Piece that can be removed and replaced using the same hole. Power drills are illegal in many areas, such as federally protected wilderness and national parks. Other places have banned bolting completely. In many areas where climbs can be seen from trails or roads, paint the hangers and hardware to match the rock; apply the paint before installing the bolts to avoid getting paint on the rock. Whatever kind of bolt you place, it is your responsibility to read and understand the

For experienced climbers, climbing into untouched terrain and discovering the route as it unfolds under the fingertips is one of the sport's greatest pleasures.

manufacturer's installation instructions. For other considerations when establishing a fully bolted first ascent, see Chapter 7, Sport Climbing.

When establishing and reporting first ascents, be aware at all times of land manager perception and rules as well as the non-climbing public's perspective. What you do during the ascent as well as what you say on Facebook, Mountain Project, or SuperTopo could influence future land regulation. Putting up first ascents is a privilege of having wild lands to recreate in— help keep it that way.

Opposite: *Heidi Wirtz and Vera Schulte-Pelkum both busy making it happen on the windy upper pitches of El Cap's* Nose *during a one-day ascent*

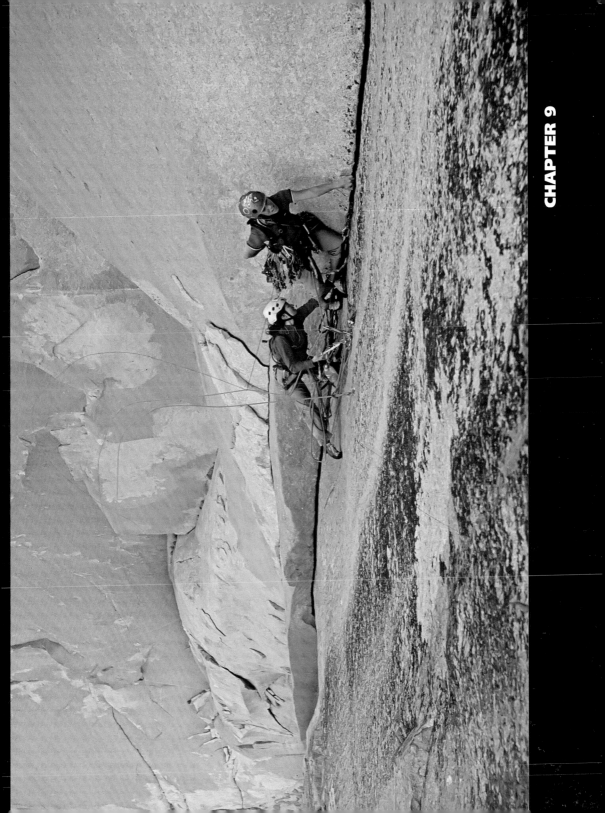

CHAPTER 9

Long Route Efficiency

"Constantly adapting—the ability to not follow the rules, but to instead adapt and be creative—is one of my favorite things about climbing big routes."

Tommy Caldwell

Putting together a long free climb at your limit is the ultramarathon of climbing (but a lot more fun). Today, there are so many great long climbs, both sport and trad, with solid protection, thrilling exposure, and a plethora of information available, that any aspiring expert shouldn't hold back from going big. Find a partner that is on the same page. Find the right climb. Practice for it. Then put it all together for one of the best days of your climbing life.

Long route efficiency techniques are important for everything from bagging a six-pitch route after work to climbing a big wall. However, climbing a big wall free is also a unique endeavor that requires its own special focus. It often takes several days to free a big wall (see Chapter 10 to read all about the specifics of big wall free climbing). The efficiency techniques explained here will help you to take on a Grade IV, V, or even VI multipitch climb in a single day—and, perhaps most importantly, to do the multipitch climbs you want to do fast enough to get down by dark, before the storm hits, or before you need to be back to work.

Whatever your goal, to improve your efficiency, consider this question: How do you go from needing all day to climb three pitches to being proficient enough to climb thirteen (or thirty-three) pitches in a single day? There may be no kind of climbing where the outcome of technique differences between different climbers is more profound than on long climbs. The same climb that takes one team several days takes another team several hours. The goal in this chapter is to reveal some of the techniques used by the team who can do a half-mile-tall climb in several hours—and thus help you to increase your own speed and safety on long climbs. By using the techniques developed by the world's fastest climbers, and using them when it is safe to do so, it is not uncommon for the average climbing team to cut their long route ascent times in half. You heard me right. Not a few minutes faster, but in half the time.

The mental approach to setting off on long climbs is a crucial aspect of gaining speed and safety, and having fun. When

I first climbed El Capitan's *Nose* in a day, the competition to do the climb ever faster was fierce. Speed climbing tactics were increasing speeds (and risk-taking) by leaps and bounds, and the speed freaks had developed an entirely new system for covering hundreds of feet of vertical rock in mere minutes. So when my partner and I were debating what tactics to use, although we were far from speed record material, we felt some pressure to use speed climbing techniques, including short fixing, simul-climbing (where both climbers move together), and leading in blocks. We'll get into each of these, but before embarking on our *Nose*-in-a-day effort, we were lucky to talk to a climber who gave us some great advice: Don't do any of that speed climbing stuff, just lead long pitches every time, free climb up to 5.11, and have the second follow quickly on their ascenders.

My partner and I took this advice and climbed the *Nose* in twelve hours. We did a little simul-climbing in a couple of strategic, easy places where the second could be on ledge-like terrain, but for the most part we just pitched it out, enjoyed ourselves, and pulled off the one-day ascent with half a day to spare. While we came nowhere near the *Nose* speed record at the time, which was about three hours for the 3000-foot climb, by being familiar with speed climbing technique my partner and I were able to experience a climbing feat that was once the exclusive realm of the elite.

The fundamental methods that dramatically raise speed and efficiency on long climbs were invented by speed climbers. But the incredible benefits of using these techniques have made them useful for the rest of us, and they form a critical component of boosting the efficiency and capability of all experienced climbers.

These game-changing methods for covering large swaths of stone quickly also make long climbs far more reasonable and even safer, as well as provide the background for the inspiring world of big wall free climbing. Before you can enjoy a hard free climb—whatever that means for you—on a big wall or even a long day route, you need to learn to perform the easier climbing and logistics extremely economically, saving time and energy for working out the crux pitches far above the ground. This style of climbing—pushing your personal limits in the midst of an enormous cliff—is one of the ultimate climbing experiences. But it gets even better. Big wall free climbing combines the power of bouldering, the exposure of aid climbing, the complexity of trad climbing, and the mind-set of sport climbing: all set in one of our planet's most dramatic sporting arenas. So we'll begin with the techniques of speed climbing and progress into applying these techniques on long climbs before moving into the next chapter on big wall free climbing.

This chapter assumes at least a rudimentary understanding of big wall methods, including ascending a rope and hauling. For an excellent and thorough education on big wall tactics, read Jared Ogden's *Big Wall Climbing: Elite Technique*.

Simul-climbing in aid terrain on the Leaning Tower, Yosemite

SIMUL-CLIMBING

"Simul-climbing (with a progress capture device) will change the sport."

Alex Honnold

Simul-climbing (short for simultaneous climbing), where leader and follower both move at the same time, is a technique that was first used in the very beginning of the sport. Mountaineers were simul-climbing long before cams, nuts, and carabiners were invented. The benefits are obvious. If both climbers are moving at the same time, the efficiency of the team effectively doubles and the time exposure to objective hazards, like afternoon thunderstorms, decreases. With the development of the sophisticated 5th class technique that we're all familiar with, simul-climbing became viewed as a high-risk technique best avoided by safety-conscious climbers. As it turns out, few things are that black and white in climbing.

Many times a bit of simul-climbing can provide these safety benefits:

- Allows the leader to reach a solid anchor rather than belaying off questionable gear
- Decreases exposure to afternoon storms, rock fall from other climbers, and other objective hazards
- Enables belays to be positioned in the ideal places for the hard pitches
- Gives the team added flexibility as to which climber leads each section
- Provides teams with an efficient way to climb with a rope in moderate terrain— an alternative to climbing unroped

There are several critical components to simul-climbing safely.

USING GRIGRIS

In simul-climbing, a Grigri is often left on the rope so the second can move faster than the leader without building up slack. Simul-climbing can be done without using a Grigri, but it is much safer with one. No matter what belay device you use, if you are going to simul-climb, *the second should not take the device off the rope when they are climbing until the leader sets an anchor and puts the second on belay.*

The second ready to simul-climb, as the leader uses all the rope on a long pitch above: A. The anchor is removed with the Grigri left on the rope. B. As the second moves up they can pull rope through the Grigri and keep a close belay on the leader. Of course, if the second falls they will pull the leader off. See Using Progress Capture Devices for a technique that can prevent this.

The second should, however, while belaying, *take out part of the anchor as the leader nears the end of the rope.* It is important for the second to begin disassembling the anchor, putting their rock shoes on, and getting everything ready to go while the leader is still climbing—you don't want the leader waiting on tiny footholds while the second dismantles the entire belay.

The second should stay clipped to a single bomber piece and only remove it at the last moment. To a beginner, removing part of the belay before the leader is finished seems like a sketchy idea. But if you consider all the gear that is placed and clipped at this point, taking out part of the anchor causes absolutely zero increase in risk. In fact, it is at this point, when the leader has placed an entire pitch of gear, that the whole rope team is at the safest point in the climbing process. This is one of many scenarios where it is better to set up belays *without* a cordelette equalized to a power point. Using a cordelette here greatly complicates the partial breakdown of the anchor while staying clipped in to a piece of it. Using an improvised semi-equalized anchor instead is a better choice; it requires less gear and offers multiple attachment points (as shown in Chapter 4, Knots and Anchor Rigging).

Then, because the second leaves the Grigri on the rope, they can pull rope through the device as they move up the easy climbing at the beginning of the pitch, meanwhile giving the leader a close belay in case she is dealing with hard climbing above. Done correctly, the leader can climb as if she has a normal belay—albeit with the entire rope stretched out between her and her belayer.

In the photo on page 219, the lower sequence of green dots is the terrain where the second can safely simul-climb. In this case, there is also a ledge 30 feet above the second. This means the second can climb, pulling rope through the Grigri (caution: *without pulling on the leader*) until the ledge where the hard climbing begins. At this point, the second can clip into one of the pieces or even place a piece of pro, and then proceed to belay normally from a standstill while the leader finishes the pitch.

USING PROGRESS CAPTURE DEVICES
"When I started using PCDs for simul-climbing, the mountains got half as big."
Tommy Caldwell

The invention of miniature ascenders and high-strength mini-hauling devices has changed the game of simul-climbing. Running the lead rope through a progress capture device (PCD)—with the device oriented so the rope can slide upward freely, but locks under a downward pull—prevents the leader from being pulled off in the event that the second falls. If the leader falls, the weight of the second, not the device, will hold the leader's fall in much the same way as a traditional belay. *Note that the PCD only adds security if the second falls and will do nothing to change the outcome of a leader fall.*

The Mini Traxion (and the even smaller but stronger Micro Traxion) was first invented by Petzl as a lightweight hauling

A. Micro Traxion PCD rigged to pseudo-belay the second while simul-climbing, with a piece immediately above to prevent a leader fall from loading the PCD directly. B. If it is not possible to place a piece immediately above the placement holding the PCD, clip the rope through a biner above the PCD so a leader fall will load the carabiner rather than the PCD.

device, with a pulley and one-way rope-locking cam integrated into a single small unit. Using it to simul-climb is one of the ways in which climbers have taken a device and used it in ways the manufacturer never dreamed. Micro ascenders such as the Petzl Tibloc, Wild Country Ropeman, and the Kong Duck can offer some added security in simul-climbing, but the Petzl Mini and Micro Traxion devices are the most commonly used. We will likely see devices built specifically for these uses; but for now, climbers who use these devices in this manner are bending the rules and care must be taken to consider the limitations and hazards of using these techniques.

While the PCD allows the second to navigate much more difficult terrain without endangering the leader, the method is not without its limitations—limitations that must be understood with crystal clarity.

The PCD backup while simul-climbing is not the same as a belay in these ways:

- If fallen on, the progress capture device's locking cams can sever the sheath of the rope with as little as 3 kN of force applied, about the strength of what a tiny nut can hold. It makes little difference if the device is tested to 4 kN if the device can shred a rope at 3 kN.
- It is not possible for the second to downclimb, to be fed slack, or to be lowered—the rope will only move in one direction.
- The piece that holds the PCD must be anchor quality. A single, bomber, multidirectional piece is commonly trusted in this application, but add an extra piece if the first is anything less than perfect.
- The PCD will be left in place as both climbers move, so there will be nobody to monitor the device or the protection it is clipped to—make sure you get it right before climbing past.
- If the stopping cam is accidentally locked open, the device will not work.

When setting up the PCD for simul-climbing:

- Clip it close to the protection point—if left on the end of a long sling, or even a quickdraw, the pivot of the sling can provide enough movement that if the second falls, the leader will be pulled downward as the sling pivots. For this reason, the PCD must be clipped close to the piece so it does not move much, and it must not cause rope drag.
- The PCD does not need to be placed at the leader's precise point when the second begins climbing, but the higher it is placed on the pitch, the farther the team can climb before needing a proper belay.
- The PCD should be set up from a good stance; take the time to make sure it is done properly and without your burning excess energy.
- Clip the PCD so it will hold the second, but place a piece for the leader immediately above it to prevent the leader from falling onto the PCD. While the device is plenty strong to hold a fall by the second, a lead fall directly onto the device would expose the sheath to dangerous forces right next to the sharp teeth of the device.

Before the invention of the Mini and Micro Traxion, other devices were used to provide a similar pseudo-belay for simul-climbing. The Tibloc for example, can be used in a similar fashion, and it is extremely lightweight. However, *particular care must be taken to thread the Tibloc so the rope is running through the biner, and not outside the biner where a leader fall would run the rope over the sharp outer edge of the Tibloc.* Also, the aggressive teeth of the Tibloc combined with the variability of the biner used—its diameter and shape—make it less predictable than the Micro and Mini Traxion. For this reason, the Tibloc should not be used in this manner as a standard technique, but only in a case where runout simul-climbing becomes unavoidable, and no other tools are available.

A WRONG—EXTREMELY DANGEROUS | **B CORRECT**

Use Tibloc as a PCD only as a last resort, and then be sure you are using it correctly.
A. Tibloc rigged wrong! This is extremely dangerous—a leader fall WILL sever the rope.
B. Tibloc correctly rigged as PCD with rope running through the biner.

ARRANGEMENT OF THE HARD VS. EASY CLIMBING

A pitch that begins with easy climbing, where the second is highly unlikely to fall or to need a close belay, is a good candidate for simul-climbing.

This is one of the key elements of simul-climbing safety: in many cases, *the leader can safely climb difficult terrain while simul-climbing because the second provides what is essentially a solid belay. The second, on the other hand, should remain on easy terrain because if the second falls, it could pull the leader off as well, resulting in an extremely violent fall.* This can be mitigated to some degree with careful use of a PCD left on a piece higher on the pitch, as described in the previous section. But this is a crucial philosophy of simul-climbing competency: It may be okay for the leader to climb hard, but the second should stay on easy terrain—and both climbers need to be aware of what kind of terrain the other is on at all times.

THE FANGS OF THE PCD

Elite climbers are taking the use of PCDs to extreme levels, but the seeming security of this method should not be overestimated. A warning for users: *Tests have shown that a toothed progress capture device can sever the sheath of the rope and begin to cut the core fibers under forces as little as 3 kN—about the tested strength of a tiny nut.* A 150-pound climber, falling 12 feet, will generate about 3 kN of force.

"If you're putting in enough gear while simul-climbing, you're probably in a safer situation without the progress capture device on the rope than you are with a device that could damage your lifeline."

Marc Piché

This potential danger can be mitigated by the second climber's use of a Grigri to prevent buildup of slack between the climber and the PCD. The critical component of safely simul-climbing in this manner is to avoid building up slack in front of the second climber.

DEVELOPING "COURT SENSE"

"Before I did the Nose *in a day for the first time, we worked through all the classics— then had a 22-hour epic (on the* Nose).*"*

Alex Honnold

Just as a good basketball player knows exactly where that out-of-bounds line is without looking at it, a good climber develops "court sense" to have a darn good idea when and where they will run out of rope, where the second may need to begin simul-climbing, and when the second will begin facing difficult terrain and need a proper belay. In the simul-climbing photo on page 219, the leader must remember that when they run out of rope, the second will have 30 feet of easy terrain before starting on the difficult climbing. The benefits of court sense apply to all aspects of climbing on long routes, but an acute sense of the rope team is never more important than when simul-climbing.

One of the benefits of developing climbing court sense is a greatly increased awareness and management of rope drag. When simul-climbing on extremely long pitches, this becomes paramount. From a bird's-eye view, it may be very clear that there are places where the rope makes dramatic bends that will require attention to prevent severe rope drag over the course of a 70- or 100-meter lead, but from the leader's perspective while on the climb, these points can be far less obvious. For most climbers first venturing into extra-long pitches and simul-climbing, rope drag management is one of the most difficult challenges. The key is to do everything you can to prevent rope

At all times you should know where you are on the wall, where your partner is, and what kind of terrain you are both moving through and into.

drag, including using safe downclimbing to backclean and incorporating strategic runouts, starting from the very beginning of the pitch before you can even feel an ounce of rope drag. (For a detailed discussion of rope drag management, see Chapter 8, Traditional Lead Climbing.)

COMMUNICATION

Communication that bolsters court sense becomes even more important when simul-climbing than when using traditional 5th class technique. In simul-climbing, there are several points where communication is critical. For example:

■ The leader, upon leaving the lower belay, realizes the initial 30 feet are easy and potentially a good candidate for simul-climbing. When she reaches the beginning of the hard climbing, and anticipates that she may extend the pitch beyond the length of the rope, she can say something like: "I think we can link these next two pitches if we simul-climb for 20 or 30 feet. Please let me know when the rope runs out and you start climbing."

▨ The second should keep the leader informed of how much rope is left so the leader has ample time to plan ahead and find an ideal spot to anchor and position the PCD if one will be used.

▨ The leader should let the second know when a PCD is placed so the second can follow with the full understanding of the system in use.

▨ The second should inform the leader when he begins climbing so the leader can adjust accordingly to the rope movements of a climber rather than a belayer. This will also allow the leader to more accurately estimate the distance of simul-climbing possible before a proper belay will be needed.

▨ The leader should let the second know when she has stopped climbing and has put the second on belay so the second can adjust accordingly and begin climbing faster and taking the shortcuts afforded by a solid overhead belay.

POSITION OF THE STRONGER VS. WEAKER CLIMBER

I'll preface this by saying that simul-climbing should only be practiced by experienced teams. But unlike other forms of roped climbing where it is best if the stronger climber leads, when simul-climbing it is often best (and somewhat counterintuitive) if the stronger climber follows. The second must deal with more things outside the scope of the traditional

5th class method, like climbing moderate terrain while possibly advancing a Grigri along the rope, moving smoothly enough to avoid holding up the leader in an awkward position, and climbing with enough confidence to not need to be lowered or require assistance from the rope.

There may also be sections of simul-climbing where it is best if the stronger climber leads. Like many things at the advanced levels of climbing, there is no one way that is best all the time. What is important is that you consider what both the leader and the second will be doing at all times, and how their actions will help—or hinder—the other, and then plan accordingly. This is one of the reasons why leading in blocks, which we'll discuss next, has become a helpful technique on long climbs, big wall free climbs, and even run-of-the-mill multipitch climbs.

LEADING IN BLOCKS

"The hardest part of swinging leads, and something that is easy to forget when assessing a long route, is that you follow one hard pitch and then lead the next without much rest."

Steph Davis

Breaking up a climb into blocks was invented as a speed climbing tactic, but it is an effective tactic for many other reasons.

▨ **Optimizing who leads what:** Leading in blocks allows each climber to lead the section of the climb most suited to their ability rather than a rigid "swapping

The belay gives the leader a chance to rest. Depending on the fitness of the team and individual leading ability, it may be best to lead in blocks, where one climber leads two or more pitches before swapping leads.

leads" approach where each climber leads every other pitch. Let's say one climber is stronger at crack climbing and the other is stronger at face climbing. Leading in blocks gives you the flexibility to always have the leader on terrain that gives the team the best chance of success.

■ **Improved rest sequence:** Each climber gets to rest after every pitch. When swapping leads, each climber follows a pitch immediately before leading, so if the climbing is hard each climber begins their lead somewhat tired from having just followed a pitch.

- **Increased gear management efficiency:** Rather than switching the rack fully between the climbers each time, one leader maintains the rack the way they want it for several pitches. This saves time transitioning the gear between the two climbers.
- **Short fixing opportunity:** This method, where the leader begins rope soloing while the second is cleaning the pitch below, is a specialized speed climbing technique that only works while leading in blocks. It is rarely necessary, but in easy aid terrain, such as a bolt ladder where the leader can aid with little chance of falling, short fixing can increase the speed of an ascent significantly.

There are special considerations for leading in blocks. This includes making sure each climber is getting the experience they want. If one climber is happy and the other is frustrated, change it up. Climbing is supposed to be fun.

Additionally, it is important for the leader to prepare the belay so the second can easily clip in and the leader can easily unclip. A single "power point" belay is usually best, but careful use of improvised rope anchors can work as long as the leader makes a plan before the second arrives at the belay.

Leading in blocks is almost essential on one-day ascents of big walls, but more importantly, practicing and understanding the idiosyncrasies of leading in blocks will change the way you look at climbing and give you an excellent tool for setting up your team for the best chance of success.

Leading in blocks and short fixing on a one-day ascent of Half Dome's Northwest Face

EQUIPMENT STRATEGY FOR LONG CLIMBS

"Identify your goals! Make the decision before you even leave the ground! Are you going to try to get up the climb fast? Or are you trying to get up the climb with both leader and follower climbing perfectly free? If your goal is to do the climb as efficiently as possible, carry a small pack, don't haul, and don't worry about following free. If your goal is for both climbers to climb every pitch free right at your limit, then haul a bag and plan accordingly."

Steph Davis

Before every big climb your climbing team needs to have a sincere conversation about what you are trying to achieve. Almost every expert interviewed for this book shared this goal-searching as a crucial part of planning and logistics for any climb. As Steph explains, achieving the goal of getting to the summit as efficiently as possible requires a very different approach than achieving the goal of a clean redpoint.

The answer to the all-important decision of what your goal is will be central to the answer of the next question: what gear do you take with you? As a beginner or intermediate climber, this question is often largely answered by a quick look at the guidebook for the recommended rack, then adding a little in case the guidebook is wrong. For an expert climber, this approach is not enough, and the question of what gear to take needs to be considered differently. The expert climber must customize the recommended gear list to match the team's goals as well as the strengths, weaknesses, and experience of the team.

THE RACK

Let's start with the rack. If you're trying to accomplish a long free ascent that is right at your absolute limit, you'll want to customize your rack to achieve this goal. Let's say, for example, that you are planning an ascent of a ten-pitch route with five easy pitches, several pitches of 5.10 hand cracks, and two pitches of 5.12 thin cracks. The guidebook recommendation is:

- Two sets of cams to 4 inches
- Extra hand-size cams
- RPs (micro nuts) and nuts
- Long runners

First, you read through some online forums, and in general the discussion indicates that the 5.10 hand cracks are pretty straightforward. Some forum posts find the hand cracks hard for the grade, and some find these pitches easy for the grade, but overall the trend is that they can be climbed fast and are well protected (which hand cracks usually are). The discussion also talks about "sustained finger stacks" and "bomber nut placements" on the crux pitches.

Second, you consider your team, your goal, and the conditions. You know that you and your partner have a lot of experience on hand cracks but have only climbed a few 5.12 thin cracks, especially in the middle of a long climb. You and your partner decide your team goal is to send the crux pitches for your first redpoint of a long 5.12 trad

Decisions about what gear to take should be based on more than a guidebook or forum report. Make the decision based on what is right for your team.

climb. The conditions aren't ideal—warm temperatures, a high chance of rain later in the day, and the climb gets sun after noon, making for a sweaty and slippery 5.12 if you reach the crux pitches too late.

Third, you customize the rack for your team's strengths and weaknesses relative to the particulars of your goal for the climb and the nature of the rock. For example, taking two sets of cams, plus "extra hand-size," makes for a heavy rack. Guidebook authors generally suggest a rack with the goal of letting climbers know what they need to protect each pitch without any long runouts where gear could be placed. If a guidebook author suggests skimping on the hand-size pieces, requiring solid jamming

skills instead, that author could end up getting people in trouble. Advanced climbers, however, should be able to assess their skills and goals and adjust the rack accordingly.

For the preceding example, a custom rack might look like this:

- One set of cams in the smallest three sizes. (Because of the forum comments about "bomber nut placements," you know the crack will not be entirely parallel, which should be conducive to using nuts and conserving cams. You also know because of the comment about "sustained finger stacks" that your team will have the best chance on the cruxes if you have extra pieces in the critical big- fingers and thin-hands sizes.

- Single 4-inch piece and hand-size cams. (Rather than carrying double 4-inch pieces as well as extra hand-size, you take only one and add a fist-size hex and a couple of hand-size hexes to the rack.)
- RPs and nuts, with a couple extra nuts in the medium sizes to help where you skimped on the small cams
- Ten long slings and four quickdraws. (Because the suggestion specifically mentions long runners, you decide to take only a few quickdraws, use tripled-up slings in place of quickdraws, and clip cams directly when possible.) Five of the slings you carry over your shoulder with a single biner; the other five you triple-up using two biners.

All this effort to carry something *different from what the guidebook suggests* prompts the question: *why?* Well, in the above scenario, here's what your team is leaving behind compared to the "recommended rack" for this climb:

- Seven cams (three micro cams, three cams in the "hand-size" range, and one 4-inch cam)
- As many as seventeen carabiners. (Many people consider ten quickdraws part of a "standard rack" at all times because they don't realize that unless rope drag is an issue, it is okay to clip cams directly; see Chapter 8, Traditional Lead Climbing. Also, the few slings with only one carabiner allow for clipping cams without leaving the cam's biner hanging unused.)
- You also know you and your partner are efficient at making bomber anchors without cordelettes, so you leave two cordelettes and two locking biners behind.

You've added three hexes and two nuts to give you a little more to work with in place of the gear you're leaving behind. Overall, you've achieved a significant savings that amounts to reducing the weight, bulk, and organizational requirements of your rack by about a third.

With more information, such as comes out of a discussion with your climbing partners, it may be possible to leave behind even more equipment. Perhaps the 4-inch section is really low angle and only 5.7, so just one wide piece would be enough with your crack climbing experience.

"I'm super-obsessive about weight; keep everything as minimalistic as possible no matter the objective."

Steph Davis

EVERYTHING ELSE

Aside from the rack, there is the rest of the gear, clothing, and supplies to consider. The following suggestions are common ways advanced climbers reduce the gear and increase their efficiency on long climbs. Note that Big Wall Free Climbing, Chapter 10, is a whole 'nother ball of wax that usually entails climbing really slowly with a lot of gear rather than paring down to the bare minimum to climb quickly.

- Leave your approach shoes behind. If the climb has a rappel descent, leaving your walking shoes on the ground can make the difference between having to drag a small haul bag on every pitch and being able to do most of the climb with the second carrying a small pack and hauling only the crux pitches.

- Carry one belay jacket or vest. Only one person (the belayer) will be sitting still at any one time, so unless it is extremely cold or you're worried about getting benighted, you can usually get away with one warm layer to keep the belayer comfortable.
- Eat and drink before the climb, then don't carry too much food or water. How much food and water you need depends on your particular biochemistry, but with experience you'll get a feel for how much you really need. Generally, climbers can get away with less food and water on long routes than they expect as newcomers to the long route game. Temperatures and the physical aspects of the climb also influence the hydration and caloric requirements of the climb. The ultimate goal here, provided there is no chance of being benighted, is to end the route with not one crumb of food or one drop of water left.

Climbing pack set up to haul. A. A good climbing pack can be stripped down on the outside to prevent catching on the rock and the lid can be removed for hauling. B. For long day climbs where the entire climb will be hauled, a lightweight haul pack is best and more durable than a climbing pack. The straps can all be tucked away and the slippery material makes for an easier haul.

- Consider taking no pack at all. Stick an energy bar in one pocket, an energy gel in the other; clip a tiny stowaway raincoat and a small water bottle to the harness. You can still haul the extra items and extra rack if you need to, clipping them directly onto the tag line for the crux pitches, but eliminating the pack creates a much faster and more capable team—provided you've assessed your needs accurately.
- Consider climbing with only one rope. A tag line can be essential, but even the thinnest second rope adds weight. If you need it—by all means bring it; but if you can pull it off with one rope you'll be a bit faster and less encumbered. *But remember: if you have to do several rappels to escape a rainstorm, you'll wish you'd brought a second rope!*

With these techniques, it can be perfectly reasonable to fire off the ten-pitch 5.12 described above before the afternoon storms roll in. Don't underestimate the long route value that every bit of saved weight from less gear gains for you. By reducing the amount of gear you need to carry, you can climb the moderate pitches quickly and without hauling. This gives you the option to simul-climb when appropriate because you are not carrying a haul pack every pitch. Carrying extra gear

DOING MORE WITH LESS GEAR

Word of warning: Doing more with less gear can get you in a heap of trouble. A surprise spring snowstorm can make you so cold you lose the use of your hands. A stuck rope during the rappel can require additional exertion, time, and exposure to free. Taking less than the guidebook recommends can set you up for dangerous runouts. The history of climbing is full of stories of people having horrific epics due to carrying inadequate equipment.

Word of encouragement: Doing more with less gear is a powerful and heady technique. For this reason, many expert climbers become obsessive about cutting gear from the rack and pack and knowing how far they can push it with little or no extra clothes, food, or water. With practice, you'll learn what you can get away with and—as mentioned multiple times in this book—the key to refining these techniques is practice. Try a three- or four-pitch climb without eating or drinking just to see how your body responds before you embark on a ten-pitch climb with minimal supplies. Done right, trimming your equipment to a bare minimum allows you to efficiently succeed on longer and more committing climbs. Efficiency has the added benefit of making climbs safer and more fun. The history of climbing is also full of stories of people having horrific epics from taking too much gear, climbing slow, and then getting caught in violent afternoon thunderstorms and/or benighted, so use your wits.

There is no way to know exactly what gear you will need, so move with confidence that what you have will work—and keep your escape route open in case it doesn't.

exponentially compounds the demands placed on climbers. There is certainly a place for carrying lots of gear, but the key is to make the decision with full awareness of how the amount of gear you carry will affect your ascent.

GET 'ER DONE MIND-SET

A willingness to simul-climb when safe to do so, establish belays outside the guidebook, and go lean on gear are all tools to achieving the right attitude for long route efficiency. Understanding and practicing

safe simul-climbing on easy terrain can change the way you look at putting together a long climb, and that outlook is perhaps even more important than the actual reduction of pitches or absolute speed and efficiency. This mind-set will greatly reduce your fear of leading long pitches that may or may not end at a good belay. In my experience, by merely preparing for the possibility of simul-climbing, I quite often find a perfect belay at the very end of the rope with no need to simul-climb. By merely accepting the possibility of simul-climbing, and knowing how to do it safely, I can frequently link pitches, increase efficiency, belay in ideal places, and climb without fear of running out of rope.

Running out of gear is another consideration, discussed in Chapter 8, Traditional Lead Climbing. But in the same way that having simul-climbing in your quiver of tools helps you, you'll discover that there is almost always a way to make do with the gear you have. The goal is to stop obsessing about running out of gear and realize that even if you run short, there are usually ways to safely handle the situation such as downclimbing and backcleaning.

Once you are comfortable with the idea of doing long pitches, you will often find that the specific location of belays marked on a topo, listed in a guidebook, or described in an online forum do not apply to you. A typical ascent using a safe application of simul-climbing often goes something like this:

You lead the first three "guidebook" pitches in two long pitches, with only a few feet of simul-climbing. Then a bit of easy terrain allows nearly a full pitch of simul-climbing, linking two more pitches into one. After that a long crux pitch slows you down and requires belaying as per the guidebook recommendation. But because of the efficiency simul-climbing afforded you on the easier pitches below the crux, you are able to take all the time you need to redpoint the crux even if it takes a few tries. After the crux, two more moderate pitches can be linked into one. You've just done an eight-pitch climb in five pitches, with extra time to work out the crux for the righteous send. Even if you don't care about sending hard, long climbs, these methods can greatly reduce the stress and increase the fun of any multipitch experience.

Achieving this mind-set may be one of the most liberating points for an expert climber: it is an incredible feeling when you realize that there are many safe ways to do the same climb, and that belaying out of sequence, belaying in different places, linking pitches, simul-climbing, and carrying less gear are choices that can be perfectly safe and fun, as well as allow you to do climbs you thought were out of your league. As with other techniques in this book, the greatest benefit of changing the way you climb is that it will change the way you *think* about how you climb—and that goes a long way.

LONG ROUTES WITH A TEAM OF THREE

A team of two is traditionally the most efficient way to take on a big climb; however, by using a few alternative techniques, a team of three can work well. The first one-day ascent of the *Nose* of El Cap was completed by a team of three—the legendary climbers Jim Bridwell, John Long, and Billy Westbay, each leading in blocks with the second two climbers ascending the rope quickly behind the leader.

Modern techniques give teams of three even more options, and although there are downsides like cramped belays and potentially time-consuming logistics, there are also benefits to climbing in a group of three:

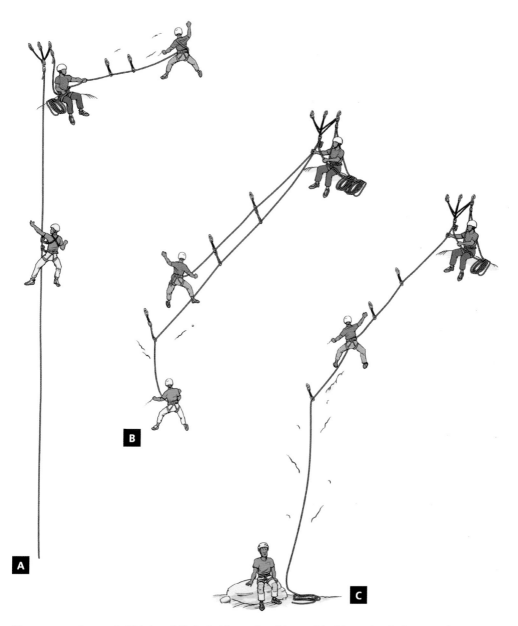

Three-person teams: A. Third on PCD B. Guide mode with autoblocking tube; C. One at a time

Teams of two are the traditional standard for climbing, but three-person teams can be a lot of fun.

more people to do the work of hauling, rope management, belaying, and leading—plus the addition of a fun social element, sharing belays with good friends in a spectacular location.

There are three primary ways to climb with a team of three, and an experienced team can switch between these methods depending on terrain, the goal of the day, and the strengths of each climber.

One climber at a time: This is the most time-consuming of the three methods, but it may be the best choice for sections with loose rock, complex terrain, or extremely hard climbing. After the leader reaches the belay, she belays the second and then the third climber, in sequence. There is little advantage to this method, and it is because this is how most people try climbing with a team of three that many climbers refuse to do long climbs with more than two people. While the next two techniques are much more efficient, one climber at a time may be most appropriate for traversing pitches where protection is needed to protect the followers from dangerous swings or where having two climbers moving at the same time would create a rock-fall hazard.

Guide mode: This method is the most popular three-person method and it employs the autoblock capabilities of belay devices that can accommodate two ropes and are designed to be attached directly to the anchor and threaded accordingly. It is the most common method used by mountain guides leading two clients—thus the term "guide mode." The downside of this method is that the leader must climb with two ropes, adding to the overall weight and rope management. Each rope does not need to be clipped to each piece, so it is critical that the leader differentiates between the

TOP-ROPE FOR THREESOME WARNING

The top-rope for teams of three method is only suitable if the climber on the top-rope solo is comfortable with advanced climbing methods and improvised self-rescue techniques. If the rope gets stuck and they must descend and reclimb, or if they encounter a section that is too difficult for them, the climber on the PCD must be able to ascend the rope, switch from ascending to descending while hanging on the PCD, and deal with most scenarios without help from the other two climbers. Additionally, *this method should only be used where there is no risk that the top two climbers will drop rocks on the third climber. Avoiding rock fall is an issue for teams of two as well, but having the third climber more than one pitch below the leader further complicates the rock-fall issue.*

A savvy team of three will be prepared to utilize all three of the methods described here as the terrain dictates. And note: like so many techniques in this book, three-person climbing methods should be practiced on moderate, noncommitting climbs before the team undertakes longer, more difficult routes.

lead rope and the second rope. The second rope must be clipped in as a directional when needed, such as on traverses or to prevent the rope from swinging into loose rock or other hazards. *Warning:* when clipping in the second rope, do not clip it into the same biner as the lead rope—the friction in case of a fall can melt through the second rope.

PCD top-rope: The progress capture device (PCD) solo top-rope method (see Chapter 6, Belaying for Mastery) gives teams of three another option. After the leader finishes the pitch and belays the second to her anchor, the second fixes the third climber's rope on the anchor. Then the third climber rigs a top-rope solo system and follows the pitch while the leader is free to lead the next pitch at the same time. The first two climbers can easily swap

leads, or lead in blocks, and by thinking ahead it is possible to move the third climber into lead position by switching the second and third position one pitch before the third will be able to switch with the leader.

This method works extremely well, and allows a team of three to operate with almost the same efficiency as a team of two, and the leader only needs to climb with a single lead rope, which is a huge advantage on difficult terrain (the second two climbers can deal with a tag line, hauling, etc.).

However, there are several unique considerations to the solo top-rope for teams of three:

■ Some extra gear may be needed because, although the second can clean *most* of the gear out of each pitch, the belays and a few directionals must be left in place to be cleaned by the third climber.

- The second climber must leave directional placements to protect traverses and keep the rope in line for the third climber.
- Belay anchors with a single power point work best, because the anchor must serve as both a traditional anchor as well as a fixed rope attachment point for the third climber.
- The third climber must remember to pass the gear they clean to the second climber every pitch, so the second can then pass it on to the leader.

Opposite: *Tommy Caldwell on the* Salathé *headwall, El Capitan*

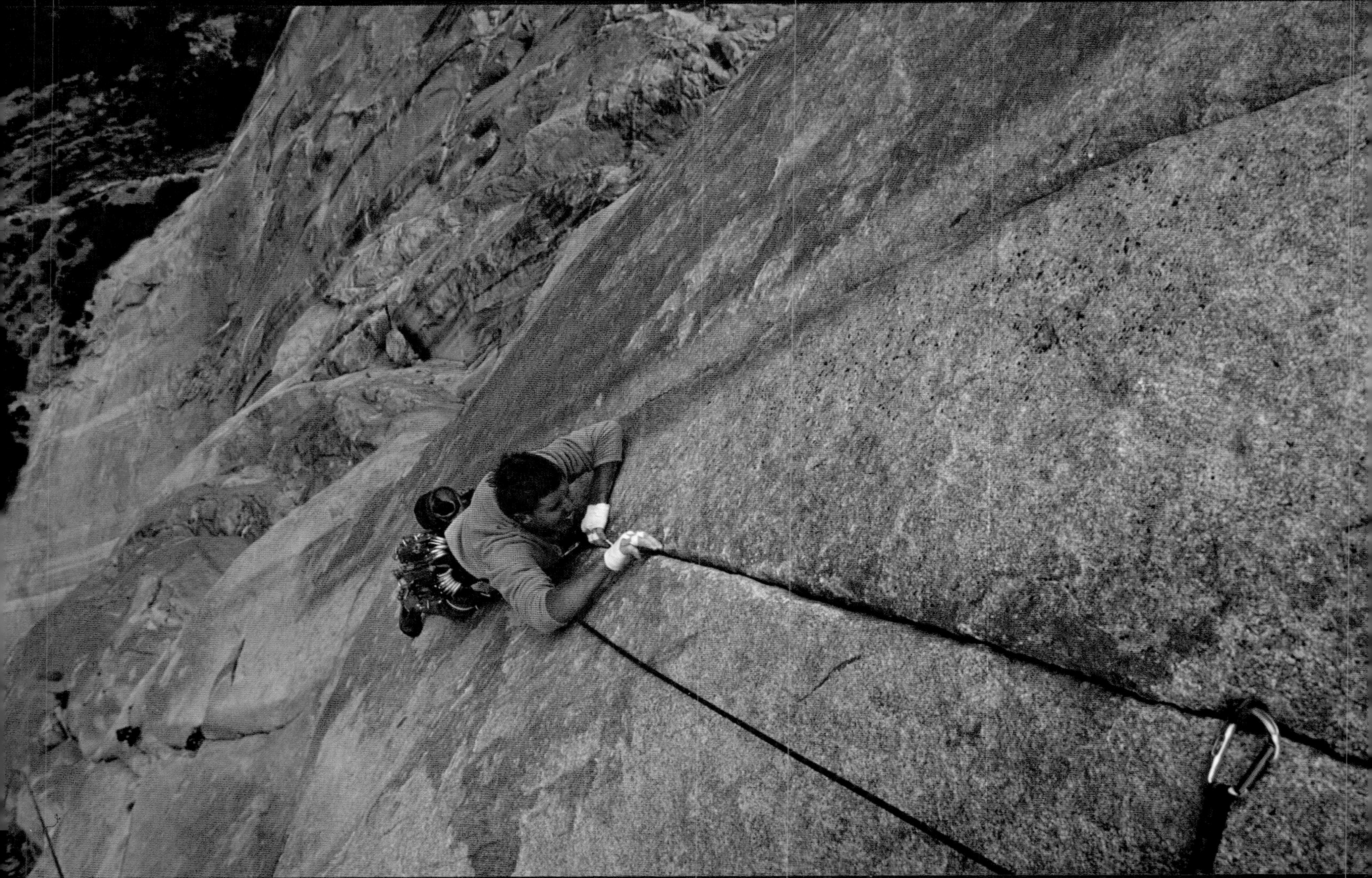

CHAPTER 10

Big Wall Free Climbing

"You have to ask yourself, 'What is the biggest thing I could ever do and how do I go about it?'"
Tommy Caldwell

A relative newcomer to the specialties of climbing, big wall free climbing is the idea of redpointing every pitch of a 1000-plus foot wall from bottom to top in a single push. Sure, as far back as the 1970s climbers were applying free climbing technique to big walls, but it was really the first free ascents of the *Salathé Wall* and the *Nose* on El Capitan in the late '80s and early '90s that opened the eyes of climbers around the word to the vast potential of free climbing on the world's biggest cliffs.

To get a taste of what a big wall free climb is like, you don't have to climb the biggest walls in the world. Over the last twenty years, dozens of "moderate" big wall free climbs have been discovered in places like Zion in Nevada, the Black Canyon of the Gunnison in Colorado, and, of course, in Yosemite Valley, California, the Mecca of big walls. Many of these are climbs that can be done in one day by a fast team, but are also commonly done with one bivouac. Across the pond, European climbers took sport climbing onto the biggest faces, and enormous "sporty" sport climbs of all

levels can be found on the bigger limestone cliffs of areas like the Wendenstocke, Switzerland, and the Verdon Gorge in southern France. Although technically not "big walls," these areas are a great place to tune the mind and body to the unique demands of climbing many pitches in a row of high-standard free climbing. Having so many great objectives to choose from has given you, the modern climber, a great opportunity to find long routes and big walls perfectly suited to your ability.

For most climbers, unless you have a partner who is an experienced big wall free climber, it is best to study books with a focus on big wall climbing, and then start with a "smaller" big wall to learn how to manage the hauling, portaledge camping, food, waste, and workload of a multiday climb before you commit to attempting an El Capitan–size objective.

The scope of this book does not include big wall basics; for our purposes, we'll focus on the unique demands and techniques used by big wall free climbers. Consult Mountaineers Books' *Mountaineering:*

The Freedom of the Hills for a basic overview, and Jared Ogden's *Big Wall Climbing: Elite Technique* for a comprehensive study of big wall technique.

FREE AS CAN BE

With today's high free climbing standards, even among average climbers, many people are capable of free climbing on big walls, and the practice is quickly gaining popularity—for good reason. There are few more thrilling moments in climbing than stepping off the edge of the portaledge roped and ready to cast off on hard climbing with birds of prey hunting in the air below, clouds swirling around the summit high above, and muscles already tired from the many pitches of hard climbing it took to get there.

To experience the world of big wall free climbing, it is not necessary to *successfully* redpoint the entire climb—although you'll need to if you want to claim a free ascent. A great way to experience this airy world for the first time is to climb a big wall with a *free as can be* mentality. This means trying each pitch as a free climb whether or not you pull off the complete send. Just as with bouldering, cragging, and multipitch climbing, your preconceived ideas about your capabilities only serve to hold you back on a big wall.

So if you're thinking about going for it, do it. Big walls are big for a reason—they're often made of some of the most solid and beautiful rock in the world. Many of the easier pitches on big walls would be the

Free climbing is hard enough; add a big wall to the game, with all the demands of living in the vertical world, and you're in for one of the biggest and most rewarding challenges in the sport.

most popular climbs around if they were at the crag. But far off the ground, these pitches are usually all yours.

To make sure your big wall free climbing experience is as enjoyable as possible, be absolutely sure your partner is on the same page. Free climbing takes more time and requires a different ethos and psyche than a traditional big wall ascent. If you are planning on free climbing as much as you can, but your partner just wants to get up the wall as quickly as possible, your climb is doomed before it starts. Usually, a free ascent will take longer than a traditional big wall ascent, and a partner who is hellbent for the summit isn't going to take kindly to waiting around for you to pull on tiny holds. Find a partner with the same goals for the climb, or at least one who is happy to hang out while you play the free climbing game.

Most importantly, you must commit yourself to the intense challenge, incredible exposure, and physical demands of trying hard on a big wall.

REDPOINTING THE CRUXES

"To send the cruxes, be patient and wait for optimal conditions."

Alex Honnold

There are many climbers who can crush the most diabolically difficult pitches at the crag, but who struggle on long climbs. There are also climbers who somehow are fueled by the inspiration of the airy exposure and dramatic commitment of long routes and somehow manage to pull of their best onsights in the middle of a huge wall. Sure, the climbers who do best on big walls often have the most experience on long climbs, but there is more to it than that. Some climbers have vast experience on long climbs, and aspire to climb hard, but they never push their limits far above the ground; meanwhile there are relative newcomers to big climbs who pull off some of their best performances a thousand feet off the deck.

So what's the difference between the two? First, climbing well on a big climb requires the ability to differentiate between real risk and perceived risk. A runout above a ledge is a real risk. Trying a hard move with a bomber piece below your feet and nothing but air between your chalkbag and the river a quarter-mile below is perceived risk. If you spend all day freaking out about perceived risk, you'll have little bandwidth left for managing the real risk, let alone putting it all together for a high-performance free climbing effort. On a big wall, surrounded by huge exposure, there are staggering amounts of perceived risk. Yet big walls are usually one of the safest venues for hard climbing. Think of it this way: on a lot of big wall pitches, you could fall an entire rope length without hitting anything.

To learn to climb well on big climbs, practice working through mental cruxes quickly. If you find yourself having mental battles trying to convince yourself to try hard, challenge yourself on cragging days to quickly push past your mental barriers. To practice this, lead extremely safe climbs, approximately one number grade below your onsight limit, without hesitation. This doesn't mean you should hurry so much that you fail to protect it well—but once you've made it safe, start moving. Don't worry about failing. *Make it safe; climb without hesitation; repeat.*

When planning a maximum-effort redpoint of a long route, do what it takes to be on the climb's crux when conditions are optimal. Sure, some people seem to be tough enough to crush hard pitches when the sun is blazing, their shoes are sliming on tiny holds hot enough to fry an egg, and their fingertips are peeling like onions on razor-sharp crimps, but even these extra-burly individuals climb better in optimal conditions. Start the climb by headlamp if that's what it takes. Then take an hour below the crux to rest up for the send. Try it

Opposite: *Take what you need to relax, recover, and climb your best on a big wall free climb.*

again if you need to. Then finish the climb by headlamp.

Also, drag a haul bag with whatever it takes to help your team relax with the idea of climbing really hard, way off the ground: an extra pair of performance shoes, extra gear, a belay seat, motivational food, a thermos of coffee or tea, and plenty of water. If cold is an issue, bring a Michelin Man belay jacket and heavy gloves. There are trade-offs with carrying extra stuff (see Chapter 9, Long Route Efficiency). But if redpointing a hard, long climb is the goal, you'll need all the goodies that will make you comfortable on the wall.

Of course the lines between long routes and big wall free climbing are blurry—but a good way to look at the difference is that on a big wall free climb you take all the time and gear you need, while a long route usually means taking a bare minimum of gear and doing everything as quickly as possible.

A decision you need to make for each pitch on huge climbs is whether or not to try really hard for the onsight, or to hangdog the hard pitches efficiently and then lower off for a quick redpoint. Most climbers experienced at long, challenging climbs will tell you that it's almost always better to go for the onsight first—you might just crush it. In part, it is simply so much more efficient to do a pitch first try, and in part it is simply so much fun to go for a maximal onsight in the middle of a sheer wall. Once you fall, however, it is most efficient to figure out the rest of the pitch while hangdogging, "cheat" aiding, or whatever

it takes to learn the moves; then lower off, rest, and go for the send.

To train for quick redpoints on big walls, practice the process every time you go cragging. If you want to climb long routes at your limit, don't just complete project climbs with the highest number grade (see Chapter 7, Sport Climbing). Instead, mix hard redpointing with quick redpoints and onsighting. The optimum way to practice quick redpoints is on climbs with a difficulty rating right at or just beyond your onsight limit.

To send a crux pitch on a big wall, use this sequence:

1. Try for the onsight.
2. When you fall, work the rest of the pitch with a priority on efficiency and energy conservation.
3. Lower off, reviewing the cruxes.
4. Let your partner have a go at it.
5. Review the sequences and gear placements thoroughly in your mind and with your partner.
6. Rest long enough—but no longer.
7. Send.

Finally, prepare your mind for the demands of climbing multiple hard pitches in a day. Climbers of all levels find themselves stuck in a rut where they only have the mental energy to try hard once each day. Once can be enough to tick your hardest pitch, but it isn't enough to succeed on a long route with multiple hard pitches. This can easily be practiced while cragging by adding a pitch or two (or more) to your everyday climbing routine. As with many aspects of improving and changing your approach to climbing, succeeding isn't the goal. The goal is to try hard on more than one pitch each day. Sure, there are times when you may be so focused on doing a long-term project that you don't want to tack on another hard pitch and tire yourself out for another burn on your project the next day. But, particularly if the next day is a rest day, practice redlining your mental and physical engine on some hard climbing *after* you've already put the pedal down on a hard pitch.

FREE ASCENT STRATEGY

To put together a complete and successful free ascent of a big wall is a feat of athletics, perseverance, boldness—and strategy. Even the wildly successful conclusion, widely followed by the viewing public, to Tommy Caldwell and Kevin Jorgeson's *Dawn Wall* ascent was in part due to a changed strategy—they opted to climb during the heart of the winter and do much of their climbing at night, when cool temperatures would help their bodies

Vertical camping is an unforgettable part of the big wall experience.

and their shoe rubber stick to the tiniest of holds.

This is where traditional big walls and big wall free climbing are entirely different. On a traditional big wall climb, getting to the top is enough. On a big wall *free* climb, the goal is to redpoint every pitch from bottom to top in a single push. This could mean camping in the same place for more than one night while working on a hard section, rappelling in from above to learn pitches high on the route, and timing each day's efforts to coincide with optimal climbing temperatures, conditions, and energy levels.

To send the cruxes, all the traditional climbing methods, including swapping leads, must be reconsidered. You may need to rest for an hour or more between attempts on a hard pitch, so the logistics need to reflect this. Who leads which pitches and whether or not you swap leads or lead in blocks can make the difference between a fun redpoint attempt and a tail-between-the-legs aid climbing session.

The locations where you set up camp also become crucial to the outcome of the climb. Ideally you want to camp where you can stay out of the way of other climbers, work on the crux pitches, and avoid hauling until a hard section is complete. For this reason, the standard bivy locations for a classic aid ascent are often different than those for a free ascent. A good strategy is to position a camp in the middle of a hard stretch of climbing, then rap down to work on the pitches below and move up to work the higher pitches. This way, only after you've done your best on that section, do you need to spend time and energy to move camp.

Big walls are hard on ropes, and the demands of free climbing require a different approach to rope strategy. On a free-as-can-be ascent of the *Nose* with a party of three, two of our four ropes suffered core shots (where a spot on the sheath of the rope is worn through, exposing the high-strength core). Consider carrying three ropes: a static line for hauling, a thin tag line (5 or 6 mm), plus a regular lead rope. If a fourth rope is needed for fixing, make it a dynamic lead rope that can be used as a backup lead rope.

The tag line is essential, so that you don't need to climb with the haul rope and kit adding weight to your already taxed body. Lead without carrying the haul gear, and instead just drag the much lighter tag line. Once at the end of a pitch, you can then use the tag line to pull up the static line and kit for hauling—as well as well-deserved goodies like comfortable shoes, water, a snack, and jacket.

MIND GAMES

"It's pretty exciting; just waking up in a portaledge that far off the ground is warm-up enough."

Tommy Caldwell

Big walls and long climbs are daunting. Even after climbing a handful of hard pitches, you still have a long way to go. There is no sprint for the finish line; there is no "Dirt me." But the level of commitment that such a climb requires also, weirdly, creates a relaxing atmosphere—you know you're not going to make it back down quickly, so you might as well enjoy yourself. Multiday ascents take the pressure off of completing the climb in a day and the experience encourages a more patient and sustained approach to the sport—like sailing across the Atlantic compared to a day on the lake.

If you get to a point on the biggest climb you've ever done, and wish you'd never started, don't feel bad; you're not alone. Almost everyone who has ever climbed a big wall has had the same feelings. Use that gear and all those supplies and have fun! Get into the haul bag when you need something. Eat. Drink. Be merry. Having what you need with you at all times, relaxing up there, and enjoying the wilderness solitude and quiet vistas are the best parts of big walling. Many newcomers to big walls don't dig into the haul bag to get a drink when they're thirsty, food when they're hungry, or a jacket when they're cold—and they end up cold, hungry, thirsty, and exhausted as a result. That's the whole thing about big walls. They're big. You can't just suffer through. Don't wait until the bivy or the top to take care of yourself. Do it when you need it.

Be willing to move around on the wall. Rappelling a rope length to a good ledge for the night or climbing an extra pitch to hide under overhangs in a storm are the kinds of things that make the difference between a comfortable climb and an absolute epic.

Climbing on wet rock: There's a part of almost every big wall where conditions are not great. Wet rock, cold or hot temperatures, and exhaustion all can conspire to make things difficult. Practice climbing in less than ideal conditions.

Big wall rule number one: take care of yourself.

Doing nothing but enduring the suffering is a recipe for disaster. Stay hydrated, fed, warm, and dry and your motivation and energy will follow.

If you're freaking out, jump off. Really! Nothing clears the mind like a short, comfortable fall, caught by a trustworthy partner. If you're nervous, and it's affecting your climbing ability, find a place where there is nothing to hit if you fall, with several pieces of bomber gear between you and your belayer—and jump off. You wouldn't be there if the rope and gear didn't work, so you might as well trust it. Besides, if you're climbing at your limit, you're bound to fall at some point anyway. Might as well enjoy the ride.

BIG WALL ANTICS

"People undervalue how important it is to have a huge base of experience. Speed climbing in Patagonia is only possible for me because I've climbed El Cap a bazillion times."

Alex Honnold

Free climbers need to be comfortable moving around on big walls. Aid techniques, such as cleaning pitches on ascenders, lowering out, tension traverses, improvised aid, and using placements that barely hold body weight, are all part of a big waller's bag of tricks. Free climbers may not use these methods as often as aid climbers or speed climbers, but these techniques are crucial to big wall literacy, be it free, aid, or speed ascents.

To free climb successfully on a big wall, these diverse skills must be well understood and ideally practiced beforehand. Jugging, or climbing a rope with mechanical ascenders, needs to be done efficiently to save energy for the hard climbing. Many big walls require some big traverses; ropework fluency to protect both the leader and the follower on these sections is crucial. Routes established as aid climbs are often not well set up for free climbing. Where aid climbers were able to simply lower out or pendulum on the rope, free climbers must desperately hang onto dime-edges. Be sure to assess each section for the safety of the leader and the follower.

An element of big wall free climbing that surprises many newcomers is the bold free climbing done by the aid climbers who have been climbing many of these routes for decades. While many aid climbers may not be able to match the gymnastic capabilities of well-trained free climbers, pioneering aid climbers traditionally used as few bolts as possible, and even the most popular big wall routes have enormous runouts and potentially dangerous sections. (Remember, don't add bolts to established climbs, aid or free. It's disrespectful, unethical, and is a step backward for our sport.)

AID CLIMBING

For forty years, free climbing has become the normal way to go climbing, and aid climbing has become a fringe technique that the vast majority of climbers don't bother to learn. There are plenty of great free climbs, big and small, and if you stay within your limits there may be no need to learn the subtleties of efficient aid climbing methods. However, if you aid climb a pitch or two and learn the basics, then apply these basics to an improvised method utilizing regular free climbing gear, you can

Paramount to any big wall send is setting up the strategy for each pitch properly, so you can climb unhindered by logistics.

be much more comfortable pushing your limits on longer free climbs and big walls in a single day, knowing you can aid through some of the crux sections as necessary.

A bit of aid climbing skill also opens the doors to the world's biggest climbs like the big walls of Yosemite and the otherworldly rock spires of Patagonia. Many of these famous long climbs are often done with 95 percent free climbing, and just a few sections of aid.

Traditional aid climbing incorporates sling ladders, daisy chains, and climbing from one piece to the next while hanging on gear for entire pitches and even for days on end. Improvised aid climbing utilizes the same gear as is used on an all-free climb, but entails many of the same principles as traditional aid climbing. For our goal, we'll focus on the improvised method.

The efficiency of aid climbing is greatly increased by adhering to these concepts:

- **Avoid "take!"** Every time you ask your belayer to hold you, you make them work harder. But more importantly, you also lose ground due to rope stretch. Instead of asking your belayer to hold you, leave a quickdraw on the belay loop of your harness and advance it on the highest piece as you move upward. With a little practice, it is far easier to avoid weighting the rope through the entire aid climbing sequence.

▪ **Spread your pieces as far apart as possible.** Every piece you place while aid climbing uses a significant amount of time. If the rock is steep and sheer, you may need to stay clipped into the piece below, but even in this case you'll want to clip in as high as possible: clip yourself directly to the stem of a cam or the wire of a nut to gain inches every chance you get. If the rock is less than vertical, or if there are some handholds, consider doubling a runner and clipping it to the highest piece for a foot loop, then grabbing a few holds or jams to stand up as high as possible on the piece below before placing the next one. This way it should be possible to reach nearly a body length between placements, saving significant time and effort.

▪ **Free climb whenever possible.** Once you're aid climbing, it's a mental challenge to get back into free climbing mode; look for places you can do a few free moves to save time and gear.

Learning how to efficiently do a few moves of aid makes attempting long routes and big wall free climbs less committing and less intimidating, and more enjoyable and relaxing. If you know that a failed free ascent will merely result in a few moves of aid rather than an epic retreat, it will feel more reasonable to push your personal limits in the outrageous big wall atmosphere.

RIGHT-OF-WAY AND ETIQUETTE

"If you need to pass another party, or another party needs to pass you, act confident and friendly and it's no big deal."
Tommy Caldwell

Many big walls are popular places, and today there are often speed climbers, aid climbers, and free climbers all playing their respective games on the same climb at the same time. To make it the most fun for everyone, it is important to remember that every climber, regardless of the climbing style they are using, has just as much right to be there as everyone else.

One issue created by big wall free climbing is that it is common to walk to the top and rappel over the wall to practice the hardest pitches before going for the ground-up ascent. One day, futuristic climbers will raise the bar with ground-up onsights of today's test piece big walls. But for now, even the best climbers usually practice some of the hard pitches before casting off on a ground-to-summit free ascent. Approaching from the top down requires added vigilance and consideration for other climbers. *Dropping gear or rocks, or getting in the way of other climbers is absolutely unacceptable.* On a popular cliff, only go in from the top if you have all of your techniques well dialed, and be prepared to change your plans if other climbers are on the pitches you were hoping to practice.

With the right attitude, the social aspect of popular big walls can enhance the experience. Tommy Caldwell, after working on free climbing the *Nose*, said that one of his

favorite parts of the climb was "meeting other climbers on their first big wall who were having the most incredible adventure of their lives."

Generally, slower parties should step aside at a convenient point to let faster parties go by. But if the climbing is awkward, the faster party may need to wait until the slower party gets to a place where passing is safe and practical. For the most part, speed climbers are the fastest, aid climbers are second fastest, and free climbers working the route are the slowest. This means that, in general, free climbers need to get out of the way of aid climbers, and both aid and free climbers need to get out of the way of speed climbers. However, all parties need to be, as Tommy reminds us, *friendly and confident*.

It is also important to consider the experience other climbers on the wall are having, and how your actions affect their experience.

- **Keep it safe.** Do not do things that will endanger or scare others, like dropping gear or doing long runouts above their heads, and do not practice sketchy safety standards for the sake of speed or style.
- **Stay humble.** Free climbing on big walls is cutting-edge, but aid climbing is equally valid and aid climbing ground up is in many ways a more adventurous way to ascend a huge cliff than redpointing a route after top-rope rehearsal. Don't cop an attitude with aid climbers just because you can hang onto tiny holds.

- **Communicate.** Talk with other parties to learn what their plans are—like how they are doing, where they plan to bivy, and how long they have been on the wall.
- **Be thoughtful in your bivouac.** If you plan to bivouac for more than one night in one location to work on crux pitches, consider setting your bivouac off to the side of the route and in a different location than the typical aid climbing bivouacs. You'll be happier, and so will everyone else.

THE SEND

A complete free ascent of a big wall or hard multiday climb is a highlight of any climber's life. Prepare for the send obsessively, and stack every card in your favor. Stashing food and water can allow you to haul a lighter bag. Leading in blocks can give each climber the pitches most suited to their strengths and weaknesses. It is mandatory to work out each day's schedule to time the optimal temperatures for the hard climbing, even if it means starting or finishing the day by climbing in the dark.

One of the most difficult parts of putting together a free ascent of a big wall is protecting skin and muscle from sun exposure and physical abuse. On the successful ascent of the *Dawn Wall*, Tommy Caldwell set his alarm to go off every four hours to remind him to apply skin cream in order to keep his skin healthy. Pay particular attention to climbing the easier pitches with

Opposite: *A big wall free ascent is an unforgettable, life-changing, inspiring, friendship-making experience.*

utmost efficiency. Relaxing on the belays and bivouacs to maximize recovery is also important. Wear leather gloves for rope-work. Take the time to set up hauls with the optimum pulley location so your weight will have the best mechanical advantage. If things are going slowly, which they usually are, set up the portaledge at belays so that you can lie down, kick back, and save your core strength in every way possible.

Well before casting off on a big wall free ascent, try climbing hard for four or five days in a row and see how your muscles, skin, and mind respond. Big wall free climbing is like nothing else; but developing mental and physical toughness for several days in a row of hard climbing will help immensely.

A prevailing message from the world-class climbers interviewed for this book was to "try hard," and big wall free climbing is no exception. Every big wall free climber has had the experience where they are so tired that a hard redpoint seems impossible—but by trying their utmost they manage to do it. With the time and energy it takes to perform a huge climb, you'll find yourself climbing better, more efficiently, and with higher motivation, and you'll do things that seem impossible—if you try hard.

World-class climbers using modern techniques and pushing their limits on the longest, hardest climbs have given the rest of us tools we can use to make our own climbing dreams more achievable. With practice, these methods will change climbs you once viewed as beyond your capability into great adventures that can be completed quickly and enjoyably with good friends.

Opposite: *Rappel access to pristine limestone in southern France*

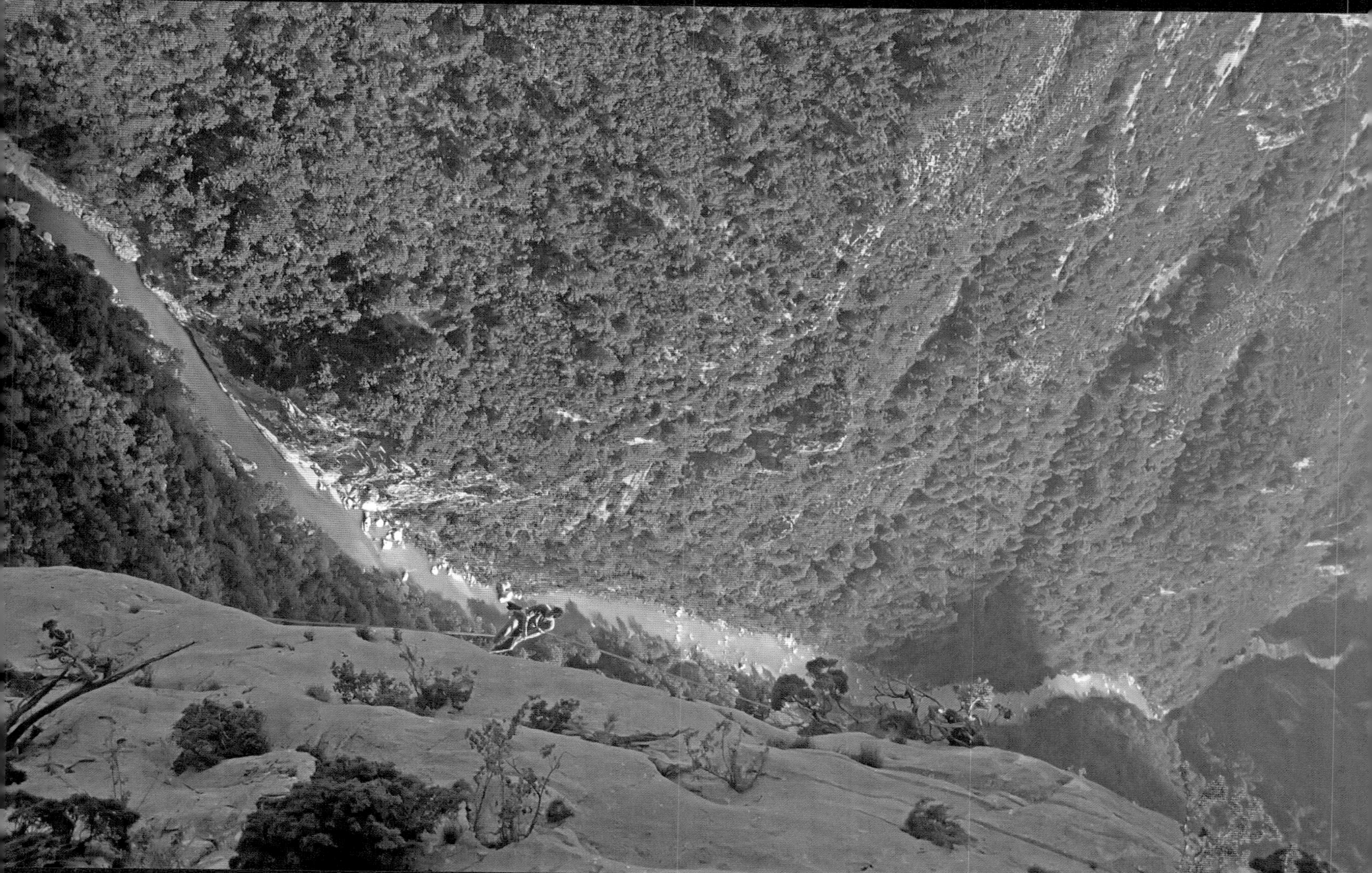

CHAPTER 11

Rappelling and Descents

"The first defense against retreat is careful planning."

Jared Ogden

If you are reading this book, you already know the basics of rappelling, including the use of an autoblock backup, tying knots in the end of the rope when possible, and how to give a fireman's belay from below while your partner descends. If you are not familiar with these techniques, learn them.

Along with belaying, advanced rappel and descent skills are some of the least developed and most underappreciated (at least until you need them) of the full gamut of advanced climbing technique. When the weather is nice, you're ahead of schedule, and the descent is straightforward, getting off a climb can seem almost trivial and like anyone can do it safely. However, when conditions change—night falls, a rope gets stuck, you have trouble finding the rap anchors—getting down can quickly become more difficult and dangerous than climbing up.

Every year, in the great climbing areas all over the world, multiple climbing parties achieve near-perfect ascents of fantastic climbs, top out ahead of schedule, celebrate on the summit—then epic huge on the descent, cutting ropes, getting benighted, leaving behind expensive anchors, and otherwise suffering a miserable ending to a beautiful climb. Of course it can end even worse, with an accident—and accidents on descents are one of the most common causes of injuries and fatalities among all levels of climbers. All-too-frequent disastrous mistakes include rappelling off the ends of ropes or clipping into the rappel rope improperly.

FINDING THE BEST DESCENT ROUTE

To begin with, it is important to remember that descending on rappel is far more committing than climbing a pitch. If you're on lead, and you go the wrong way, all you need is a solid piece of protection and you can lower back to the belay and go the right way. If you rappel off the wrong side of a spire, you can be left dangling in space with no anchor. And if you pull the rope from the first rappel, then end up hanging in space on the second, you may find yourself suddenly (and embarrassingly) in need of a rescue.

TAG LINE SIZE FOR DESCENT

As lead ropes get skinnier yet still pass UIAA tests for single lead rope performance, the second rope, or tag line, has remained a matter of individual preference. While climbing, a tag line as thin as 5 mm can work for hauling a small bag, although care must be taken to avoid tangles. While rappelling, however, the slimmest tag lines become a liability. Not only do they tangle terribly when the rope is thrown down from above for a rappel, they are also far too skinny to climb on or ascend if your lead rope gets stuck on a rappel and you need to lead a section to free the stuck rope.

Many experienced climbers have experimented with ultra-skinny 5 mm tag lines, but have then switched back to a more robust rope that is easier to handle and can be doubled-up and led on if the lead rope gets stuck on a rappel, for example. To be useful as an emergency lead line, a 6.9-mm to 8-mm dynamic rope is just about optimal for a tag line on long routes and for descents. Together with one of today's thin lead ropes (down to 8.9 mm), the pair allows for both a light pack and a robust combination of ropes.

To find the best way off of a climb, do your homework and research beforehand. Consult the most recent guidebook and internet forums, and study the feature you plan to climb from a distance so you have a mental picture of the line of ascent and how it relates to the line of descent. On the approach, snap a photo if possible; a quick zoom in on a digital photo can reveal much that cannot be seen while on the rappels.

One of the most important philosophies for becoming an expert climber is to balance all the information you can gain beforehand with a fresh and critical eye for the climb. Approach the climb as if yours is the first team to ever do it. Finding the descent is a perfect example of how this philosophy is critical. On many big climbs there are various ratty old anchors that can lead you astray.

Often, the first climbers to reach the summit rig natural rappel anchors and make a series of rappels off the summit, building minimalist anchors as they go. Subsequent parties back up these natural anchors— but then may not be able find the original anchors so they leave even more anchors. Both versions may result in a sketchy down-climb of a loose gully at the bottom with some of the anchors less than perfect.

There is a second stage in the evolution of a descent. Climbers or guides looking to simplify the logistics and increase safety will put in a few bolted anchors to create a rap route directly down clean rock; but the original rap anchors are overlooked and sometimes not removed. So, it is not uncommon to reach a summit and find an out-of-date anchor consisting of a tattered sling around a horn and an old slung hex.

The transition from climbing up to descending is a time when many accidents happen. Make a point of consciously shifting gears from summit success to the careful ropework management of descent.

If the climb is popular, with a well-used climber's trail to the base, and the first anchor you find at the summit is made entirely of faded, neglected-looking webbing, this should be a warning that you may not have found the best anchor.

Today, with modern climbing history stretching four decades, many climbs have several generations of descents, not all of them properly marked or recorded in guidebooks or even on the internet. Long ledge systems are a frequent place for other's mistakes to lead you into a rappel epic. In many climbing areas, it is normal to find anchors along ledge systems where a previous party committed to a rappel too early. Perhaps it was dark, they were lost, or they just made a poor decision. If you then use their anchor, you're also committing to whatever experience they had. *Just because there are fixed anchors doesn't mean you're going the right way.*

Before you commit to backing up a ratty-looking anchor and using it, have your partner put you on belay and take a careful look around for another descent option. With the security of a rope it is much easier to lean over the void and, frequently, spot two shiny stainless steel rappel bolts showing the way down.

THINK ABOUT GETTING DOWN— EVEN WHILE GOING UP

"In most rock types, the terrain repeats itself: the ledges, terrain patterns, crack systems. Getting a handle on the geology can make descents a lot safer."

Angela Hawse

Opposite: *Unlike climbing up, once you commit to a rappel line it can be impossible to reverse.*

To make sure you find the best way down off your route, on the way up, continually assess the options for getting off the climb, even if you plan to simply walk off the top. Remember, too, there's always the possibility that you won't quite make it to the top. Regardless of the plan, a wise climber will assess the descent possibilities at every opportunity.

Look for any of these:

- Are there ledges you could traverse that would get you closer to the ground?
- Are there gullies reaching high onto the wall that may offer easy terrain to scramble down?
- What are the distances across blank sections of rock? This helps you judge rap length.
- Are there sheer or overhanging walls longer than your rope that you must be sure to avoid on the descent?
- Are there sheer or overhanging sections that are exactly a rope length between ledges that would be good places to rig rappels in case you need to descend the way you are going up?
- Do you see any ledges or easy terrain that would allow you to poke around a corner and take a look at other faces? Sometimes rap anchors (or heinous piles of rubble you want to avoid) can be seen, giving the team a huge advantage when it comes time for the descent.

Once you are descending:

- Just because you found a fixed anchor doesn't mean you've found the best way down. Take a few minutes to look around further to be sure.
- Swing delicately and slowly back and forth as you rappel, looking into corners and learning the terrain below you. Be careful not to dislodge rocks with your rope, but a bit of research as you descend can pay dividends in finding hidden anchors. Sometimes the next anchor is hidden in a corner facing away from you, and if you don't look around you'll miss it.
- If you finish a rappel on a ledge where there are no anchors, look around and find the next anchor before you pull the ropes from above. Maybe you missed the anchor and it's on the wall 50 feet above the ledge—and if you pull the rope, you're stuck.
- Measure your progress against the climb you just did as well as the surrounding features. Distances can be very deceptive while rappelling, and keeping tabs on features nearby can help you calculate how many more rappels you have to go and if your rope will reach the ground on the last rappel.

IMPROVISED RAPPEL ANCHOR BACKUP

Due to a combination of a deeply rooted environmental ethic and a cheapskate culture fundamental to the dirtbag history of our sport, climbers evolved to abhor leaving gear behind. This is a good thing. It keeps our cliffs cleaner and is a hedge against

Safely executing a descent from a big climb can be demanding. Take the time to check out the options, look around for the best anchors and route, and plan on using more energy and time than you might expect.

the materialism of our society. But when it comes to rappel anchors, this minimalist approach can be dangerous. Even with the skyrocketing popularity of climbing, there are thousands of substandard rappel anchors in climbing areas all over the world that people use nonchalantly. When you encounter one of these anchors, it is not the time to be thrifty.

Sometimes the anchors are really bad, and it is easy to make the decision to leave additional gear as a backup. Other times the anchor is borderline—"it will probably hold just fine," you think. But you want to be sure, not lackadaisical. There are three ways to improve a rappel anchor.

The first option is to simply remove and then replace and better reposition the same gear in the same spot. Over time, the freeze/thaw of winter combined with wind can cause fixed nuts to shift slightly, dislodging the nuts from the spot where they were originally placed. If the nuts are wire, it's often a simple matter of removing them and replacing the same nuts in their original slots. If the slings are extremely faded or worn, cut them off and replace them with new ones. Obviously, a knife will be needed to do this job properly.

The second option in the case of a really bad anchor is to remove it entirely and build a new anchor that is both stronger and better positioned. If this is not possible, you'll want to evaluate the rappel carefully. Sometimes a sling over a subtle horn can be a strong rappel anchor—provided that you don't lift up on it as you lean back over the edge. Trees with sturdy root systems reaching into cracks in the rock are also secure rap anchors; make sure they are alive. In the ideal world, rappel anchors would be as strong as belay anchors, but in reality since a rappel anchor isn't holding dynamic falls and will be used in a very predictable vector—down—there are times when you can get away with rappel anchors that are less burly than belay anchors. That said, how can you be sure how much a subpar anchor will hold? *When in doubt, make it stronger.*

The third, and often the best, option is to simply back up the anchor. Nuts are the cheapest to leave behind, but don't ever hesitate to leave a cam if that's what it takes to make an anchor solid. In a well-formed constriction, a jammed knot can be an excellent backup (see Chapter 14, Improvised Rescue and Epic Avoidance, for the Elbsandstein method for jamming knots).

Finally, consider the future of the anchors. If a series of poor anchors is the only way down from a climb, particularly a popular climb or one you plan to do again, and you find yourself jamming knots or replacing tangled nests of rotten webbing, consider going back with a drill and establishing a proper bolted rappel route that will last longer and will not require future climbers to leave behind even more webbing that merely deteriorates into trash. If you can't return, or don't feel experienced enough to make the decisions required to establish a rappel route, at least post the anchor issue on an online forum so that other climbers will become aware of the need for an improved descent. If you decide to take it upon yourself, read on.

ESTABLISHING RAPPEL ROUTES

As with the scenario described earlier, where there may be several generations of descents off the same climb, the popularity of a climb changes the demands placed on descent routes and at some point many experienced climbers are faced with the responsibility of rigging an established rappel route for others to follow. If you will be placing bolts, make sure to consult with locals before drilling holes to assure the rappel route will be welcomed and not be offensive to the area's ethics.

Planning a rappel route is similar to establishing a new ascent route and should be considered with utmost care. A good rappel route will:

- Not threaten other climbers or hikers below with rock fall
- Avoid routes of ascent to prevent teams on rappel from getting in the way of climbing teams
- Use the least amount of fixed hardware while still being bomber and durable
- Avoid rope-eating flakes and sections of loose rock

Soft rock can be worn dramatically by rope friction, so whenever possible place anchors below the lip so the rope can run free and avoid this scenario over time.

- Be rigged for teams with 60-meter ropes
- Be visually discreet from a hiker or sightseer's perspective, but obvious and visible to climbers looking for the descent

ADDING AND REDUCING FRICTION

Not all rappel friction is created equal. The diameter of the rope, how much rope is hanging below the descent device, and the type of device each contributes to friction. Sometimes there is so much friction that it is necessary to push the rope through the rappel device; other times there is so little friction that it becomes difficult to control the descent. There are several things that can be done to add or reduce friction to a rappel.

To reduce friction:

- If you are using an autoblock friction hitch backup, remove one rope wrap from it—you can easily add the wrap back once you are lower on the rappel and the rope weight below the device eases.
- Thread the rappel device backward. Most modern rappel devices have one orientation that creates more friction than the other. If you are rappelling on double fat ropes, threading the device in the orientation that delivers the least friction gains you a smoother rappel.

Most climbers don't mind a little too much friction, but not enough friction on a rappel can be a horrifying experience. To increase friction:

Increase the friction on a rappel, such as when descending a single rope, by redirecting the rope through a biner clipped to your leg loop.

- Add a second biner to the belay loop and thread it alongside the primary rappel biner. The increased diameter will pinch the rope more tightly where it runs through the device. Not all devices will have the same result from adding a second biner, so experiment to see how your device interacts with the rope and second biner.
- Redirect rope through a biner attached to the leg loop of your harness, then back up to a biner clipped to the ropes above the device, then down to the autoblock (see photo above).

- If you're already on rappel and want to increase friction, run the rope behind your waist and clip it through a redirecting biner on a gear loop on the opposite side, or even to the belay loop, for maximum friction. Run the rope along the harness to prevent the rope wearing against your skin or clothing.

TO KNOT OR NOT

In general, to prevent the possibility of accidentally rappelling off the ends of the ropes, it is best to knot the ends of the ropes before tossing them down for the rappel. There are, however, times where knotting the ropes creates an additional hazard, increasing the chance of the rope ends jamming behind flakes, for example, or deep in cracks where retrieval is impossible. In complex terrain, where there are many flakes and deep cracks, experienced climbers often prefer to leave the ends of the ropes free of knots and instead use an autoblock backup. As they near the end of the rope they use the autoblock to securely stop, pull up the remaining rope, and tie stopper knots in both ends, before finishing the rappel.

Most of the time, it is strongly recommended to tie knots in the ends of the ropes. To minimize tangles and let each end spin and swing freely, it is best to tie two knots—one in each rope end—rather than a single knot tying both ends together. The best knot for this purpose is half of a double fisherman's tied snugly (see Chapter 4, Knots and Anchor Rigging).

The first person down should always clip the ropes into the anchor; it makes it easier and safer for the second person down. (Also, it is easier to rappel with a pack clipped in below than it is to wear it.)

RAPPELLING WITH TWO ROPES OF DIFFERENT DIAMETERS

Rappelling on two ropes of significantly different diameters, for example a 10-mm lead rope and a 6-mm tag line, creates an awkward situation—one rope needs more friction while the other rope needs less. If the thin rope is threaded through the anchor, it gets even more complicated because the skinny rope slides through the device faster than the fat rope. This pulls the rope through the anchor as you descend, creating uneven ends at the bottom and potentially setting up the dangerous potential to rappel off the end of the skinny rope. This is one of the primary reasons that, while many climbers experiment with ultrathin tag lines, they often return to more manageable-size 7-mm and 8-mm tag lines.

If you are using two ropes of different diameters, there are two options for threading each rappel—both have positives and negatives.

You can thread the thin rope, so the fat rope is pulled for retrieval.

- Pros: Once you are pulling the ropes, if the falling rope jams, it will be the thin rope that jams, and you will already have the fat rope down and available to lead on to free the stuck rope. Pulling the fat rope is also physically easier than pulling the skinny rope.
- Con: If you thread the thin rope through the anchor, the rope will slide through the anchor unevenly as you rappel due to the differing friction between the two different diameter ropes running through your belay device.

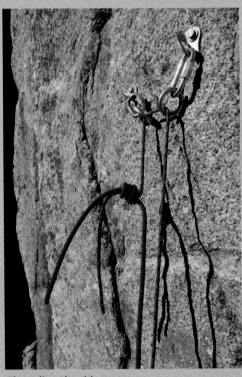

Threading the thin rope

Continued

RAPPELLING WITH TWO ROPES OF DIFFERENT DIAMETERS (CONTINUED)

You can thread the fat rope so the thin rope is pulled for retrieval.

- Pro: The rope will not slide unevenly on the rappel because the knot will jam against the anchor ring—essentially creating a scenario where most of the climber's weight is on the fat rope.
- Cons: It is now the fat rope that is falling after you pull the ropes, and it is most likely to get jammed; if it jams, you will be left with only the tag line to re-lead on to free the stuck rope (if you must lead on a skinny tag line, double it). Also, pulling the skinny rope can be difficult, especially if the rope runs over edges.

The best solution is to evaluate each rappel and rig the ropes accordingly. If the ropes run freely through the anchors and directly to

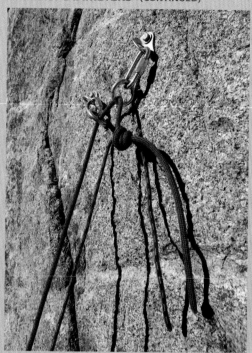

Threading the fat rope

the ground or the next anchors, it is usually best to rig it so the skinny rope will be pulled, leaving the knot to jam against the anchor and prevent the rope from slipping during the rappel. If, however, the rope runs over a rough edge where the rock will help keep the rope from slipping, and that rock friction will make the pull difficult or could cause the rope to get stuck, it can be best to rig the rappel to pull the fat rope.

Make a separate evaluation and decision on every rappel, even if it requires retying the knot each time. By using the barrel knot (see Chapter 4, Knots and Rigging) to attach the ends of rappel ropes, it is easy to retie the ropes. Be sure to secure the ropes to the anchor temporarily while retying the knot to prevent your dropping one or both ropes, leaving you stranded.

When rappelling on ropes without knots in the ends:

- Always use an autoblock backup.
- As you near the ends of the rope, stop and pull the ends up to you and knot them—in this way you can control the knots and prevent them from getting jammed as well as avoid rappelling off the end of the rope.
- If the rappel is threaded to pull the fat rope, be aware of the thin rope sliding down through the anchor as you descend—sometimes this will make one end of the ropes hang a dozen feet or more lower than the other.

RAPPELLING IN HIGH WINDS

Mountainous regions can be some of the windiest areas on Earth, and even when there are no winds in the forecast, updrafts from the day's heat can create strong gusts on big cliffs. Climbing in the wind can be distracting, but rappelling in the wind gets downright dangerous.

Climbers in notoriously windy regions, like Patagonia, have developed techniques for rappelling as safely as possible in high winds. The bottom line is to avoid throwing the ropes, because even moderate winds can blow the rope around the corner to tangle far out of reach. There are two options for getting the ropes down without throwing them.

- Lower the first climber on one rope as they pull down the second rope.
- Coil the ropes backpack-style, with short loops to prevent blowing in the wind, and sling them bandolier-style to clip one on each side of the first climber to descend. Take special care to start coiling with the bottom loops slightly longer and shorten the loops as you go. This way the top coils can feed from the slings without tangling in the bottom coils.

These methods can make it reasonable to get down the rappel in the strongest winds, but there is little that can be done to control the ropes while pulling them down in high winds. Once in Torres del Paine, when pulling the ropes after a long rappel, the very end of the rope jammed near the anchor. I re-led the pitch and found the end of the rope jammed in a crack 20 feet *above* the anchor. The wind had tied the rope in a perfect knot then flung it above the anchor where it jammed in a crack. In the same storm, two teams of two with double ropes each joined forces after getting their ropes stuck. They returned to basecamp with one rope remaining.

The only way to minimize stuck ropes while pulling them in high winds is to do short rappels. This way when they do get stuck, and they inevitably will, it is easier to climb back and free them, and you will have more remaining rope to do so.

RAPPEL GURU SAFETY TIPS

"The first person down should always tie a bight in the rappel rope and clip it into the lower anchor, securing the end of the rope in case the second climber down loses control—I've seen it work."

Steph Davis

FIXED ROPE CONSIDERATIONS

Some popular descents may be equipped with fixed ropes, and if you are using a rappel to approach—such as in Colorado's Black Canyon of the Gunnison or in France's Verdon Gorge, where the climbs are approached from above—you may leave a rope in place to facilitate access for several days in a row.

While rappelling a fixed rope—even if you fixed it yesterday—don't assume it is safe to rappel. It only takes a split second for a falling rock to ravage a rope, and a rope left fixed is a sitting duck for rock-fall damage. So when rappelling a fixed rope, the first climber on the rope should slow down and take time to view each section of rope as it becomes visible below them while descending, making sure the rope has not been damaged before they rappel over each section. Most importantly, if you didn't fix the rope, and you can't see what it's attached to, don't trust it.

Leaving fixed ropes more than a certain amount of time is illegal in many national parks, and fixed ropes are frowned upon in some climbing areas. Fixed ropes also deteriorate quickly in the elements and become useless trash. When you are finished with your fixed rope, remove it and take it with you.

From below, this fixed rope appeared to be in good condition. A climb up to check out the anchor revealed it to be attached to a single ancient, rusting piton.

Opposite: *Rappelling in high winds with the rope coiled*

Many of the most experienced climbers have developed strict safety habits dictating how they rappel. Everyone develops their own style. There is more than one way to rappel safely, so find your own method and be open to learning from your partner. Also, there is certainly nothing wrong with politely explaining to your partner if you are uncomfortable with how they are rappelling. Usually, when you explain nicely, your partner will then adopt your methods for their own, increasing their own safety margin and passing on the wisdom to their other partners. Below are some good routines to follow:

- Use an autoblock backup, especially as the first person down. (The second person down can be secured by a fireman's belay from the first climber down, so an autoblock may be unnecessary.)
- At the top, weight the rappel device *before* unclipping from the anchor. Make this routine, so you *feel* the rappel device working before you commit to it. Steph Davis, a veteran of many long rappels, will extend her attachment to the anchor if need be to allow her to weight the rappel before unclipping from the anchor.
- When the first person arrives at the anchor, they clip in and feed slack through their device, then clip a figure eight on a bight, using both ropes, into the anchor. This will allow the second to rappel without an autoblock if they choose, because the anchor below will stop them if they lose control. It also prevents the horrific scenario of the second

climber making a mistake, falling, and taking the ropes with them as well.

- Before starting the rappel and all along the way down, make sure the ropes stay side by side and uncrossed and in the ideal location to pull them. Before you begin pulling, consider extending the anchor so that you can pull the ropes in the ideal trajectory to avoid getting them stuck on flakes or in cracks as they fall.

Rappelling, like belaying, is one of those skills that seems easy but is difficult to do well consistently and without error or mishaps over many years of climbing. Put as much effort into learning the idiosyncrasies and finer points of rappelling as you do into the rest of your climbing, and you'll dramatically reduce your chances of having accidents or minor and major epics during your climbing career.

RAPPING FOR SUCCESS

When we think of rappelling, it is often in just two contexts: we rappel to descend after a successful climb or to retreat from an aborted effort. Either or. But what if the notion of rapping is seen as a tool in the quiver? Staying honestly aware at all times of rappelling as an option can increase your chances of succeeding on committing climbs.

The key mind shift is this: *particularly during the ascent, use an ongoing assessment of your descent options to develop a more accurate perception of your level of commitment at all times.* For example, if you are within a single 60-meter rappel of the ground or close to an established rappel line, and you

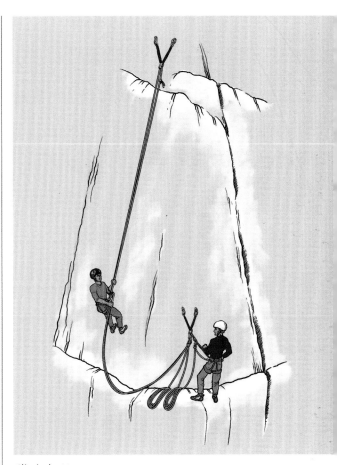

Clip in bottom rap rope

have two ropes, you are at little risk and not really very committed. You can always rap down. Become comfortable with the option of a rappel anytime it is reasonable and suddenly many places become a lot less committing, allowing you to push yourself harder with the knowledge that it's no big deal to rap off.

All the ingredients of a safe rappel: ropes tied together with a barrel knot, both hands on lower side of device, autoblock in place monitored with one hand while the other brakes

Many climbers live in fear of having to rig their own rappel anchor and leave behind a few pieces of gear. You shouldn't. If you're afraid to leave some gear behind, you will be less likely to try climbs that you are not sure of being able to finish. Difficulty, bad weather, a partner's lack of enthusiasm, and impending nightfall are all good reasons to avoid getting committed to a climb; refusing to consider the safe option of a rappel is not. What if you were able to try the climb and feel reassured that you could easily retreat at any time? Feeling bolder already?

This philosophy can change everything. I'm not talking about foolhardily climbing during a lightning storm; but if the worst-case scenario is that you have to leave a couple of pieces of gear, then go for it! If your partner isn't feeling as gung ho as you are, try explaining to them that you don't mind if you have to leave some gear and rap off. If you often feel intimidated in the face of climbs near your limit because of concern for getting off the route should you get stuck, leaving gear behind might be the best thing you could do for your climbing. Here's why: merely being willing to leave your gear behind allows you to climb with more confidence. And although you will occasionally have to pay the price and replace a cam, a couple of nuts, or a few biners and slings, usually you'll send the route in fine style without leaving anything. Don't get so attached to your rack that you don't go climbing for fear of having to leave some of it behind!

DOWNCLIMBING

In Chapter 8, Traditional Lead Climbing, we talked about downclimbing as a tool to be used on lead to help fix routefinding mistakes and reassess or recover from cruxes. Here, downclimbing is discussed in the context of descent. There is one monumental difference between the downclimbing done on lead and the downclimbing we do while getting off of a climb: the fall potential. On lead, the protection system is usually well set up to protect you in case of a fall. On descent, however, even the most conservative climbers end up doing unroped scrambles at times, and many serious accidents have occurred in such places. The key to downclimbing safely is to be brutally honest with yourself before you move into the terrain, and don't take it one inch past the point of comfort.

UNROPED DOWNCLIMBING

"If you need the rope, don't hesitate to use it, but committing to the rope in the wrong place can be a big mess, get you committed to going the wrong way, and waste a lot of time."

Alex Honnold

A common misunderstanding about expert climbers is that when they are not using the rope they are taking greater risks. In many cases, especially on big, low-angle slabs and loose, mountainlike terrain, it can be safer to take the rope off rather than let it drag between the climbers.

Downclimbing without a rope is a perfectly acceptable technique (provided you don't take it too far), and much terrain blurs the lines between climbing and scrambling. The descent from El Capitan is a perfect example. There are acres of slabs where, if you stepped on a shoelace and did a cartwheel, you might fall for an eternity. If you rope up, however, there are almost no anchors anyway and there is the rope management to consider, so you could easily end up looking at a fall that would be long enough to kill you anyway, even if the rope eventually held.

Once across the slabs on the El Cap descent, there is a series of ledges. Along the ledge there are old anchors leading over the abyss and into complex, rope-stranding terrain. By continuing to downclimb to the very limits of the ledge, you reach an easy couple of rappels on clean rock that lead to a fat trail. For a climber who is not comfortable with even a single easy move of unroped downclimbing, the descent from El Cap is a difficult, dangerous, and slow undertaking. For a climber who can move with caution and confidence without a rope on easy downclimbing, the descent from El Cap is quick, easy, and safe.

Rappels from dubious anchors and through loose terrain can be much more dangerous than a bit of calculated downclimbing without a rope.

ROPED DOWNCLIMBING

At the end of a huge day, it is easy to decide to skip the rope and just do a few more moves without the rope. This is when accidents happen. If you downclimb without a rope, or do any exposed climbing without a rope for that matter, and go one step too far, the results can be fatal.

A good way to decide if you should rope up or not is to ask yourself this: *if the rope was already uncoiled and tied into our harnesses, would it increase our safety?* If the answer is yes, then you probably should rope up. Don't let the fact that the rope is in your pack keep you from making the smart decision.

Roped downclimbing in complex terrain

Roped downclimbing requires a slightly different way of looking at consequences and where you place protection. The biggest difference is that the first person down places the protection with the benefit of an overhead top-rope. This means the first person's instinct for self-preservation cannot be relied upon to find protection in the right places. The person going first must assess what it will be like for the second person to descend, *and for them to descend protected by gear they did not place.*

In general, look for protection immediately below harder or more exposed sections. Also consider that the climber descending last will not be able to see the protection they are relying on, so it is always nice to yell back and keep them informed as much as possible. For example, the first person down might yell, "I found some bomber gear here!" or "I can't find any good protection here, but there are good handholds to the right!"

When orchestrating a section of roped downclimbing, it is almost always better to err on the side of short pitches. It is also extremely helpful to see your partner and to communicate through the entire process of a roped downclimb. Climbing out of sight and earshot will almost always result in wasted time and awkward and potentially dangerous situations. One of the primary reasons for short pitches is that when you are belaying the top climber down, you must be extremely careful when pulling in the rope, and it's easier to be careful with shorter amounts of rope out. Pull too hard and you risk pulling the climber off; don't pull enough and the rope may pile up on a ledge without either climber noticing. If the bottom climber keeps a sensitive hand on the rope, feeling each movement of the top climber, this scenario can be avoided even if the climbers are out of sight of each other. But if the rope slips behind a flake or into a crack, the increased friction can prevent the belayer from "feeling" what the top climber is doing.

DOWN JUMPING

Surprisingly, to descend and clean the steepest climbs if the second doesn't want to follow to clean (the steepest pitches are often better led than followed), it can be easier to use a combination of downclimbing and down jumping to clean the pitch rather than lowering off and tramming (clipping into the rope below to pull in to clean the pitch while being lowered). Some climbing areas, such as the mixed trad/sport caves in Australia, even have a tradition of not leaving fixed anchors on top of the steepest routes simply because it is not practical to clean the route by lowering anyway. This method sounds absurd to anyone who has not tried it, but it is amazing how quickly and efficiently even difficult terrain can be reversed with a combination of downclimbing and taking short falls (jumping). The caveat: the climb must be well protected.

To learn to down jump: next time you are on a cave-like climb, rather than lowering off, try to downclimb it. What you'll find is that some sections are surprisingly easy to downclimb, and the difficult sections can easily be passed by simply jumping off and grabbing the belay rope below the piece that catches you to pull yourself into the wall.

When the terrain gets this steep, to clean a pitch after leading, it can be easier to downclimb and down jump than it is to lower off.

At each piece or bolt, first hang on it before unclipping and cleaning it, then downclimb as far as you can before jumping off again. It is best to communicate your plans with your belayer before down jumping: After I had descended a route over a river using this method—to prevent pulling the rope into the water after cleaning the route— my partner scolded me. I deserved it—it's always best to explain your plan to your partner first.

To make down jumping as easy and safe as possible:

- Don't take huge falls (30 feet or more) while down jumping.
- Don't take any falls at all when you're really close to the belay—even short falls hit the belayer hard when there is little rope out; if you can't downclimb without jumping near the belay, leave a piece or a leaver biner on a bolt.
- Hang on each bolt or piece as you descend and assess the section below to plan how far you can downclimb before cleaning the piece and jumping.
- When you unclip a bolt or clean a piece, give the belayer time to pull in rope before jumping.
- On the steepest rock, to prevent being stuck in the air after jumping, have your belayer pull in rope as you swing from your arms; this way they can pull in as much rope as possible before you let go.
- Communicate with your belayer at every step along the way so they can be prepared.

A secondary benefit to down jumping, if done safely, is that it develops an incredible sense of confidence for going for it and trusting your gear. Rather than looking at climbing as a linear game of starting at the bottom and going to the top, down jumping will teach you that the gear and rope are tools for creativity, freedom, and exploration.

Opposite: Dean Potter nearing the point where bouldering ends and free solo begins

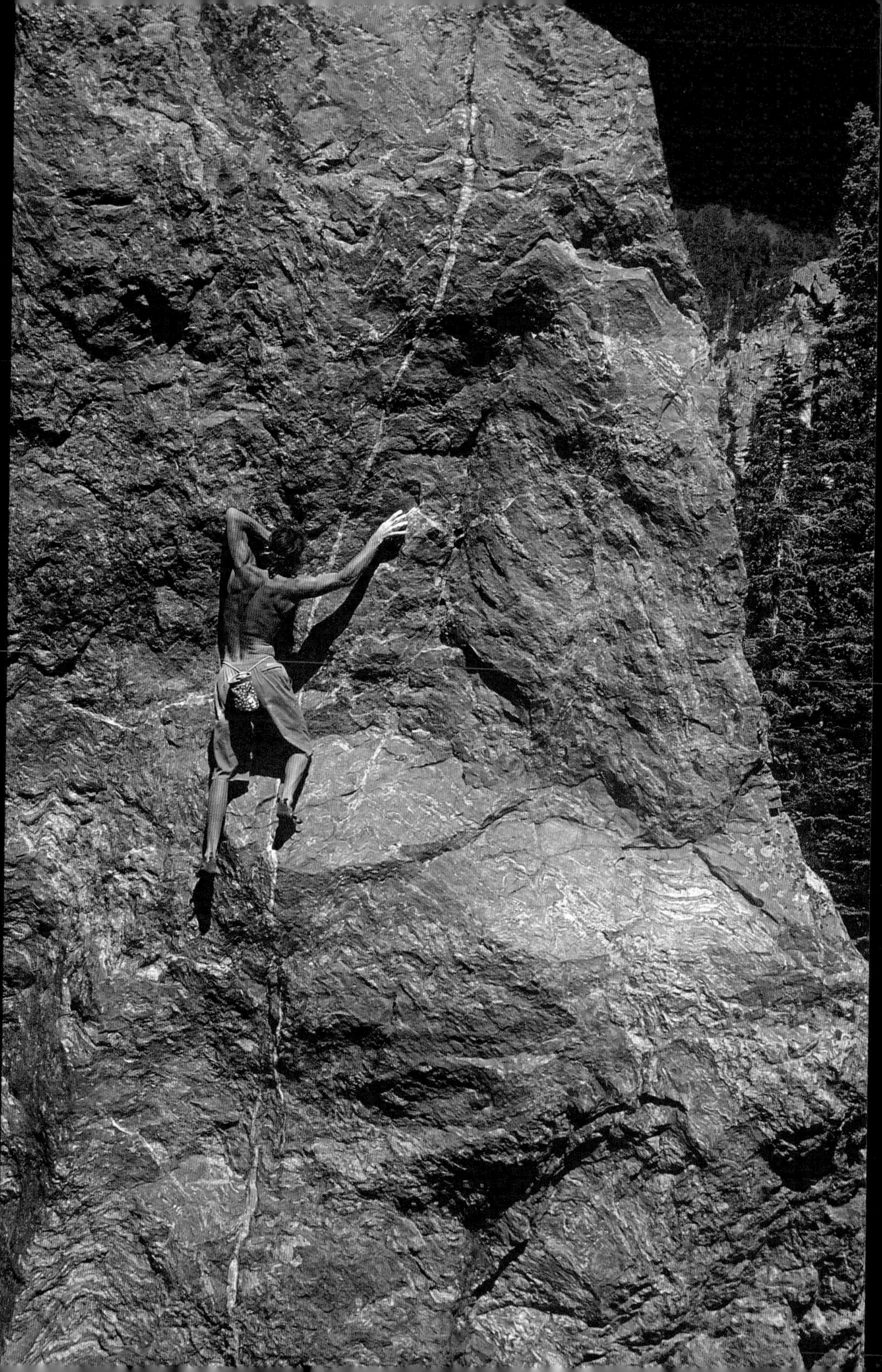

CHAPTER 12

Bouldering

"Climbing's not brain surgery; you can learn the basics in a weekend. It comes naturally. Climbing hard, however, is a different story. It comes down to the psychological part and making it a pursuit—finding that burning desire."

John Sherman

The history of bouldering is colorful, bold, sexy, and inspiring, developing in parallel on the angular blocks of Colorado, the globular slopers of Fontainebleau, and other places. Modern bouldering took the sport all around the globe, to the most beautiful rock in the world in the Rocklands of South Africa, the glacier-polished arêtes of California, the steep caves of Hueco Tanks in Texas, the glacial erratics scattered across Himalayan valleys, and anywhere solid, steep rock can be found.

If there is one chapter in this book that deserves to be its own book, this is it. Bouldering is as complex, interesting, varied, technical, and specialized as all the rest of climbing combined. This is why it has developed into almost its own sport entirely, with many boulderers never using a rope at all and yet becoming highly skilled climbing athletes with many years of experience. Yet climbing and bouldering are inseparable.

Bouldering is where the hardest moves that have ever been executed happen. The gymnastic standards in bouldering are typically a full grade or more beyond the hardest moves being done with a rope. It's been this way for half a century, ever since John Gill pushed bouldering to hard 5.13 or V9 (although the bouldering V-grade system had yet to be invented then) way back in the late 1950s, at a time when the hardest roped 5th class climbs were only about 5.10.

There are typically two kinds of boulderers: those who started out rope climbing and ended up bouldering because it is a great way to improve as a climber (that, and it's just so much fun), and those who boulder as an end in itself. I was the first kind, and enjoyed bouldering but never really understood it until I hooked up with a group of the second kind.

First, I took a couple of scary falls while bouldering. I took a high school friend bouldering and asked him to spot me on a problem. I fell and he was too close to me so my feet landed on his shoulders. I toppled over and rolled down the hill. Luckily both of us were relatively uninjured. A few years later, a trad climber friend was spotting me when a hold broke and I fell right between her arms and landed flat on my back. That hurt, oy. Second, I didn't know how to embrace the learning curve of solving a boulder problem. I either did the problem quickly—or didn't do it at all. So even though I'd climbed for many years, it wasn't until I climbed with a modern bouldering posse that I learned how much fun it could be; I climbed way harder, felt safer, and truly experienced the sport of bouldering for the first time.

Many of the movement and technique lessons from earlier in this book apply to bouldering, and many of the lessons in this chapter also apply to roped climbing, so this chapter does not stand alone. Boulder problems are getting bigger, roped climbs are getting smaller, and the lines between it all are blurring. If you're a boulderer and want to develop a stronger head and more diverse technique, go sport climbing. If you're a trad or sport climber and you want to develop better power and improved creativity and technique on hard terrain, go bouldering.

WARMING UP

"Initially I start on the easiest boulder problems I can find. I then progressively increase the difficulty of the boulder problems I climb as my body starts to feel ready to pull harder moves and my fingers feel ready to pull on smaller or sloping holds. I know from experience that injuries happen when my body is not properly warmed up. I use the warm-up time to stretch on the rock by easing into the body positions that I know I will use

Take time to warm up even if you're champing at the bit to climb. Your session will last longer and you'll climb harder with less chance of injury.

throughout my climbing day. I also like to practice the best techniques possible, emphasizing or even exaggerating the movements during my warm-ups so I reinforce good body positioning that will carry over into the harder climbs. I practice relaxing and work on feeling confident during the warm-up period, especially on tall, easy climbs. I find that what I do in my warm-up period will set the stage for the rest of my climbing session."

Lisa Rands

Some bouldering areas have a plethora of easy problems, making the warm-up process fun and easy to do right. Others have just a few hard problems and it can be challenging to get the body ready to pull down. Temperatures also change the warm-up process. The best bouldering conditions are when it's cold. In many parts of the world, it is not uncommon to head for the boulders in subfreezing temperatures wearing down parkas, mittens, and long underwear under climbing pants. Low temperatures provide optimal conditions for rubber and skin friction on the rock; but cold weather also makes it difficult to get warmed up.

In areas where there is not a good selection of easy problems to warm up on, consider the following warm-up techniques:

- Warm up at home or in the gym. Even a fingerboard at home can deliver a good hand warm-up, and top climbers sometimes use the gym to warm up for outdoor projects. Be sure to warm up at a very light level—maybe 20 percent of your normal climbing or training output.

- Carry a rubber therapy band with your climbing gear and use it as part of the warm-up process.
- Use a couple of light rocks as free weights to do presses, curls, and fly reps to provide a back, arm, and shoulder warm-up.
- Walk through moves with your feet on the ground, pulling lightly and then increasing pressure as you warm up. This can allow you to get your fingers ready to pull on small holds without holding full body weight.

SOLVING COMPLEX SEQUENCES

"Try to execute your vision while remaining open to other methods that surface in the moment. If you fall, then start from the last position and continue to work each move until the end. When the path becomes clear, attempt to stitch the moves together into a seamless flow. It's also helpful to watch others to get ideas and understand the body positioning, movement and sequence—especially fellow climbers with similar strengths and proportions."

Abbey Smith

When you step up to something that is at or a little beyond your limit, one of your first goals should be to explore the options. It's easy to get tunnel vision on one potential solution and try it again and again, toasting your muscles and skin without trying any other way. To be sure you experiment with different options:

- Reach up to the holds you can grab from the ground and grasp them every

Experimentation gets harder the higher off the ground you get. A calm mind, acute awareness of your power reserves, and disciplined movement are critical for solving highball problems.

way you can, with both hands and in different orientations, so you'll have a feel for the options from the very beginning.

- Once you've given a problem a couple of good tries, try it a couple of completely different ways: switch hands, lean the other way, try a bizarre foot sequence.
- Consider stacking or folding pads, or even asking for a friendly knee or shoulder stand from your spotter, so you can feel the higher holds and visualize what it will take to reach them.

THE SEEMINGLY IMPOSSIBLE

"When the holds appear to run out, be creative before getting discouraged. Look for micro-edges, unusual pinches, textured slopers, and ways to compress or stem between features. To navigate the blank space may require powerful and dynamic movement, funky contortion, or delicate, technical moves on seemingly impossible features. Try all combinations imaginable."
Abbey Smith

Some hard problems look possible, but require a high level of power or technique. Others look just plain impossible. To become a great boulderer it is important to try all different kinds of hard problems. The smooth, blank, impossible-looking problems develop a particular kind of skill that will help you break through both mental and physical barriers. To work through a problem that appears impossible at first glance:

- Climb by braille. Feel the holds and body positions rather than looking at them. The solution to these kinds of problems is often revealed through tactile and kinesthetic feedback rather than visual feedback.
- Ask your spotter to hold some of your weight. This can reveal the solution so you can then develop the momentum or power to execute the move without their help.
- Use all of your body. Knees, shoulders, elbows, hips, and everything else can be used in subtle or significant ways to crack the code of the impossible.
- Try the impossible. Sometimes a huge reach, an overhead heel hook, a tiny edge, a toe smear on a rice grain–size sloper, or a wild dyno can work far better than you ever imagined—but you'll never know if you don't try it.
- Don't obsess over grades. As John "The Verm" Sherman, inventor of the V-grade system, says: "People obsess over numbers and that's why they get stuck at a certain grade. Unless you're the very best climber in the world, numbers shouldn't define you as a climber."
- Learn to try really hard. Nobody climbs hard without trying, and only by practicing the art of maximal effort will you be able to tap your deepest well of energy and power.

MOMENTUM

"Good climbing technique involves moving with controlled, dynamic movement. It takes practice to learn how to coordinate

Push back the impossible by climbing right up to the edge of the possible every chance you get.

a more dynamic style of move because it requires using a very specific amount of power—enough to move the body into the right place, but not too much to cause a swing or put extra strain on the hands. Understanding how to apply power at the right time and in the right amount is crucial to help you move efficiently between holds. Purely 'static' moves can't really exist, because you have to move to climb— but a nearly static move may be necessary to maintain balance when holding extremely poor holds and moving to a very

poor, or difficult to grasp, handhold. Most people starting out climbing tend to adopt the slow, static style, which is generally inefficient, and they need to learn to use momentum and other techniques to move between holds rather than 'locking off' every time."

Lisa Rands

Climbing, as slow as it can be sometimes, is a sport of movement and there is no better way to learn how to move on the rock than through bouldering. As a beginner on the boulders, it is important to focus on positioning: how to place feet and weight them with the rubber perfectly still against the rock, how to find quiet balance between both feet and one arm in order to let go and move the other arm, how to hold still in a strenuous place while figuring out what to do next.

"To climb hard you have to redefine success; you have to learn to find progress in the smallest of successes. Some days you have to look really closely to find progress; but there can be a lot of success within failure if you look at it right."

Angie Payne

Next, as you move into intermediate and advanced bouldering, it becomes critical to look at motion as much more than where you put your hands and feet and to study how to carry your momentum between the moves. Learning foot and hand placements is akin to learning how to play the right notes on a musical instrument. Adding the movement and momentum creates the complete song; just playing a note correctly does not make a song.

To learn to use momentum:

- Monitor speed. Experiment with how fast you climb, not just which holds you use.
- Loosen up. When repeating easier problems, add more motion to your method.
- Channel Sharma. Try adding momentum by cutting one arm or one leg free and using it to give you a swing in the right direction.
- Do it your way. Look beyond the obvious "beta" of where you put your hands and

feet to study the rhythm and dance of the problem.

DIFFERENT ROCK TYPES

"Anytime I go to a new area with a different type of rock or style of climbing, I need a day or two to build my confidence to the different style of movement and to get used to the friction of a new rock type under my hands and feet. The great thing is that the more types of rock you climb on, the better your climbing will become."

Lisa Rands

Climbing on different rock types is, for many climbers, the best part of the sport. Learning the friction coefficient, the movement, and the aesthetics of the almost infinite variety of stone is a fascinating process. When we climb in one area, we tend to get really good at one particular type of climbing. Then when we visit somewhere new, we tend to suck. This is normal. It takes time to learn the language of a new rock type and if your expectations get in the way on day one, you may set yourself up for a psychological hindrance that could limit you for your entire trip. When you go somewhere new, open up your beginner's mind; it's by being a beginner again that you will become better than you ever were before.

- Forget grades. Grades are, at best, a clumsy way to compare one climb to another; they have nothing to do with you.
- Get mileage. The best way to learn a new area is to do a ton of easy climbing.

You'll climb harder in the end if you start off easy.

- Get out with the locals. Even the world's best climbers often learn tricks from the climbers who know the rock better than anyone else.
- Train for the destination. If you're going somewhere with high altitude, add a bit of cardio to your training program. If the holds will be small, practice crimping. If you're heading to slopersville, get on sloper problems in the gym.
- Get your head in the game. When you're topping out, don't just hurry over the top. Relax and learn to think clearly and move in perfect control even when you're super pumped.

SPOTTING

"Sometimes I like spotting even more than climbing."

Dean S. Potter

Spotting is to bouldering what belaying is to roped climbing and many of the same philosophies apply. It's easy to spot but hard to spot well. A good spot can make the difference between a successful send and yet another failure; spotting should be taken just as seriously as the climbing. Just as with belaying, thank your spotter when they give you a good spot (regardless of if you fall or not), spread the word in a positive way about how much difference a good spot makes, and help educate others about spotting technique. There are several strategies for spotting, and many

Dave Graham on a V12 first ascent with a perfect spot by Dean S. Potter and the boys

times every strategy will be used on a single problem.

In any scenario, visualizing the physics of the fall should be at the forefront of any spotter's mind. Not only do the moves and gravity affect the fall, but different people tend to fall in their own way. Some flail to the ground like an injured bird while others land like a cat.

BOULDERING FORCES

"Take the spotter's role seriously—as seriously as belay duty. Start with the right stance: stand close behind the person with your hands by their waist, dominant foot forward, and legs engaged with nimble readiness. Pay attention to where the climber might fall, be ready to move quickly, watch the hips, but ultimately, protect the head. Also, focus: don't scope beta when you should be spotting."

Abbey Smith

There are several all-too-common mistakes made in spotting, the first of which is the half-assed spot. A spotter should either spot with conviction or not spot at all. The second is the overoptimistic spot, where the spotter is at risk of being injured by the climber. The forces generated in a fall are significant and it is critical to be realistic about how much a spotter can do. For perspective, here are some weight and height numbers according to a fall force calculator:

- If a 150-pound climber falls 15 feet and is given the textbook perfect spot, which decelerates them for approximately the last 3 feet of their fall, the climber will generate about 900 pounds of force.
- If the same climber falls flat on their back from 15 feet with no spot to decelerate them and only 1 foot of body and pad compression, they will generate about 2400 pounds of force.
- If the same climber falls off a proper horror-show highball at 30 feet and lands flat on their back with only 1 foot of deceleration, they will generate about 4650 pounds of force, a likely lethal scenario.

These numbers do not take into account the absorption of force by a person's legs or the complexities of physics caused by an angled or rolling landing. But there are two very clear takeaways from these calculations. One, the spotter can make a huge difference in the impact force if they can help to decelerate the climber as early as possible. And two, for highball problems a spotter is taking a great risk by getting in the way of a falling climber. It is usually best to tell the climber before they start up a highball that you will spot them only up to a certain point—and after that you are stepping out of the way.

NO SPOTTER

"Sometimes it's best to have just the pad and no spotter."

Chris Schulte

There are times when a spotter is more of a hazard than a help, and other times when a spot would be ineffective. These situations include:

- Lowball problems, sit-starts, and liedown starts where the climber is too close to the ground
- When the fall is particularly perfect onto a well-padded, flat landing and the spotter will just get in the way of the climber's fall
- Highball problems where the climber is pushing into the realm of a free solo. An advanced or tall spotter may be able to help guide a falling climber from a high problem, but don't expect miracles.

While the climber should alert the spotter if she prefers not to have a spot, the spotter

If the fall is clean and the landing flat, it may be best to have no spotter in the way.

should use his own judgment as well. For really low sit-starts or when the spotter could get slammed between a falling climber and a spike of rock or other hazard, the spotter should make it very clear through verbal and body language that they are *not* spotting.

ONE SPOTTER

"A good spot is like tai chi—directing the momentum perfectly with the minimum amount of force and contact. As the climber, once you get a spot like that, you try harder."
Chris Schulte

Many bouldering sessions happen with just two people, leaving one to spot, but an experienced single spotter can be far more effective than a posse of newbies. It is best to consider spotting not as "catching" a climber as you would with a roped belay, but rather "directing" the climber's momentum and correcting their body position so that they land in the most anatomically correct position possible. When bouldering in popular areas or with other experienced boulderers, take note of how great spotters prepare for and execute a catch. This includes:

- Body position—The spotter should be positioned just outside the climber's landing zone. You want to help the climber land in the safest possible position without getting in the way of their natural catlike abilities.

- Hand position—The spotter's hands should be as close to the climber as possible without touching them. When the climber falls, the sooner you can begin directing their fall and helping them decelerate, the less overall force they will generate and the better their landing will be.
- Stance—Assume an alertness and stance like you would for starting a martial arts or wrestling match, with all your joints slightly bent and ready to react, not like you would for holding a pizza.
- Self-preservation—Be aware of where the falling climber's force will take you and avoid places where you could be injured, pushed over edges, or knocked into objects. Broken legs and arms can and do happen to spotters.
- Anticipation of fall trajectory—Straight down, with gravity, is the obvious trajectory. But due to the powerful, dynamic nature of bouldering it is very common to fall to one side or the other or even to explode straight back off of the rock. The spotter should watch the climber and position themselves in anticipation of the type of fall and direction the climber is likely to take.

MULTI-SPOTTER

"As a climber, never assume someone is spotting you. Communicate with the spotters before starting up—you'll spend less energy worrying about the landing and more on climbing."

                                        Abbey Smith

Having a group of experienced spotters is the best way to send high, hard problems with funky landings. But it is possible for a large number of spotters to create a hazard—the phenomenon of everyone thinking someone else was spotting. Just about anyone who has bouldered much has had the experience of crashing hard in the middle of a circle of people and lying there on the pad looking up at the spotters, each of them looking sheepishly around at the others: face, body, and voice all saying the same thing, "I thought you had him." On the other hand, you don't want to set up a stage-dive scenario either, with everyone in a disorganized crowd right under the climber.

It is usually best to designate a primary spotter and a couple of secondary spotters to spring into action as the climber is getting ready for a burn. Often the tallest climbers with bouldering experience are the best choices; but an experienced shorter spotter will almost always give a better spot than an inexperienced giant. The other climbers can then support the primary and secondary spotters in several ways:

- Be in the outfield ready for unexpected fall trajectories.
- Move the pads to match the climber's movement and fall potential.
- Spot the main spotters: supporting the spotters as they direct the climber is more effective and safer than crowding the landing area.

CRASH PAD STRATEGY

"How you set up your pads really depends on the terrain. A lot of bouldering happens in talus fields, so you really must pay attention to padding. Keep the seams of the pads

If you're going bouldering in a talus field, the more the better when it comes to crash pads.

together and monitor them; just a little shift each time you fall and suddenly you have a 4-inch gap between the pads."

Chris Schulte

Hang out around boulderers for long and you'll inevitably see somebody on crutches, usually from falling onto the edge of a crash pad and twisting an ankle. These falls are quite often not the heroic highball dismounts but rather everyday jumps that land precisely wrong. The shortest fall I've ever seen result in a sprained ankle was perhaps 3 inches and resulted from, you guessed it, landing and twisting down onto the sheer edge of the pad.

Most experienced boulderers are aware of this, and place their pads with great care to avoid bad falls. Crash pad strategy depends on how many pads are available, the terrain, and the size of the boulder.

"Align the crash pads in the direction of all possible falls with the biggest and thickest pad in the main drop zone or covering the most dangerous areas. Watch for sharp objects, gaps, tangle-prone straps, and stiff edges."

Abbey Smith

Padding for a hard send in a talus field is a feat of engineering and risk management

Crash pad strategy

Here, three pads are used to pad the places the climber is likely to fall, and a fourth pad is placed to protect the spotter from falling into the cooler-size rock in the grass behind her.

that boulderers take as seriously as trad climbers placing protection. To pad a rugged, uneven landing:

- Multiple pads are essential.
- Place small pads, sometimes folded closed to make them thicker, in the gaps between the obstacles.
- Use packs, clothes, or other items to pad sharp rocks or log or stump ends.
- Build up the downhill part with more pads to make the landing as flat as possible.
- Once a foundation is in place, lay an organized layer of bigger pads over the top, keeping the seams aligned.

Done right, careful padding can make the difference between a full-throttle fun-fest and an ankle-spraining horror show.

Manage your bouldering sessions in a way that is both inspiring for the climbers and sensitive to the beautiful natural environment where the sport happens.

MOVING PADS

"If the pads need to move mid-climb, then discuss a game plan amongst the group beforehand to avoid confusion."

Abbey Smith

Ideally, you set up the crash pads so that they don't need to be moved during the climb. Reaching down to move a pad just as the climber falls is a good way to get smashed, so do everything you can to get it right the first time.

Sometimes, however, on traverses or angling or steep problems it can be necessary to move a pad or pads. To move pads:

- Stay in tune with the climber's movement and points where they are more and less likely to fall. There are natural pauses on the better holds and times when the climber is particularly solid— these are the times to move the pad.
- Keep your eyes on the climber even as you reach down to move the pad. If they

Bouldering areas are often stunningly beautiful; keep them that way. Share the environmental ethic with other climbers every chance you get in the most positive way possible.

BOULDERING ALONE

Bouldering alone can be one of the most peaceful and meditative of climbing experiences, but the fall potential and the risk of being out there without a partner to help if something goes wrong must always be considered.

> *"Every time I go bouldering I experience a subtlety I've never felt before—and climbing hard is all about subtleties. That's one of the things I love about bouldering; the less equipment you have to deal with, the more you can focus on the movement."*
>
> Angie Payne

Many people go bouldering alone, and while it is certainly safer than free solo climbing far above the ground, there is still an added risk that comes with doing anything outdoors alone. Break a leg bouldering on a cold evening in a remote spot without a partner or cell service and you could be in for a fight for survival.

Continued

BOULDERING ALONE (CONTINUED)

That said, running a favorite circuit in the flowing, efficient, Zen-like, quiet style that climbing alone tends to encourage is many a climber's favorite part of the game. The obvious, tricky part is that once you are climbing, you can't move your own crash pad. To help with this issue, be aware of these factors when bouldering alone:

- Use your biggest crash pad—more space means less need to move the pad.
- Be aware when you move into a position where your fall will miss the pad.
- Practice climbing in perfect control rather than pushing the difficulty.
- Force yourself to rest—it's harder to rest when there is nobody climbing between your burns.
- Watch for loose holds—breaking a hold is a common story behind really bad bouldering falls.
- Fall with intent—try to jump off onto the center of the pad when you feel yourself losing control rather than falling willy-nilly.

fall you'll have a fraction of a second to react and give them a good spot.

- If there are several spotters, assign somebody to moving the pad so the primary spotter(s) can stay focused on the climber.

Make a plan with the climber before they start up for when and where they will want the pad moved.

ENVIRONMENTAL IMPACT

"Pay attention to the plants around the boulders, and not just while bouldering; be careful where you put your gear, where you eat lunch, and how you move around. Keep as small of a footprint as possible."
Chris Schulte

Bouldering may or may not be the most environmentally impactful form of climbing, but from a non-climber's perspective it certainly appears to be the most harmful. Land managers have been working on how to manage climbing for the better part of thirty years. They have only just begun to manage bouldering. The ways in which we take care of our bouldering areas will have a great effect, either positive or negative, on how bouldering is managed and regulated in the near future.

Crash pads are one of the more environmentally stressful parts of the bouldering routine. They can smother and crush plants and cryptobiotic soil crusts. Many problems can be climbed safely without pads. If the ground area is particularly lush with plant life, try to avoid using pads at all, or minimize their use, and just climb well instead of always relying on the pad as a mental crutch.

Protect the vegetation. Any cutting of trees or other such dramatic, intentional damage to the ecosystem is an absolute no-no. We are not alone in the areas where we climb. Hunters, birders, hikers, photographers, land managers, and others will see any damage you cause. For the sake of our sport, climb in a leave-no-trace, minimal-impact manner.

Be aware of noise. Noise from bouldering sessions affects other wilderness users. Not everyone likes to hear techno music, yelling and cheering, or your favorite I'm-trying-really-hard scream.

Maybe you don't care what other people think, but the feedback land managers get makes a big difference in how they perceive user groups. If climbers are viewed as loud, obnoxious, and inconsiderate of their surroundings, land managers are more likely to put more restrictions in place than if they view climbers as quiet, thoughtful, and environmentally aware.

"Clean your holds! Not just for visual impact, but for your own climbing. Clean holds stick better. Keep a clean pad, clean shoes—a clean workplace. Stepping onto soft rock like sandstone with grit on your shoes wears down the rock much faster. If you climb clean, the rock lasts longer and you climb better."

Chris Schulte

Clean your shoes. It usually goes something like this: You get really excited and step up on the first hold with muddy feet. Then you slip off, laugh or throw a wobbler, clean your feet, and get back on to try again.

What you don't realize is that every time somebody steps onto that first hold with muddy feet it grinds a few more grains of rock off the hold, reducing the friction and making the hold harder and harder to stand on. This is true not only for softer rocks like limestone and sandstone: even granite becomes polished and harder to climb with use, particularly in bouldering areas where the holds are used with gritty, dirty shoes that just left the ground. The same kind of holds 50 feet off the ground on a popular roped climb show much less sign of wear because the grit is worn off the shoes by the time the climbers get there.

Remove tick marks. Leaving tick marks is no better than graffiti, and because bouldering happens so close to the ground—mostly at eye level or a little above—bouldering tick marks are even more noticeable to non-climbers than tick marks on roped climbs. There are simply far too many climbers and far too many other users of our natural areas for tick marks to be left. Carry a toothbrush and brush your holds when you are done. To reach higher holds, tape the brush to a stick, clean the holds, then remove the brush and tape from the stick you'll leave behind. Climbing visionaries have been recommending the removal of tick marks as standard practice for years, but still, very few climbers are doing it. It's time to change our ways. If we don't reduce our impact, our sport is likely to face far more severe restrictions.

Opposite: *Getting mind and body in tune on Taft Point, Yosemite*

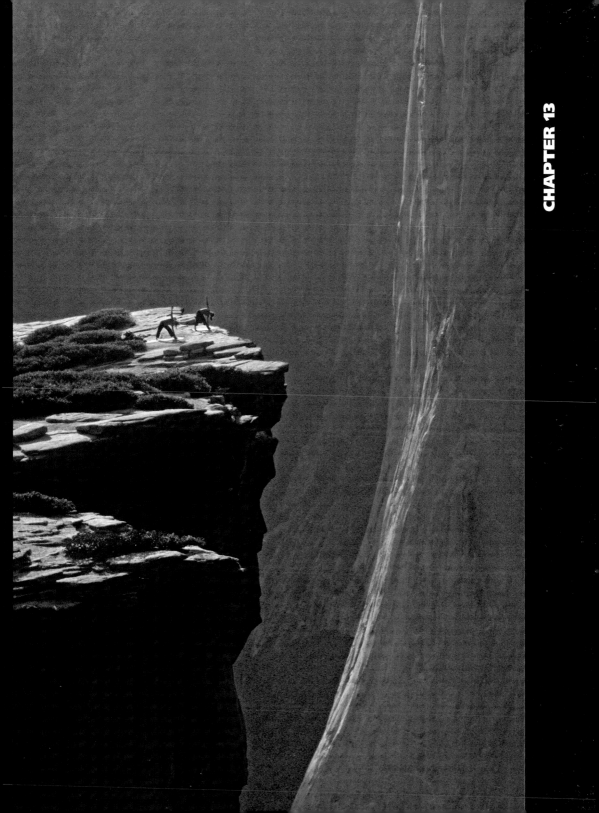

CHAPTER 13

Performance

"To model for photos on Realization *(the world's first 5.15) where Chris Sharma was taking those huge whippers, Alex Megos would just downclimb the crux so he didn't have to batman back up the rope. It's a whole new level."*

Sonnie Trotter

In the old school of climbing instruction, this chapter would have been titled "Training." But as I researched the best practices and interviewed top climbers, coaches, and personal trainers, it became clear that training is only one aspect of the overall quest for athletic improvement in the vertical arena. There is far more than training involved in optimizing the athlete inside you. All the other chapters in this book are primarily about how to execute the sport of climbing *externally*. This chapter is about how to perform internally—the physiology and the psychology of climbing.

When I set out to write this chapter, I wanted to provide a recipe, a collection of best practices that anyone could use as a training plan to become a better climber. From talking to coaches, trainers, and athletes, it quickly became apparent that this is not the way improved athletic performance works when it comes to climbing. Each climber is unique, and any canned, one-size-fits-all training program is indeed a recipe—a recipe for disaster. Go online and pick a training program for hangboarding, campus boarding, power-endurance, power, finger strength, or any other element of climbing, and—unless you tailor it for your needs, strengths, and weaknesses—there's a good chance that you're setting yourself up for injury, burnout, and disappointment.

"Actual physical change from training begins immediately, but progresses slowly. It's a lifestyle thing if you want to really get into training. It takes years to get to the point where advanced training is appropriate."
Chris Wall

Not one climbing expert I interviewed recommended even a single training method that would work universally. In fact, they all were adamant that athletic improvement in climbing must be based on only one thing: *you*. Your physiology, strengths, weaknesses, past injuries, history, and attitude balanced against your goals and dreams.

Many self-directed training programs fail to consider that dreams and goals are a critical element of training. If you are preparing for the back-to-back huge days and endless hand jams of the Bugaboos in Canada, the training program should look very different from one to prepare you to fondle tufa and fight the pump in the Greek caves of Kalymnos.

This is the secret sauce of athletic performance in climbing: look inside yourself at what you are made out of, ask yourself what you most want to do, and then figure out how to build your inner athlete to the point where your can achieve your goal.

BASELINE

"Self-assessment is a really big challenge. People get tired and confused and they lose their objectivity. Hire a coach and/ or trainer to help you find your challenges and figure out a baseline to start from. Almost every climbing gym has a coach or a trainer who can help."

Chris Wall

The first step to performance climbing, whatever that means to you, is to very precisely and honestly determine your athletic baseline. In the individualistic culture of climbing, we are loath to hire experts to tell us what we should do. But there are two times in climbing when it is highly advisable to spend a little money to get expert advice: the first is when you decide to lead trad, and the second is when you decide to train. You can learn more from an expert in one day in both of these phases than you will in an entire year on your own. As an added benefit, you will also dramatically reduce your risk of injury.

If you do hire a trainer for a baseline athletic evaluation, remember that they don't know you. If you have fragile shoulders, they don't know it. If you have a history of elbow tendonitis, they don't know it. You need to tell them. Also, only you know how you have responded in the past to training or athletic challenges. The things you tell your trainer or coach are critically important to the kind of program they design and how beneficial it will be for you.

If you choose to pass on hiring an expert for baseline evaluation, the next best thing is to conduct a careful and honest self-evaluation. Assess your own:

- Power
- Endurance
- Power-endurance
- Flexibility
- Mental strength

If looking at this list brings up more questions than it answers, you can see why hiring an expert can be worthwhile. With or without a professional trainer, you'll still need to develop the self-awareness to continually assess these basic elements of climbing performance. So read on.

POWER

"The three most important things in training for climbing are: power, finger strength, and managing your weight. But power is the ultimate—if you have extra power everything else is easier."

Sonnie Trotter

It may require taking time away from climbing to increase power, but the results can be a power increase beyond your wildest dreams.

Power is the name of the game in hard climbing. In fact, power is so critical at the top levels of the sport that many of the climbers gunning for the world's hardest climbs actually take time away from climbing to train specifically to dramatically increase power.

The age-old wisdom in climbing is that if you are lacking power, go bouldering. It is still the most enjoyable way to gain climbing-specific strength; it is also an ideal way to assess your own power level. For

your self-assessment, go bouldering and pay close attention to the following:

- If you don't enjoy bouldering, that's probably an indication that you are lacking in power and/or finger strength.
- When you do a hard move, do you feel like it is your technique limiting you or that you simply can't pull hard enough? (Poor technique can easily be mistaken for lack of power, so be brutally honest with yourself here.)
- Video yourself climbing—what does your body language say?

Power has a large genetic element. Some people can reel off pull-ups to the point of boredom without any training at all; others have trouble doing just one. Some level of power is needed in climbing, and many breakthroughs, as well as injuries, have resulted from the quest for power. Campus boards, hangboards, system boards, training with weights, and working hard bouldering circuits are all good ways to build power— they are also good ways to get hurt. Read on for advice on each of these methods.

ENDURANCE

"I climb better when I'm also running."
            Steph Davis

Climbing isn't the most cardiovascular of sports. Sure, a nice 50-meter off-width can have you breathing like a 400-meter runner; but cragging, sport climbing, bouldering, and the kind of climbing most of us do most of the time is not highly cardiovascular. In fact, we can be in relatively dismal cardio-vascular shape and still be able to climb really hard. That said, the root of endurance is recovery, and the root of recovery is building your cardiovascular fitness. Thus, a reasonable cardiovascular base will help any climber.

One of the best ways to determine your cardiovascular fitness is to measure your heart rate recovery. Using Digifit or a Fitbit connected to your smartphone is an added plus for gathering data. The basic idea is this:

1. Use a stationary bike, running, or other cardio exercise that is easy to stop and start.

2. Bring your heart rate to about 80 percent of your maximum (100 percent is roughly determined to be 220 minus your age, but this varies by person also).

3. Take your pulse for 10 seconds and multiply by 6 (shorter duration gives you a more accurate starting point).

4. Rest for exactly 1 minute and take your pulse again. The difference between your first pulse check and your second is your heart rate recovery.

Endurance training, in moderation, will improve recovery.

According to Heart Zones, the heart rate recovery results are as follows:

- Less than 10 = Extreme caution
- 11–20 = Low
- 21–40 = Good
- 41–50 = Excellent
- 50+ = Athlete

To extrapolate these numbers into climbing, you should be "good" or better. If not, consider adding some gentle cardio-training into your weekly schedule.

"A 15-mile run is not a rest day from climbing. The cardiovascular, nervous, and endocrine systems are still being stressed, and this stress can become cumulative. The activities might be different, but the athlete only has one body to accomplish all the recovery."

Chris Wall

If you determine that cardiovascular fitness is holding you back from achieving your goals, devise an exercise routine that supports your climbing schedule, not detracts from it. It has been long understood among trainers that when you train for endurance, your power will suffer; so realize that you will need to allow adequate rest periods after your last endurance workout before you step into the ring with your nemesis.

POWER-ENDURANCE

Power-endurance is a cornerstone of rock climbing fitness. We all know the feeling of not having adequate power-endurance. It's that moment when we realize that even the biggest hold in the world isn't big enough. There are few sports that tap into the power-endurance reserves in the same way as climbing. To assess your power-endurance, go to the gym or to a sport crag with sustained, steep routes. After warming up, pick a climb that is a full number grade below your best redpoint and have at it. On the way up, don't think about success or failure, but instead focus on how quickly you lose power. When you get to the last good jugs on the wall, do a pull-up.

- Can you still do a pull-up?
- How pumped are you?
- Can you recover while hanging on the finishing jugs or do you just get more pumped?
- When you begin to weaken, does the countdown to failure tick slowly or with blazing speed?

Again, it's personal. What you want to do is determine if power-endurance is a weakness, or if it is a natural strength for you. How long does your natural level of power last? One of the biggest mistakes climbers make with self-assessment is to compare themselves to other climbers. You want to compare your own power, endurance, and power-endurance, and build upon the weakest of the three.

FLEXIBILITY

"Some range-of-motion exercises are important, but you don't have to be able to throw splits between two chairs à la Jean-Claude Van Damme to be a good climber. I've never seen the absolute need

Yoga can be a great complement to (or warm-up for) climbing, building mental calm, physical strength, and flexibility—provided it is done in a way that doesn't add excessive stress to your body.

for an extended flexibility program in climbing. Some people may need more than others, and some not so much."

Chris Wall

When I was 16 years old, I went to Devils Tower to climb the legendary *El Matador*, a perfect stem box that goes for 50 calf-burning meters. At the bottom of the pitch, I tried to spread into the stem and couldn't make the span. I went home and stretched for several weeks, then returned and climbed it easily. Flexibility matters, but not as much as the yoga pants strutting in every gym might suggest.

Some climbers will extol the virtues of flexibility all day long, while others can hardly touch their toes and yet climb 5.13+. Like most things in climbing, it's personal. I know a climber who has such naturally flexible joints (she is practically double-jointed) that when she stretches too much she ends up dislocating her shoulders while climbing. I know others who are so stiff that they find it difficult even to step higher than their knees.

> ## BREATHING
> There are four kinds of breath: belly breath, power-endurance breath, screaming breath, and holding breath. You want to adjust your breathing to the type of move you are doing.
> - **Belly breath** gives you recovery, relaxation: This breath fills your lungs to capacity, pulling from deep within the belly, as if you are about to hold your breath underwater.
> - **Power endurance breath** gives you endurance, commitment: This is the breath you would use running up a hill—fast, strong, and with conviction.
> - **Screaming breath** gives you power, focus: This breath isn't just called screaming breath, *it is screaming*. This is the *kiai* of martial arts.
> - **Holding breath** gives you tension, stillness: Even a breath can detract from perfect form. For absolute tension or complete balance, don't even breathe.
>
> Justen Sjong

This is when it can be helpful to measure your flexibility against others. Watch other people climb. Can you put your body into the positions that most climbers seem to be able to achieve? Or do you see climbers moving their bodies in ways that yours just won't go?

If you are above average in flexibility, know that increasing flexibility is probably not going to be what makes you a better climber. If you are below average in flexibility, know that adding a gentle stretching program to your life will likely improve your climbing significantly. Yoga can help, but be forewarned there are now therapists who specialize in treating yoga injuries. As climbing coach Chris Wall explains, it is easy to get distracted by other aspects of training and forget that the sum total adds to your stress load. Even though yoga is known as a therapeutic pursuit, it also increases the demands placed upon your body.

MENTAL STRENGTH

"What I try to identify is not weaknesses, but strengths. What makes you awesome? What makes you confident? What makes you strut?"

Justen Sjong

Mental strength in climbing is just as critical as physical strength, and no performance program will be successful without also building mental strength. Self-assessment of mental strength is largely about, as Justen explains, identifying your natural strengths. Find them, then extend your strengths into areas where you are less comfortable. To target your strengths, look back at all the climbing you've ever done and ask yourself these questions:
- What is the thing you are most proud of about the way you climb?
- When you sent your hardest climb, what stands out as the thing you did best to make it happen?

Climbing is at least as much a mental game as a physical one. Build a strong mind as well as a strong body.

- On your best days, what is it about your attitude that causes you to be fierce and on fire?
- As Justen asks, "What makes you strut?"

In today's world of muscle-sculpted bodies, training machines, wearable fitness devices, and weighted fingerboard routines, mental strength is dramatically underappreciated and often underdeveloped. And while some climbers have naturally strong minds, most of us do not. Instead, it's tempting to compensate for lack of mental strength by training harder, spraying tick marks all over the rock, redpointing more methodically, and generally viewing climbing as a mechanical game rather than a melding of the mind and body.

To develop your own mental strength, put as much effort into training the neural pathways in your climbing system as you do in training the mitochondria in your muscles. This means working toward a stronger mental game every time you climb—indoors and outdoors, good days and bad, on climbs that you do well on and the ones that give you the beatdown. To improve your mental game:

- Don't throw wobblers (tantrums) when you fall—this prevents the development of a mature relationship with your motivation and is a sign of poorly managed energy output.
- After every pitch you climb, consciously assess the things you did well, both mentally and physically.

THE SENSES OF CLIMBING

Eyes: There are two gazes, soft and hard—soft is the big-picture decision-making, and hard is the pinpoint focus on crystals and grains—and both are essential. The thing is, once people go into the hard gaze, they have a hard time getting out of it to look at the big picture again. One moment you want to be a West Coast beach bum (soft gaze), and the next moment you want to be an uptight East Coaster (hard gaze): you want these coast-to-coast extremes.

Ears: Listen to your breath. Are you breathing efficiently and appropriately? Or is your breathing in fits and starts, panting and struggling?

Listen to your body's interaction with the rock. Are you moving like a stealth ninja, or clumsily stubbing your toes against the rock and slapping with your hands?

Listen to the noises you make climbing. Are they roars of confidence or whimpers of uncertainty?

Touch and Feel: Not just the rock, but your inner movement. Did the move feel good or did it feel like there is a better way to do it? Practice this by repeating moves—learn not only to do the moves, but to do them in a way that feels right for your body.

Justen Sjong

- When you finish a pitch, don't just grab the anchors desperately—instead, keep your composure, look for the best finishing holds, and calmly clip the anchors as if you were going to continue climbing.
- When the climbing is safe and you are properly warmed up, practice climbing to failure, rather than giving up.
- Minimize the use of tick marks—learn the moves with your mind and body rather than dot to dot.
- At the end of a big day, do one more pitch; when your body is tired, only a strong mind will get you through.
- Develop a performance curve with your mind just as you do with your body—warm up, perform your best, cool down—and complete these phases every time you climb.

"We naturally dwell on the negative, but we don't spend enough time reflecting on the positive—what is it about you that allows you to be a badass?"

Justen Sjong

When you climb with partners you are comfortable with, it is easy to get into a conversation about the things that you (or they) do wrong, the negative. Try to steer the conversation toward the positive. Ask them to watch you climb and to tell you the things they see you are doing well so you can build on your strengths. Ask them to describe the best parts of your climbing. At the end of the day, ask them what was the best climbing moment they had that day, and maybe they'll do the same for you. Point out the parts of the day when they were climbing really well. Even on the worst days, we have moments of brilliance. Make a point of noticing those moments in yourself and your partners and everyone will benefit. Consciously build your mental strengths.

TRAINING TOOLS

"It's nice to train because it's more fun to climb when you're climbing better. Just the fact that you're going climbing is reason enough to train."

Steph Davis

Up to a point, you can train for climbing by just climbing, and this is certainly the most enjoyable. But you can only get so good through climbing alone. Training becomes an essential element of progression, and it gets far more complex than just working on your weaknesses. To train for the 8-foot dyno on the *Dawn Wall*, Tommy Caldwell used a tape measure and the inclinometer on his iPhone to precisely measure the actual move 1700 feet off the ground on El Cap, then went home and built a model in his garage.

"When you're first aspiring to climb hard, you can improve without training, but if you really want to excel, you have to train."

Alex Honnold

For the rest of us, the most popular tools for training to climb are the campus

Climbing-specific training tools, like the campus board, are a great way to get strong—or get injured.

board, hangboard, system board, and treadwall. Each device has countless potential workouts, and when factored into your unique physiology, it is impossible to give a textbook recommendation for what makes a healthy workout for you. That said, there are a few basic considerations for each tool.

CAMPUS BOARD

"Campus boarding develops upper body strength and power, as well as finger strength and power. But not everyone is ready for campus boarding. If done in the classic way with feet off, it is an enormous amount of stress."

Chris Wall

The campus board was invented by climbing legend Wolfgang Gullich in an effort to develop the mutant finger strength and explosive power needed for *Action Directe,* the world's first 5.14d. It worked. He sent. Now no climbing gym, home or commercial, is complete without one.

"If you want to be a powerful climber, campusing is the best thing you can do—if you do it properly."

Sonnie Trotter

Recommendations for the campus board vary, but consensus is that it should only be used in small doses. A danger of the campus board, as well as other high-intensity finger-training techniques, is that an athlete's muscle strength develops much more quickly than their tendon strength.

As a result, you will make great strides in muscle strength while your tendons lag behind. Base your training cycles on tendon strength, rather than muscle strength, and you will reap great rewards in your training. In designing your own campus board training, consider the following:

- How old are you? Younger tendons (say, those under thirty) recover more quickly. Once a week is a good start for mature fingers, and younger fingers can handle more stress, perhaps a couple of days per week, but should still be monitored carefully.
- Only campus for two or three weeks before taking at least two weeks off to let your tendons fully heal and strengthen.
- Start with your feet on a chair or other support—there is no need to support full weight to get great benefit from campusing.
- Avoid "go agains," where you leave one hand low and "go again" with the other hand to higher and higher rungs. This puts your shoulder in an increasingly compromised position with each higher move.
- Do not feel the need to copy what other people are doing: what is good for someone else is not necessarily good for you.
- Remember, the goal is to climb better, not to do more rad moves on the campus board.

"When hangboarding and campusing, don't use the smallest holds, or you just end up sick of it—or injured."

Tommy Caldwell

HANGBOARD

"One of the biggest mistakes people make is that with any supplemental training, like fingerboard or weight training, people add too much too quickly. Add layers of these things slowly—keep the frequency low and make sure your climbing isn't suffering."

Chris Wall

Also called a fingerboard, the Metolius Simulator hangboard was one of the first training tools to be commercially produced when it hit the market in 1985. With the invention of the campus board in 1990, and the proliferation of climbing gyms, the hangboard fell out of fashion. Then recently, thanks to the dramatic finger strength gains made by top climbers using the hangboard, climbers have rediscovered the hangboard specifically to increase hand and finger strength, which for climbers is perhaps the most challenging part of training to climb hard.

These newer hangboard programs usually involve adding weight to the climber's body in small increments. The method, while effective, must be done correctly, carefully, and with adequate rest.

"Training with extra weight is a dangerous game, but you can only go so far by lifting your own weight."

Sonnie Trotter

Training recommendations for hangboarding are similar to campus boarding, and it is highly recommended that you consult with a trainer familiar with these methods before embarking on a training program. If you want to do a little supplemental hangboarding, follow the recommendations for campus boarding outlined earlier.

SYSTEM BOARD

"System boards are the most underutilized training tools, but most are set up wrong. They should be set up for variety of movement, mirrored left and right, but not repetitive. It's a great tool for refining movement."

Justen Sjong

The system board, another German contribution to climbing, was invented by Thomas and Alexander Huber, the brothers known for free climbing on El Capitan as well as difficult sport climbing in Europe. Using the system board can be a great way to study the idiosyncrasies of movement as well as to increase climbing power. The best design for a system board includes:

- Mirrored holds on the left and right, so the exact same movement can be practiced on both sides to develop symmetrical results and movement patterns
- Variable orientation and types of holds, to force different body positions
- Variable angle of the entire board, to allow the climber to develop the muscles required to execute the moves at different angles

System board best practices are, you guessed it, an individual thing. If the

Opposite: Use the climbing gym as a place to strategically train specific parts of your athletic system, not just as a venue to get pumped and socialize.

movements feel overly strenuous, lower the angle of the board or consider working with a training partner who can support some of your weight while you execute the moves properly. This will help you develop both the power and muscle memory to do them on your own. Know too, that developing perfect form is more important than fighting through desperate movements. If the moves feel too hard, back off a little and do more reps of slightly easier movements until your form and strength improve.

As with hangboarding and campusing, system board training should be considered a heavy workout, with up to four days of rest (depending on your fitness base) needed for full recovery. Plan your climbing accordingly.

TREADWALL

Aside from free soloing, the treadwall is the only way you can climb straight up for a thousand feet without stopping—and you can do it in a small room. A number of top climbers have installed treadwalls in their own homes or garages, and the training benefit is unquestionable. However, with a cost of $5–10K, buying a personal treadwall will set you back the equivalent of several trips to Europe. Many gyms have treadwalls, but the ultimate benefit of a treadwall is for an in-home application where you can train power-endurance without going to the gym or traveling to the crag.

Treadwall tips:

▪ The best training benefit is to "tread" at a grade well below your limit. You want to get pumped, but be able to hang on and keep going. It's a way to develop power-endurance.

▪ Use medium-size holds and adjust the angle beyond vertical rather than using only small holds that limit the angle to near vertical.

▪ Hit the stop button and practice resting on the wall rather than just stepping down.

▪ Adjust the angle occasionally to give your elbows and shoulders a break from pulling away from the wall at exactly the same vectors.

▪ Like any training, count the treadwall course as a climbing day. If you want to climb hard on the weekend, don't do a long treadwall session on Thursday, do it Tuesday or Wednesday—give yourself a couple of days' rest before you pull down on your project.

E-STIM

Legendary Spanish climber Dani Andrada was the first well-known climber to experiment with electrical stimulation of muscles as a recovery aid. Electrodes are placed on the skin, and the current causes the muscles to twitch. The idea is that the stimulation will help flush lactates (lactic acid) from the muscles, allowing the athlete to recover quickly and train harder, sooner.

The practice has since caught on among some top-level climbers, and many claim that the practice is helpful. But the limited data behind the technique, at least so far, shows that E-Stim works about as well as traditional recovery methods. According to a study reported in the *Journal of Strength*

Conditioning and Research, E-Stim provided some subjective benefit. There was no evidence, however, that the practice reduced blood lactate levels any better than traditional recovery methods like a massage, easy jogging, or cycling—although it did show improvement over doing nothing at all. Certainly, in the mind game of climbing, if you do something that you *think* will make you perform better, there's a good chance it will.

One issue with the technique is that there is enormous variability—surprise, surprise—in how individuals react to the electricity. An electrical impulse too little for one person will be too much for another, causing either no recovery benefit on one extreme, to excessive muscle breakdown rather than recovery on the other. Once again, training has proved to be a very personal thing. For these reasons, the study concluded that E-Stim data did not convincingly demonstrate that the technique would enhance performance.

YOUR TRAINING PLAN

"When you put together a plan, unless something goes wrong, stick with the plan from beginning to end. Then evaluate it. Adjust it. Make meaningful changes and then do it again. Trim away the useless and add the useful. It's a trial and error process."

Chris Wall

Having completed an honest and revealing self-assessment, and carefully considered what training tools will help you the most, the next step is to develop a training plan. Remember, training for climbing performance is a tricky combination of working on your weaknesses while bolstering your strengths. To improve your mental

GENERATING POWER

One of the big things that challenges climbers trying to move beyond the 5.11 or 5.12 range is the way in which they generate power. Many of these climbers are incredibly strong, but they generate power with only their shoulders and arms, moving in abrupt lunges between handholds. If only your upper body generates power, you will be limited to the biggest holds and tire quickly.

You want to generate power with your whole body, starting with the toes, legs, and hips, before recruiting your upper body: think of your hips and butt like a big wrecking ball—you want it going the right direction and you drive that wrecking ball with your toes, not your shoulders and arms. Ask yourself, are you generating power with your whole body or just your shoulders and arms?

Justen Sjong

game, technique, and attitude, you want to build on your strengths. To improve your power, endurance, power-endurance, and flexibility, you want to identify your weaknesses and train the part that is limiting you the most.

Most importantly, you have to develop a training plan that is right for you. The young superstar Alex Megos climbs hard four days in a row, then takes one day off. On the other end of spectrum, older climbers who are not already well trained may do best to plan just the opposite—one day of full-throttle climbing followed by four days off. It all depends on you.

At the most basic, if you find that power is holding you back, go bouldering. If endurance is holding you back, do two or more pitches in a row at the climbing gym before swapping with your partner. Or do longer, more sustained pitches on real rock, and spend a little time on the bike. If power-endurance is holding you back, ascend more sustained climbs and be sure to get on more pitches each day that are closer to your limit. If you suck on slabs, go slab climbing—but only as much as you can tolerate while still staying positive mentally. If you suck on overhangs, get after some monkey business in steep caves—but again, only as long as you can keep the experience positive.

"You have to step back and ask yourself the tough questions. Most people don't like to look at their issues; it's kind of scary. Every time you step into the cage with your weaknesses, you realize that these are the things that you suck at, that scare you, and that you want to avoid. But if you are serious about addressing your weaknesses, you have to put your ego aside, stop making excuses, and get to work."

Chris Wall

SETTING GOALS

"A lot of people get confused as to what their goals are when they start training. There are specific strategies to achieve your goals. If you want to be stronger, find out the principles of strength training. If you want more endurance, it's the same thing. But take the time to clarify what your goal really is. Then draw the straightest line toward it."

Chris Wall

A critical part of training that is often missed is asking the simple question: what inspires you? Training is hard work, and without the inspiration, it is even more difficult. Some people are inspired by the training as an end in itself and that's great. But training alone will not make you a better climber; only in conjunction with climbing motivation and improved technique will training help you successfully climb harder. Others are inspired by trying to break into a new grade, and that's great too; but what kind of climbing will it be? The training needed to advance your climbing on a vertical granite face is very different than the training needed to powerfully climb across pocketed, overhanging limestone.

By considering your self-assessment alongside your goals, any training you do will be much more effective than undertaking a training program that is not personalized to you and your needs and dreams. Athletic training is a well-understood concept these days, and there is a program that will be ideal to help you achieve your goals.

MAKING CHANGES

"One of the big ruts I see people get into is to get all bent out of shape about hitting a plateau. When you hit a plateau, rather than viewing it like the doldrums where you just need to double down your workouts and beat yourself up, you should take the time to address the details of the work you are doing. Are all of your efforts where they should be? If you get to a certain point really quickly, it probably means that your current ability exceeded the demands of the tests you've put yourself through. Real progress is slow to evolve. It takes time for everything to come into line: a critical mass if you will. And then . . . BLAM! You break the plateau. You evolve."

Chris Wall

I'd wager that never in the history of the sport of climbing did anyone set a single goal, with a single training plan, then achieve that goal in a perfectly linear fashion. An element of flexibility and adjustment must happen for training to be effective in this diverse and individualized game. It is important to sustain training for long enough to ascertain what worked and what did not—for example,

The most important part of developing a training plan may be looking inside yourself and asking this question: What do I most want to accomplish, and how can I get there?

simply getting on the campus board once will have next to zero training benefit (and perhaps a negative effect). Let your program play out, but then adapt and make adjustments as you see results.

One of the ways to know your training program needs to be adjusted is when you hit the dreaded plateau. It's a natural part of climbing, so don't freak out when it happens. There are multiple factors that can cause a plateau, including technique, fitness, motivation, and the time you have available to pursue the sport. Luckily, there are ways to break out of the doldrums.

"Many people develop bad movement patterns, which reinforces bad technique and wastes strength. To break the habit of bad movement patterns, identify your weaknesses and work on them."
Lynn Hill

Changing how you climb and changing how you train are paramount to climbing improvement. Don't limit yourself to the kind of climbing you aspire most to do. For example, in their quest to change their own game, modern world-class climbers:

- Use bouldering to train for big walls and alpine climbing
- Go trad climbing to improve their mental and analytical strength at sport climbing
- Ride a bike or run to improve overall fitness
- Try other sports and visit new climbing areas to refresh the beginner's mind
- Stop climbing for extended periods to regain their psych or train a particular power

INJURY PREVENTION

"The idea that you're always supposed to train until absolute failure is a mistake. There are only a few specific times in a training program where you should push to this point."
Chris Wall

Injury prevention should be a conscious part of any training plan. Many athletic careers are cut short or sorely stunted due to injuries caused by training, most of which could have been prevented by changes in behavior. With our current understanding of physiology, a slight adjustment of training and technique can prevent the vast majority of training issues—provided you actually change your behavior when your body gives you the message.

"Pay attention to the science."
Tommy Caldwell

To prevent injury as you pursue your personal hardest climbs requires a special version of the self-assessment program we've already talked about. Your movement patterns, training habits, lifestyle, and genetic makeup all conspire to either cause or thwart injury. Avoiding injury is largely about listening to your body, and doing maintenance while you're healthy to prevent injury in the first place. According to

The single best way to avoid injury: Listen to your body. As an added benefit, you'll climb way harder.

climbing coach Justen Sjong, preventative maintenance on the primary joints used in climbing includes:

- For the fingers: Practice stretching and extension exercises.
- For the wrists: Do wrist curls, back and front. (Climbing strengthens fingers, but not wrists—it is important to build wrist strength along with climbing muscles. This can also help prevent inflammation of the carpal tunnel.)
- For the elbows: Increase triceps strength and small muscle rotation strength.

- For the shoulders: Use Therabands and free-weight exercises with light weights to build range of motion and opposition muscles.
- For the knees: Spin for 20 minutes on a stationary bike three times per week.

"When you see a breakthrough and you're climbing your very best, take a week or two off and chill. You can climb, but take it easy and stay on moderates. It's when people push past breakthroughs that I see people get hurt."

Justen Sjong

Then there is the holy grail of injury prevention: *rest*. Many times a chronic injury can be avoided, and a minor tweak healed rather than irritated, simply by taking a couple of weeks off of climbing and training. Embracing rest for a few weeks now is far better than being forced into a few months or years of recovery later. This approach has the added value of letting other body parts recover as well. More often than not, you'll return from a rest period stronger and more motivated than before.

"Climbing is a unique sport because you need to have a strong body, a strong mind, and also have the motor coordination and good technique to be able to move your body through a variety of body positions. These attributes can only come from climbing, so all of my 'training' is climbing based. I make sure to keep my whole body strong, balanced, flexible, and healthy by training on different styles of climbs and, very importantly, different wall angles from slab to roof. In my everyday workout I address as many types of movements and techniques—such as heel hooking, manteling, stemming, and finger strength (both closed and open handed)—as I can on the given terrain."

Lisa Rands

Opposite: *Avoiding a rescue in the Swiss Alps*

Improvised Rescue and Epic Avoidance

"People completely underestimate the need to practice this stuff before they need it. Just seeing it in a book isn't good enough."

Marc Piché

Sometimes the lines between a retreat and rescue are blurred. One of my first tastes of the big time started while standing on top of Fitz Roy in Patagonia, and involved descending the mountain's mile-long North Pillar, mostly rigging our own anchors for each rappel. Our ropes got stuck and we had to ascend the ropes to free them, 4000 feet off the ground, in the dark. We left all our slings then started doing shorter and shorter rappels as we cut the ends off the ropes for anchors. On the last rappel we left the remaining 70 feet of our lead rope hanging over the bergschrund and walked across the glacier using our last 40-foot piece of tag line to keep us out of any crevasses. We avoided making the news because we used epic avoidance techniques to avoid the need for rescue. We lost most of our gear, but we walked away happily and under our own power. Sound epic? Not near as epic as getting stranded half a mile off the deck. . . .

The vast majority of climbers do not know basic rescue techniques—even many of today's sponsored climbing athletes have never practiced simple pulley systems or improvised rope ascension. This is a testament to how being competent with fundamental skills and conservative with risk-taking is a great way to avoid a rescue in the first place. But it also reveals a weak point in our climbing culture: we are simply not prepared for things to go wrong. It is irresponsible to do multipitch climbs without knowing these techniques, yet the average climber who does multi-pitch climbing has never practiced a single rescue technique. This deficit in rescue skills is due partly to the way we learn to climb—usually cragging within half a rope length of the ground, where, when something goes wrong, we simply lower to the ground. It is also thanks to the fact that when we become advanced climbers there is a tendency to think that our climbing skills will prevent our ever getting in trouble or needing rescue. This is a false bravado.

Good climbing skills can, and do, help prevent accidents and the need for rescue. But if your rescue plan is to always carry a cell phone and hope you always have service and battery power, that's not enough. You shouldn't consider yourself a solid climber until you have practiced and can employ at least a few rescue techniques. *Rescue techniques are effective not only for self-rescue, but for avoiding rescue in the first place.*

Every chapter until now has been designed to start where other instructional books end. This chapter is different; the whole discussion around self-rescue for advanced climbers is about simplifying the process and doing what is needed with less equipment—not more advanced techniques requiring more than basic knowledge and equipment. Advanced rescue techniques are great, and it is worth consulting a comprehensive rescue book to get a solid understanding of the physics and considerations of roped rescue. But the reality is that when something goes wrong, and we really need to get up or down a climb, we rarely have enough equipment to perform most of the techniques shown in self-rescue literature. What then?

With this minimalist approach in mind, this chapter is devoted to improvised rescue and epic avoidance, including getting off a climb at all costs. This includes improvised aid climbing, for times when it is best to push on to the top rather than descend; emergency retreat methods, such as mid-pitch retreat on dicey gear; and methods for using improvised anchors and ways to ascend a rope with minimal equipment, such as when you are carrying only quickdraws. It also covers simplified improvised

When it gets dark and cold, and you're a long way from the top and going down is even worse, having practiced the skills and means to avoid the need for rescue can save the day.

self-rescue methods that utilize the least equipment, including block and tackle, Garta hitches, releasable knots, and, for rigging a Z-pulley, a high friction tube or assisted lock device.

IMPROVISED AID

Aid climbing was once an essential skill for any climber, but with the sexier, more accessible sport of free climbing stealing the limelight, aid climbing has become a fringe pursuit (just the way most aid climbers like it). Yet when conditions turn poor and the chips are down, knowing how to do a bit of aid climbing can make the difference between finishing a climb and turning into rescue bait. Aid climbing can also open the doors to astonishingly fun adventures like doing the *Nose* of El Cap in a day and other big routes composed mostly of enjoyable, moderate free climbing connected by a few short aid sections. Finally, knowing a little aid technique makes it much easier to attempt a trad climb a little beyond your ability level. Should your fingers fail, a few quick aid moves can often make short work of the hardest free climbing crux. But for this chapter, think about aid technique as applied to epic prevention.

Improvised aid climbing consists of five steps:

1. **Clip in.** Do not "take" or have the belayer hold you. When you weight the rope, you sag down a little, losing precious inches and causing your belayer unnecessary effort. Instead, clip a quickdraw to your gear loop and clip it into the highest part of the piece. *In the most efficient aid sequence, the climber never weights the belay rope.*

2. **Move up.** Climb as high as possible on the piece you are hanging on before placing the next one. This can mean clipping into the top piece with a single biner from your belay loop or, even better, clipping a doubled-up sling or two enchained draws into the top piece and standing up in the

resulting loop—what aid climbers call "high-stepping." When high-stepping, once your waist is above the piece do not remain clipped into the piece with a quickdraw or daisy chain: if you fall you want the rope's dynamic qualities to catch you, not the static sling. The point is not to just hang on the piece but use it to climb as high as possible. Use a foot tucked under your butt, à la Layton Kor, to allow you to extend as high as possible if the rock is too steep to high-step.

3. **Place high.** If you have good protection below you, it is better to place a mediocre piece at the limit of your reach than it is to place the perfect piece mere inches above your previous piece. You want enough bomber gear to prevent bad falls, but when aid climbing, fiddling with each piece to make it perfect is a waste of time. Depending on the terrain and fall potential, only every third or fourth piece needs to be bomber. Efficiency is the name of the game.

4. **Clip with care.** Once you have placed a piece high, if it is a bomber piece, go ahead and clip it as if you were free climbing. If it isn't bomber, clip in with a sling and move onto it without pulling the rope up to clip it. This way, if it fails as you move onto it, you won't fall the extra distance of the rope you pulled up to clip.

5. **Bounce test.** If the piece is anything less than perfect, clip into it and bounce on it to test its integrity. Test

A bit of improvised aid can make the difference between a fun adventure and a miserable epic.

it while you are at the level of the piece below, so if it pops your fall will weight the piece below while you are still even with it, minimizing the shock load onto the piece.

The best way to learn how to do a little improvised aid when needed is to spend a single afternoon doing a pitch or two of aid. As an added benefit, a few hours spent aid climbing will also make you much, much more accomplished at placing trad gear while free climbing.

MID-PITCH RETREAT

There is a scenario that unfolds in every climber's life at some point: You've gone as high as you can on a pitch, and you just can't make it any higher. Maybe you're off-route and maybe you're simply in over your head. Either way, you need to get down. The easiest way down is to leave a couple of bomber pieces of gear as an anchor and lower off. If you're more than half a rope length above the belay, you may need to rig a rappel to retreat. Develop a mind-set that it is possible to retreat from just about anywhere; that way you won't feel forced to continue upward when it is not safe to do so. Many rescues could be avoided each year if more parties simply bailed off when conditions deteriorate or the climbing is too hard.

The situation gets more complicated if you don't have enough gear or good enough gear to rig a bomber anchor. If you have a tag line, a good solution in this case is to rig a rappel with the tag line on the best piece (or pieces) of gear you can find. Rappel on the tag line while leaving your lead rope clipped through all the gear below, having the belayer pull it in as you descend, and clean the gear as you go, just as if you were downclimbing on belay through the gear you placed on the way up. This way, if the dubious piece you are rappelling on were to fail, you will take a normal leader fall onto the gear below you.

USING IMPROVISED ANCHORS

There are alternative options to standard protection and pieces if you are in a situation where you need to create a solid anchor with minimal gear or to back up a dubious anchor. Climbers are an amazingly creative lot when necessity calls. Jamming a rock in a crack with a sling around it, creative use of knobs, threading hidden holes, and slinging subtle features are opportunities to back up or build anchors with minimal equipment. Sometimes, of course, you'll happily leave anything behind to get down, like the guy who pounded his camera into a crack for an anchor on a desperate descent. But if you're trying to build rappel anchors with as little gear as possible, or are forced to use less than perfect anchors, consider the following:

JAMMED KNOTS

In Elbsandstein, a popular climbing area of Germany, jammed knots are still used for protection on lead, and in the right placements they can be strong enough to hold a fall and more than strong enough to hold the weight of a rappelling climber. Most of the time, there is little need to use a jammed knot. But knowing how can allow you to back up dubious anchors as well as safely utilize minimalist anchors in an emergency retreat from a big climb where you may not have enough gear to rig a full, textbook anchor for every rap.

To jam a knot, according to German climbing legend Bernd Arnold:

1. Find a significant constriction that is not much wider than the thickness of your sling at the narrowest point.
2. Tie an overhand knot in the webbing—either single strand or double strand, depending on the size of the constriction.
3. Leave the knot loose so it is soft enough to conform to the shape of the crack.
4. Wiggle the loose knot into the crack above the constriction. Use a cleaning tool or wire to stab the knot into the ideal and most secure point in the crack.

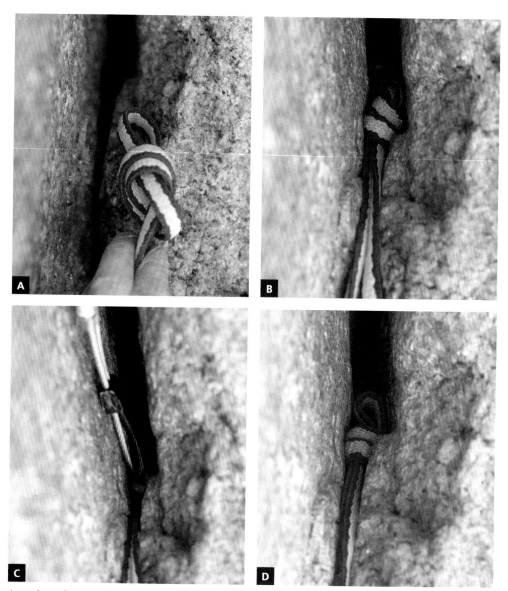

Jamming a knot: A. Tie knot loosely in sling or cord. B. Place knot above constriction. C. Poke knot into constriction using a wire or nut tool. D. Pull knot tight.

5. Pull hard on the sling to tighten the knot in place—this step is crucial to creating the strongest knot placement.

6. Consider tying the remaining sling so that the back strand of the knot holds the weight, then pull or "set" the knot using the strand coming from the deepest part of the crack.

7. Equalize the jammed knot with the rest of the anchor.

For jamming knots, it is useful to carry more than one width of webbing and cord. Consider using a chalkbag belt, prusik cord, cordelette, or even a piece of your rope to fit different-size cracks.

BROKEN, OLD BOLTS

Keep at least one nut on your rack that has a head that can be slid down the wire. Many nuts are now swaged at the head,

Wired nut cinched over bolt stud

preventing this improvised technique. Aside from carrying a specialized keyhole hanger, this is the best way to utilize a bolt stud protruding from the rock without a hanger. The smallest nuts with greater than 4 kN test strength work best for this use; too small and the wire strength is inadequate, too big and the nut tends to lever the wire off its placement around the bolt. Remember to clip the nut with a long sling to avoid lifting up on it as you climb past.

A similar method can be used to bypass or back up the welded or open cold shuts and other shoddy hanger designs that were used mostly in the 1980s and '90s. Often, the bolt itself may be reasonably strong, but the hanger is the weakest link in the chain. If the bolt stud can be looped with the wire of a stopper or a sling, the hanger can be effectively backed up.

IMPROVISED SELF-RESCUE

A rescue was called in the Bugaboos of British Columbia when a team of four made a minor mistake on the descent and was unable to solve the problem before a snowstorm rolled in. The first rappel was supposed to be short, only 10 meters. The first person down missed the anchor and kept going, 20 meters past the anchor before realizing the error. According to Marc Piché, technical director for the Association of Canadian Mountain Guides, who was on the rescue, the climber recalled the epic:

"I started to prusik back up the rope. It went well for the first three hours, and then it started to snow. Because of the snow, I

Wired stopper backing up a cold shut hanger

Sling backing up a cold shut hanger

gave up. My partners made a 12:1 to pull me up, which took another four hours."

In three hours, anyone who has practiced improvised rope ascension should be able to climb a thousand feet of rope. Thirty meters, even without the optimal-length slings or other cords, should take less than half an hour, including setting up the system. Next, they rigged a 12:1 pulley system, a complex and gear-intensive system that, unless done with pulleys and advanced understanding of rescue rigging, could easily be built to the point where the system pulls on itself rather than raising the needy climber. "If they had just used a 3:1, they could have pulled him up in half an hour," Marc explained.

In the end, the entire party had to be rescued. The team was experienced, had done multiple ascents in the Bugaboos, and had enough people, power, and equipment to quickly solve their original problem. But because they had not practiced improvised rope ascension, and knew only theoretical rescue technique, what should have taken an hour (at most) resulted in a seven-hour ordeal culminating in an expensive and truly unnecessary rescue.

IMPROVISED ROPE ASCENSION

"Don't be a one-trick pony. When you drop one of your devices fumbling with cold fingers, everything changes. All the different materials work in different ways

THREE METHODS FOR IMPROVISED ROPE ASCENSION

In these photos, a belay device, climbing webbing, and quickdraws are used to illustrate an improvised method for rope ascension with only the most common climbing equipment. Using a round cord for the friction hitch will make some friction hitches perform better, and of course a lightweight ascender would make the job easier. If an ascender is available, use it in place of the upper friction hitch. NOTE: For visual simplicity, the backup figure eight on a bight in the rope that is clipped to the harness at intervals when possible, is not shown in these photos.

Belay device in autoblock mode on waist with friction hitch for foot. Grigri or other assisted lock device on the waist also works well with this method.

Garta hitch on waist with friction hitch for foot. NOTE: Because the Garta is not a belay-quality system, a second sling is clipped to the upper prusik to provide backup should the Garta fail.

Two friction hitches—one for the foot and one for the waist. As with the Garta method, a single friction hitch is not belay quality; so clip both of them into your waist, with slack in the lower one to give it room to move as you step up.

(for friction hitches). When you're hanging on the rope with only one or two pieces of gear—that's when knowing a bunch of tricks will save you."

Marc Piché

Climbing a rope is easy, and there are a dozen or more techniques that get the job done. The trouble is, when we need to ascend a rope, we rarely have precisely the right gear to do it without some improvisation. It's possible to improvise with *minimal* gear, but you do need *some*. A bare minimum is a shoulder-length sling, a couple of biners, and a belay device, ideally with auto-blocking or assisted lock capabilities. When you realize you have to ascend a rope, there is one critical element of the improvised rope ascension process that you must do no matter what specific method you use: *Stay clipped into a backup of some kind.*

There are two scenarios that typically unfold when faced with needing to ascend a rope:

▦ The rope is well secured above you (Typically this scenario unfolds when a rappel rope gets stuck while it is still through the anchor and you can ascend both strands at the same time, or the rope is fixed properly to an anchor, as in the Bugaboos incident above, or you've fallen off of steep rock and the belayer can hold you while you ascend the rope to get back on the rock.)

▦ The rope is *not* well secured above you (Typically this scenario occurs when a rappel rope is pulled through the anchor and gets stuck on some flake or jammed in a crack with unknown holding capacity.)

In the first scenario, backing yourself up is easy. Simply tie a knot like a figure eight on a bight in the rope below you as you are ascending and clip yourself to it, repeating and redoing this every 10 to 30 feet (how far you can go between backup knots depends on the fall potential if your ascending hitches or devices were to fail). Because you are backing yourself up, there is no need to use locking biners on each part of your improvised ascending rig. Regular biners are adequate; use your locker or reversed and opposed nonlockers for the backup knots.

In the second scenario, the rope may be simply looped over a small flake or twisted into a crack. Such a jam may hold several hundred or even thousands of pounds, but it also may fail under body weight as you're halfway up the rope. This is an extremely dangerous scenario, yet there are usually ways to provide some backup. Usually when this happens, you have already pulled one of the ropes, so you have a rope to work with. If at all possible, lead the pitch on the other rope without ascending the stuck rope at all. If this is not possible:

- In a last-ditch effort to free the rope, bounce on it, with both you and your partner pulling as hard as possible. The good news: if it is still stuck after this test, it will *probably* hold your body weight.
- Tie into the free rope as if you were going to lead.
- Have your partner put you on belay.

- Attach your ascending devices or friction hitches to the rope and begin ascending as gently as possible, without bouncing.
- Carry the rack and, as you go, place gear and clip it into the rope as if you were leading, but instead of climbing the rock, you are ascending the stuck rope.
- If the rope comes unstuck while you are ascending, you will take a leader fall onto your last piece of gear.
- Carry a knife—if the rope twisted into a knot and jammed in a crack, you will likely not be able to free it after hanging on it. Be careful: sharp knives used on ropes under tension can cut like hot blades through butter.

The scenario gets even worse if there is not a second rope or enough rope already pulled down to use for a belay. In this case, *you are facing an extremely dangerous situation; consider calling for help rather than ascending the rope.* If rescue is not an option, pull as hard as you can on the rope (this either frees the rope or gives you some idea that it will hold) and ascend the rope using neatly tied prusik hitches (prusik hitches will work in either direction). As you move up, place gear below you whenever possible. If there is extra rope to work with, tie the bottom into a strong multidirectional anchor and clip off knots frequently as you go, so if the rope releases from whatever it is stuck on, the pieces you place along the way, and your backup knots, have a chance to keep you from falling too far.

In both scenarios, place protection as frequently as possible and be extremely careful as you near the point where the rope is jammed. As you near the stuck point, the angle of pull will change and it is quite possible for the snag to release just before you reach it (with catastrophic results if you are not on belay with gear placed nearby).

IMPROVISED RAISE TECHNIQUES

"You don't need much; understand load transfer, keep everything simple, and make every knot that is weighted releasable under load."

Angela Hawse

In nearly forty years of climbing, there have been two situations when I needed to pull my partner up the wall below me. Once my partner broke an ankle, and once my partner fell from a climb that traversed the lip of a huge roof and he did not know how to ascend a rope. In neither case did I have enough gear to rig a complex haul system. In both cases, a 3:1 or "Z-pulley" was adequate, even though my partners outweighed me in both cases.

Block and Tackle

"If you know how to use a block and tackle, you can do just about anything— and all you need is a long sling and a couple of biners."

Angela Hawse

Block and tackle

Block and tackle tied off with releasable knot

333

Creating the 3:1 pulley. A. First, attach friction hitch on load strand of rope—tie it off short, as shown, to maximize haul distance with each stroke. B. Second, redirect rope through a biner near the Grigri and pull.

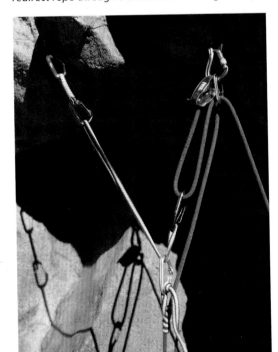

Changing the 3:1 to a 5:1 pulley. For visual clarity the 5:1 anchor point is placed off to the side in this photo.

The block and tackle, in combination with a friction hitch, is one of the most versatile tools in any well-prepared climber's quiver. This method can get you out of a variety of situations because it creates a mechanical advantage separate from the rope itself. Situations where a block and tackle can be useful include:

- Raising a climber a small distance
- Unweighting a heavily loaded auto-blocked belay device
- Unweighting a loaded knot that is not releasable
- Lifting a climber who is injured or stuck in space after falling from steep or traversing terrain
- Adding mechanical advantage to any raise system

Load-Releasable Knots

The only way to release most climbing knots under load is with a knife—not the best plan. Thus, knots that hold firmly but release easily after the job is done are core to every improvised raise method. For example, use either the Munter-mule or the slipped buntline when tying off in any scenario where you anticipate needing to release the knot while it is loaded. See Chapter 4, Knots and Anchor Rigging, for a selection of load-releasable knots.

Simple Pulleys

Simple pulley systems are easy-to-improvise, powerful aids to lifting larger loads. In the photos opposite, how to rig a 3:1 and 5:1 pulley (both commonly called Z-pulleys) is shown using minimal climbing hardware and cordage. For simplicity, the climber attachment point isn't shown, *but it is essential for all climbers to stay attached to the anchor at all times.* Also, the more you can spread the system vertically, the more distance you can haul with each stroke. The system shown here is compact, which may be necessary on a cramped belay, but to whatever extent possible, extend the lower friction hitch as low as you can reach to begin each stroke.

If additional leverage is needed, increase mechanical advantage by converting the 3:1 to a 5:1. For additional mechanical advantage to any raise system, or in an awkward stance where it is hard to pull, add a block and tackle to the pull side of the rope.

HOW TO PRACTICE

If all you ever want to do are single-pitch sport climbs, then you may be able to get away without knowing these skills. But if you aspire to any other kind of climbing, do yourself and your partner a huge favor. Practice. The ideal improvised rescue prevention session should include two parts: first, improvised aid and rope ascension on a steep crack with good protection, and second, raising and lowering on low-angle terrain with easy communication and within sight of your partner.

Here's how to practice aid and rope ascending:

- Pick a steep crack with good protection. Climb it using improvised aid technique, hanging on each piece as you go.

- On top, fix the rope and rappel down, cleaning the gear as you go.
- Ascend the rope using friction hitches, and rap again, using an improvised rap method like a carabiner brake or Munter hitch.
- Ascend the rope using a different combination of friction hitches.
- The key to both aid climbing and rope ascension is to figure out how to make lots of progress with each move. With each move, you want to move up 2 feet or more, not 2 inches.
- Take turns with your partner so you both practice and learn.

Raise/lower session: Even a single session of practicing a simulated rescue with your partner will supply a lifetime of basic rescue skills. Here's how to practice raising and lowering:

- Build an anchor on top of a slab—a 30- to 40-foot section of low-angle rock; this way you can communicate with your partner easily and work through the learning process without having the "victim's" full weight on the rope.
- One climber should play the role of victim, while the other manages the belay and the raise/lower system.
- The climber should start at the bottom, climbing on belay as normal. When you are 5 feet off the ground or so, hang on the rope.
- The belayer should then convert the belay to a raise using a Z-pulley or block and tackle and lift the climber 5 or 10 feet.
- Switch the raise back to a belay and lower the climber gently to the ground. (Hint: the transition is really easy if you employ a releasable knot where

---

EPIC AVOIDANCE: WHY IMPROVISED RESCUE SKILLS MATTER

- *Get a rope tangled below you while belaying?* No problem. Rap down, free the jam, and ascend the rope back to the belay.
- *Your partner falls off of an overhang and can't get back on the rock?* No problem. Put a block and tackle or 3:1 on the rope and pull them up until they can reach the rock.
- *Miss the anchor during a series of rappels?* No problem. Use slings to put friction hitches around both ropes and ascend back up to the anchor.
- *Drop a mechanical ascender during a big wall or other fixed rope ascent?* No problem. Use a French prusik or similar hitch in place of the ascender.
- *Get caught in a snowstorm leading the last pitch and realize it's better to go up than rap off?* No problem. Aid your way to the top.
- *Get caught in a snowstorm following the last pitch and the rock is too slippery to climb?* No problem. Slap a couple of friction hitches on the rope and get out of there.

If you want to climb in adventurous areas, it is critical to learn improvised rope ascension and other rescue prevention and self-rescue methods.

the friction hitch that holds the load between pulls attaches to the anchor.)

▪ Take turns with your partner so you both learn.

Investing an afternoon in these two sessions will give you a solid set of tools to keep you out of trouble for the rest of your climbing career. It will also help you to become a better climber at all times. Through the gear placement improvement that comes with aid climbing as well as the big-picture thinking and skill set that are developed during raise, lower, and rope ascension practice, you will develop vastly greater mobility and versatility in the vertical world.

The comfort that comes with knowing how to ascend ropes, pull your partner up if needed, and move around on the wall using aid or rope trickery will give you far greater competence in any roped climbing scenario. And even if you are so talented (and lucky) that you never need any of these techniques, just knowing how to handle minor epics and unplanned tangles makes climbing more relaxing and much more fun.

Contributor Profiles

Tommy Caldwell
Tommy has done as much to raise the bar as any climber in the world with ascents ranging from *Flex Luthor*, the first 5.15 in the United States, to the 5.14+ *Dawn Wall* on El Capitan, the hardest big wall free climb in the world and the most followed ascent in modern history. Tommy's athletic style of hard work and perseverance was particularly well illustrated after he cut off his index finger with a table saw in 2001 and returned to world-class performance standards. His work ethic and friendly nature make him a great role model for the younger generation. Tommy can be found at www.tommycaldwell.com.

Steph Davis
Steph is one of the most well known and best respected adventurers in the world. An articulate advocate for outdoor sport, Steph made her mark on the climbing world through high-standard free solos and big wall free climbs. She runs climbing clinics in Moab, Utah, where she teaches her method of climbing developed over thousands of pitches all over the world. Her free ascents of the *Salathé Wall* on El Capitan and *Inshallah* on Shipton Spire stand out as some of her finest ascents. Visit Steph at www.stephdavis.co.

Emily Harrington
Emily first set climbing standards as a child prodigy, winning five US National Sport Climbing Championships and two North American Championships before she graduated from high school. With an adventurous spirit, Emily shocked the climbing world by taking her gym-trained background and going on to summit Mount Everest and free climb El Capitan. Always game to help other climbers work through their fears, Emily is one of the friendliest and most humble world-class climbers ever to take a dip in a chalkbag. Visit Emily at www.emilyaharrington.com.

Angela Hawse

Angela is part of the new school of American guide, who has embraced the inclusion of the AMGA into the Union Internationale des Associations de Guides de Montagnes to allow her to guide in Europe, Canada, and other parts of the world. This exposure means Angela can share the lessons from guiding cultures around the globe. She is known for meticulous preparation before a climb and maintaining a personable and friendly manner while keeping a level head during even the most horrific weather conditions or complex mountain scenarios. Angela can be found at www.alpinist007.com.

Lynn Hill

Push the standards during the golden age of free climbing as a teenager in the 1970s. Check. Be the first woman to climb 5.14. Check. Make the first free ascent of the *Nose* on El Capitan. Check. Grade it 5.13b when it's really 5.14a. Check. Dominate World Cup climbing competition for years. Check. Onsight 5.13. Check. Inspire thousands of climbers on every continent. Check. Be trained by the American Mountain Guides Association to teach her skills to other climbers. Check. If there were a Climbing Hall of Fame, Lynn would be on the top of the roster. Find Lynn at lynnhillclimbing.com.

Alex Honnold

Alex is known for free solo climbing, including the 5.12+ big walls of *Moonlight Buttress* and *Sendero Luminoso*, but his grounded approach to climbing is perhaps his greatest contribution to the sport. Rather than speak to his elite level, Alex prefers to normalize world-class climbing adventure through his frequent interviews for both climbing and mainstream media as well as appearances in feature films. He has used his success as a climber to develop the Honnold Foundation, a charity organization that advances sustainable infrastructure. Visit Alex at www.honnoldfoundation.org.

Craig Luebben

Craig Luebben contributed spiritually to this book as the author of *Rock Climbing: Mastering Basic Skills*, the book that inspired this title, as well as through a close friendship with this book's author. Craig invented the Big Bro expandable tube chalk as part of a master's program, and went on to become well known for hard off-width climbing and a generous smile as well as an exceptionally clear teaching and writing style on the subject of climbing instruction. With his death in 2009 the climbing world lost a great mentor and inspiration.

Angie Payne

Angie is a respected visionary in the world of modern bouldering. A self-proclaimed gym rat, Angie has used her training discipline and mental strength to excel in competition climbing, including bouldering, roped, and psicobloc contests as well as double-digit bouldering feats from Greenland to Rocky Mountain National Park. Angie is a poster girl for the new generation of climbing athletes; she maintains a full-time profession outside of climbing, trains hard, then sends V13 during her time off. Angie can be found at www.angiepayne.com.

Marc Piché

Marc is technical director for the Association of Canadian Mountain Guides. With experience in all aspects of mountain sport, he is a sought-after expert in technical elements of skiing and ice, alpine, and rock climbing. When he is not guiding and climbing near his home in the Canadian Rockies, Marc consults for guiding organizations from other countries to help them achieve international certification. He is also an accomplished mountain photographer. With his finger on the pulse of the ever-changing standards of professional guiding, Marc is an excellent resource for the cutting edge of mountain safety. Visit Marc at www .marcpichephotography.com.

Lisa Rands

Lisa was the first American woman to win an international bouldering event and was ranked number one in the world. Taking her skill into the realm of danger climbing, Lisa did the first female ascent of *Gaia*, a gritstone E8 that requires 5.13 climbing with ground fall potential. Lisa now shares her love for the sport through guiding and managing the High Point Climbing School in Tennessee. Find Lisa at www.lisarands.com.

Chris Schulte

Chris is a well-respected spokesman for hard bouldering, as adept at hanging onto the worst holds imaginable as he is at getting his climbing partners to do the same. He shares his passion for the mental side of climbing by contributing often to the climbing media as well as establishing sloper boulder problems up to V14 that will puzzle elite climbers for many years to come. The perfect day for Chris involves exploring a boulder garden and cranking off dozens of lines he's never seen before. Chris can be found occasionally on Instagram at chris _schulte, or more frequently on the farthest sculpted sandstone block.

John Sherman

John is most famous for inventing the V-grade system for bouldering, and his contributions to climbing magazines have inspired a generation of climbing writers. One of the sport's most outspoken visionaries, John helped to make bouldering a sport of its own. A proponent of the idea that climbing is not about numbers, John holds a deep respect for the forefathers of climbing, from the great alpinists to the early big wall climbers. He redpointed 5.13 at fifty and plans to use his new titanium hips to do it again at sixty. Find John at www.vermphoto.com.

Justen Sjong

Justen began coaching in 1994 and has helped people of all abilities push their limits. He specializes in evaluating a climber's movement and developing customized drills to improve strengths and weaknesses. Justen is also a vastly experienced climber, having established first free ascents on El Capitan up to 5.14. He's most proud, however, of his coaching achievements, including helping some of the best climbers in the world—such as Daniel Woods and Emily Harrington—since they were kids. Reach Justen at www.climbingsensei.com.

Abbey Smith

Abbey Smith is a freelance writer, producer, and professional rock climber who values the friendships in climbing as much or more than the athletic element of the sport. She is best known for adventure bouldering, taking her passion for adventure, writing, and exploratory bouldering to the extreme altitudes of the Indian Himalayas and the Peruvian Andes. Her international exploits have been featured in several feature-length films, online web series, and commercials, and in the pages of *ESPN, Men's Journal, Outside, Backpacker, Climbing, Alpinist,* and other international print and online publications. Abbey can usually be found enjoying life with her favorite bouldering posse.

Sonnie Trotter

Sonnie is one of those people who fell into just the right niche in life. After his first twenty-one months of climbing experience, spent in a gym, Sonnie hit the road on his first outdoor climbing trip and ticked four 5.14s. He then went on to push the standards on sparsely protected 5.14 trad climbs and 5.13 runouts on El Cap free climbs, as well as in world-class sport climbing. Sonnie is an example of how hard climbing, when supported by natural talent, disciplined

training, and intentional experience on a variety of rock types, can be a whole lot of fun. Find Sonnie at www.sonnietrotter.com.

Chris Wall

Chris is a trainer and coach cut from the cloth of the greatest trainers of all time. Committed to the idea that training is a lifestyle, Chris shares his methodology as the Boulder Rock Club's head trainer and coach. He has a master's degree in physiology and is an NSCA-certified strength and conditioning specialist. In addition to coaching and training, Chris works with exercise scientists and coaches to develop training programs and philosophy for the next generation. Chris can be found at www.boulderrockclub.com.

Resources

Recommended Reading

Anderson, Michael L. and Mark L. Anderson. *The Rock Climber's Training Manual: A Guide to Continuous Improvement.* Broomfield, CO: Fixed Pin Publishing, 2014.

Beal, Peter. *Bouldering: Movement, Tactics, and Problem Solving.* Seattle: Mountaineers Books, 2011.

Cauthorn, Dan and S. Peter Lewis. *Climbing From Gym to Crag: Building Skills for Real Rock.* Seattle: Mountaineers Books, 2000.

Loomis, Molly and Andy Tyson. *Climbing Self Rescue: Improvising Solutions for Serious Situations.* Seattle: Mountaineers Books, 2006.

Luebben, Craig. *Rock Climbing Anchors: A Comprehensive Guide.* Seattle: Mountaineers Books, 2007.

Luebben, Craig and Topher Donahue. *Rock Climbing: Mastering Basic Skills,* 2nd edition. Seattle: Mountaineers Books, 2014.

Mountaineering: The Freedom of the Hills, 8th edition. Seattle: Mountaineers Books, 2010.

Ogden, Jared. *Big Wall Climbing: Elite Technique.* Seattle: Mountaineers Books, 2005.

Pease, Kent. *The Crack Climber's Technique Manual: Jamming with Finesse.* Broomfield, CO: Fixed Pin Publishing, 2015.

Samet, Matt. *Crag Survival Handbook.* Seattle: Mountaineers Books, 2013.

Sherman, John. *Better Bouldering,* 2nd edition. Guilford, CT: FalconGuides, 2011.

Guide Certification Programs

Britain: BMG, www.bmg.org.uk/index.php/eng/Guide-Training

Canada: ACMG, www.acmg.ca

New Zealand: NZMGA, www.nzmga.org.nz

France: ENSA, The French National Ski and Mountaineering School, www.ensa.sports.gouv.fr

Germany/International: UIAGM/ IVBV /IFMGA, www.ivbv.info

Spain: AEGM, www.aegm.org

United States: AMGA, https://amga.com

Information and Technique

Animated Knots
    www.animatedknots.com

The British Mountaineering Council
    www.thebmc.co.uk

Climbing
    www.climbing.com

Epic TV
    www.epictv.com

Indoor Climbing
    www.indoorclimbing.com

Mountain Project
    www.mountainproject.com

Rock and Ice
    www.rockandice.com

Safe Climbing
    www.safeclimbing.org

SuperTopo
    www.supertopo.com

UK Climbing
    www.ukclimbing.com

The Whipper
    www.thewhipper.com

Competition and Assessment

Alpine Mentors
    www.alpinementors.org

American Bouldering Series
    www.absnationals.org

Climbing difficulty database
    www.8a.nu

International Federation of Sport Climbing
    www.ifsc-climbing.org

Psicobloc deep water soloing competition
    psicocomp.com

USA Climbing
    www.usaclimbing.net
    www.usaclimbing.org

Index

Page numbers in bold type refer to photographs.

About the Author

Topher Donahue began guide training at age eight, leading his first guided ascents at age fourteen. By his late teens, Donahue was guiding alpine routes in Alaska and establishing 5.12 first ascents on rock. Today, with more than forty years of climbing experience, he continues to push his own limits (when the gear is good). His resume includes world-class climbs on several continents and first ascents ranging from alpine big walls and cutting-edge ice climbs to hard off widths and sport climbs.

He lives in Nederland, Colorado where he balances his time between writing, photography, playing in the mountains with his young family, and getting out on the rock with good friends. For more of Donahue's work, visit www.alpinecreative.com. This is his fourth book.

MOUNTAINEERS BOOKS

SKIPSTONE   BRAIDED RIVER

recreation · lifestyle · conservation

MOUNTAINEERS BOOKS is a leading publisher of mountaineering literature and guides—including our flagship title, *Mountaineering: The Freedom of the Hills*—as well as adventure narratives, natural history, and general outdoor recreation. Through our two imprints, Skipstone and Braided River, we also publish titles on sustainability and conservation. We are committed to supporting the environmental and educational goals of our organization by providing expert information on human-powered adventure, sustainable practices at home and on the trail, and preservation of wilderness.

The Mountaineers, founded in 1906, is a 501(c)(3) nonprofit outdoor recreation and conservation organization whose mission is to enrich lives and communities by helping people "explore, conserve, learn about, and enjoy the lands and waters of the Pacific Northwest and beyond." One of the largest such organizations in the United States, it sponsors classes and year-round outdoor activities throughout the Pacific Northwest, including climbing, hiking, backcountry skiing, snowshoeing, camping, kayaking, sailing, and more. The Mountaineers also supports its mission through its publishing division, Mountaineers Books, and promotes environmental education and citizen engagement. For more information, visit The Mountaineers Program Center, 7700 Sand Point Way NE, Seattle, WA 98115-3996; phone 206-521-6001; www.mountaineers.org; or email info@mountaineers.org.

Our publications are made possible through the generosity of donors and through sales of more than 600 titles on outdoor recreation, sustainable lifestyle, and conservation. To donate, purchase books, or learn more, visit us online.

OTHER MOUNTAINEERS BOOKS TITLES YOU MAY ENJOY!

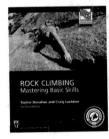

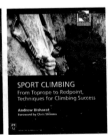

Mountaineers Books is proud to be a corporate sponsor of the Leave No Trace Center for Outdoor Ethics, whose mission is to promote and inspire responsible outdoor recreation through education, research, and partnerships. • The Leave No Trace program is focused specifically on human-powered (nonmotorized) recreation. • Leave No Trace strives to educate visitors about the nature of their recreational impacts and offers techniques to prevent and minimize such impacts. • Leave No Trace is best understood as an educational and ethical program, not as a set of rules and regulations. • For more information, visit www.lnt.org or call 800-332-4100.